# THE
# SILENCE
# SPEAKS

# THE
# SILENCE
# SPEAKS

MAJOR GENERAL (RETD) PRAN KOUL

PARTRIDGE
A Penguin Random House Company

**To order additional copies of this book, contact**
Partridge India
000 800 10062 62
www.partridgepublishing.com/india
orders.india@partridgepublishing.com

# CONTENTS

**Foreword**

**Introduction**

# FOR

My parents, Sh. Nand Lal Koul and Smt. Lajwanti Koul

My Uncle & Mentor, Sh. Triloki Nath Ticku

My wife, Kunti

Navin, Smriti, Nikhil, Rishi and

All near and dear

# Acknowledgements

*I don't boast of this being my book,*
*rather I consider it the result of fond memories and the*
*support of my well wishers.*

Lieutenant General (Retd) S M Chadha, former
Surveyor General of India, for the 'Foreword' and his
guidance.

Mr. Andre Unger, for being the main force behind this
book and for his valuable inputs.

Ms. Preeti Mishra, for her constructive and
patient editing.

Navin, my son, for reading the first draft,
in spite of being down with chicken pox and
his persuasion to take this project ahead.

Smriti, my daughter, for her encouragement and
critical feedback all along.

Nikhil and Rishi for their occasional suggestions.

'Oraclequest Education Foundation' and 'Indian
Antarctic Program-Wikipedia the Free Encyclopedia'
for enriching my knowledge on 'The Least Known
Continent-Antarctica'

And above all,

My mother, for her blessings, all through.

My wife, for her continued support and patience.

Last but not the least, the Team at Partridge Publications for their support throughout.

# FOREWORD

Koul is a natural and prolific story teller. The lucid narration of his memoirs from childhood in Sopore to a professional Army officer, engineer, surveyor and cartographer is full of thrilling experiences, interesting facts, history, anecdotes, adventures and morals. It covers a vast expanse of the country from Kashmir in the north to the 'Seven Sister States' in the east, with a vivid description of their changing physiography and cultures.

It further takes you to Antarctica, China, Russia, Bhutan and the United States.

Born and brought up in Sopore, the 'Apple Town of Kashmir', Koul aptly describes the ethos of 'Kashmiryat' and how the colourful shades of this culture got embedded in him during the years of his innocence.

Koul came under my direct acquaintance when he was posted to the Directorate of North Eastern Circle, Survey of India, in 1981. I had the chance of observing him closely while he executed the topographical surveys in Nagaland, plains of Assam and in the high hills of Arunachal Pradesh, mostly under extreme weather conditions and in areas infested with insurgency.

The picturesque description of his 'Voyage to Antarctica' will interest many a reader for some interesting facts and the challenges in exploring this icy continent. Koul surveyed the first Indian map in Antarctica which received a lot of recognition and publicity.

The narration of his interaction with the Pakistani counterparts on the well known boundary problem: 'Sir Creek', is informative and makes interesting reading.

In the end I would like to warn: that once you start reading; you are spellbound and it becomes difficult to put the book down.

Noida

Lieutenant General (Retd) S M Chadha

Date: 02nd December, 2013

Former Surveyor General of India

# INTRODUCTION

A child, born and brought up in the 'Apple Town of Kashmir', has many stories to share; more so, after having keenly observed, experienced and in many cases adopted various aspects of the social ethos, which weaved together the social fabric prevalent in the valley those days. I held some of these personal experiences close to my chest during my transition from childhood to adolescence, adolescence to adulthood and beyond. In my heart of hearts, I always felt that people, especially those from other parts of this vast and varied country and beyond deserve to know the salient glimpses of this unique culture of 'Kashmiriyat' from one who has experienced it at close range. My attempts here are to depict some glimpses in a simple form through personal narratives that may interest you, the reader.

Through my growing up years I had always cherished the desire to pen down these salient memories which unfortunately, till now, never went beyond a few poems in English, one of which was selected for publication in 'Sabzar,' our college magazine when I was in my teens. Though encouraged by the concerned Professor, I couldn't take this hobby forward first as an engineering student and, thereafter, as an officer in the defence forces, mainly due to exigencies of service.

This latent desire to 'record' kept simmering silently within but apparently went unnoticed. This desire was inadvertently satisfied, to some extent, by writing and presenting technical papers related to my profession in various national and international seminars/workshops, some of which have been published or are archived in reputed journals including the technical literature of the prestigious 'International Society of Photogrammetry and Remote Sensing'.

Though commissioned in the Indian Army as a sapper officer I had the advantage of being a professional surveyor as well. The dual profession provided me the springboard to survey far-flung places of our country located in plains, deserts, moderate and high hills of the North East, laden with permanent snow features, which at times even went beyond 15,000 feet above sea level. Life, for me, has generally been adventurous leading to some valuable experiences, thus enabling me to address situations under trying circumstances, not only at various levels in my profession and command, but also in my personal life.

Another desire that simmered right from my childhood was to visit the neighbouring countries of China & Pakistan. This was probably to understand for myself the mindset of the people in these two countries. Destiny would have its way and my second visit to Rawalpindi, Pakistan in 2007, as part of the Indian Delegation on the issue of 'Sir Creek' even brought me face to face with General Pervez Musharraf, the then President of Pakistan. Besides Pakistan and China, my profession provided opportunities to visit and sometimes even work in other countries including Bhutan, the United Sates and Russia, in various official capacities. Tibet was one such place I had the fortune to tour extensively as part of the group of GIS experts from 'Asia and Pacific Countries'. The tour took us much beyond the townships of Lhasa and Gyangze, up to heights of about 16000 feet.

In 1991-92, I was lucky to participate in the prestigious 'Indian Scientific Expedition to Antarctica' leading the 'Survey Team', as a Sub Team Leader, to survey and map an area of our interest in Antarctica. The news about the map, published in 1993, was broadcast on 'Doordarshan National News', the only national TV News channel that existed then.

The 'Film Division of India' also produced a film on the expedition, specifically highlighting the work of my team during the expedition. The film went on to win the prestigious National Award in 1992-93 and was exhibited in Sri Hari Fort Auditorium, New Delhi, along with other National Award winning films. In fact cinema halls all over the country showed this film as a prelude to the commercial films giving our work appreciable visibility. I have tried to include some salient glimpses of this 'Least Known Land' in forthcoming chapters of this book.

On superannuation from the Indian Army in June 2011, the silence that was simmering deep within, knocked at the door of my mind and called upon me to vent it out. To begin with, I wrote a few English poems and in the process, I discovered that when the 'silence within speaks' it churns the mind and resonates deep. Thus I found myself compelled to give this desire flesh and blood which has now taken the form of this book which I call 'The Silence Speaks'.

# PART I

## Nostalgia

# Chapter 1

# EARLY MEMORIES

W hen I look back, the earliest memory that comes to mind is that of my mother who had just given birth to my twin brothers. I must have been about three years old then. I faintly remember her frail face when she asked me, in a low voice, to go and buy her two eggs. I guess that was because she felt very weak and in those days it was not easy for us to afford eggs as a regular luxury.

Another memory that comes to mind is of the day when my grandfather took me to a Government School for my enrolment in Class 1. I must have been about five years old then. Sporting a proud countenance he carried me, holding a school bag in one hand and a bag of sweets in the other. The class teacher, Sh. Rajab Sahib, entered my name in the school register and the sweets—*Shireen,* (sugar balls) and *Khazeer,* (dry dates)—were distributed to the teachers and students. I vaguely remember that my grandfather was extremely excited and literally on top of the world. After distributing the sweets, he left me in the school. I was too innocent to realize that a new phase in my life had started, probably a serious one.

My mother says that when I returned from the school, I threw the school bag and went to play with my friends whom, probably, I had missed through the day. This made her angry and she complained to my grandfather that on the very first day I had flung the school bag and dashed out to play. My grandfather, in his calm way, said, "Look, he is a child, let him play and don't expect him to become an engineer or a doctor the very first day".

It was a great lesson for my mother. Even today she remembers it very fondly and narrates it to her grandchildren. Elders say that my grandfather Sh. Mahesher Nath Koul was a very learned man, had a good sense of humour and could write poetry in Persian as well. They also say that he was a genius, immensely interested in Urdu literature. He was a reputed teacher and headmaster of a Government school located in our town, called 'Babayusuf', which is still well known. After his superannuation, with too many responsibilities to fulfill, he continued to work in the local court. I still have a faint memory of him taking me to the temple garden on his return from the office.

I was born and brought up in Sopore, located in District Baramulla, Kashmir. The town is about 40 Kilometers

North of Srinagar, the summer capital of Kashmir. It is situated on both banks of the famous Jhelum river that flows through Kashmir. The river is known by multiple names. In Sanskrit, it is called 'Vitasta', while Kashmiris called it 'Vyth'. However it is now more famously known as Jhelum. The Jhelum river originates from the beautiful spring 'Verinag', located near the township of Anantnag and subsequently confluences with the Krishanganga river, before flowing into Pakistan.

Coming back to my hometown of Sopore, the genesis of its name has an interesting background that is related to the river Jhelum. Folklore has it that many centuries ago the river faced one of its worst floods, which gave King Avantivarman of the Utpala Dynasty many sleepless nights. The king was finally advised to call the genius engineer 'Suyya' to save the place. 'Suyya' identified the bottleneck in the river flow and attributed it to the accumulation of silt along the riverbed. This had obstructed the free flow of water and was thus the reason for the crisis. 'Suyya' was clear that to save the deteriorating flood situation there was no alternative but the removal of the silt from the river bed. However he couldn't find men who were prepared to plunge into the river to remove the silt.

He briefed the king about the impending situation and requested him for plenty of *Ashraffis,* gold coins, and sought permission to throw these coins into the river. The king accordingly provided vast sums of the gold coins and gave him the freedom to carry out his plan. 'On Suyya's orders the coins were thrown into the river. On seeing the gold coins, people were tempted and plunged deep into the river along with *kranjuls,* willow baskets, in their hands. They removed huge *kranjuls* of silt to retrieve the coins and thus huge quantities of sand and stones were physically dredged out from the river. As a result, the river became deeper and the water gushed out. The water level receded appreciably, thus saving the township. The town was named as 'Suyyapur' to commemorate *Suyya* and over the ages, it became 'Sopur'. It is now known as 'Sopore', though in Survey of India topographic maps it continued to be spelt as 'Sopur' for a long time. The township of Sopore has rich lands and is famously nicknamed the 'Apple Town' of Kashmir.

Being my birthplace, I have a lot of affiliation to this town and love it sincerely. I know it's every street, it's every rubble that is embedded in its soil, it vicissitudes and why not for, it has contributed to the growth of my flesh and blood.

Chapter 2

# THE FORMATIVE YEARS

## The First Enrolment

I was enrolled by my grandfather in the Government Primary School Sangrampora, Sopore, which was not very far from my house. The teachers were extremely strict and in those days, one could not imagine a teacher without a stick in his hand. On a lighter note the stick, in many ways, was the first identification of a teacher.

I recall there were strict instructions issued by the Headmaster not to go swimming in the Jhelum river during recess breaks, which lasted for half an hour, as there had been many cases of drowning. However, some students would love to break the rule and teachers always caught culprits, who were then beaten black and blue.

To overcome this, teachers, through experience, devised a method of imprinting legs of the students with the school stamp at the exit gate during the time of recess. After the recess break, the teachers would check the impression of the stamp on the students' legs and any student who went swimming was identified immediately. Even then, there were defaulters and scenes of culprits being thrashed, while we could hear forlorn cries, "Sir, we will not do it again", were pretty common. At times we enjoyed it, primarily because we knew that they would do it again.

I remember a teacher with a long grey beard, 'Janab Nab Sahib', who had an irritating habit of addressing us by our father's names. He was fond of using his stick at random and at times for no rhyme or reason. It thus goes without saying that we were scared of him. He always came like a thunder and one never knew where he would strike. Here, it may be worthwhile to mention that these teachers were very hard working and commanded well-deserved respect. Looking back, I owe them a lot.

There were a few incidents, which took place around the time I was in one of the initial primary classes. I have deliberately included these incidents as they reflect the approach of an elder or a teacher in correcting a child with the intention of keeping them on the right path. Children are very sensitive and deserve to be corrected with utmost sensitivity, not by thrashing them or creating fear in their minds.

As a young child, I was scared of walking alone at night. My father realised this and one night when everybody in our joint family was about to sleep, he told me to close the main gate of our house, which was on the extreme side of our compound. My father or one of my uncles generally did this every night.

On the given night he encouraged me to go alone and said, "As you go ahead, I shall call your name loudly and you reply loudly". I agreed, and came back running after closing the gate, while pretending that I was not scared at all. Every one present at home then, including my grandmother, patted me and called me a brave boy, though I knew in my heart of hearts that it was not entirely so. My father gave me a rupee coin as a reward, which was not a small amount in those days. He thereafter made this a practice and encouraged me close the main gate of our house for a couple of nights till he was convinced that any vestiges of fear were removed from my mind.

Another incident worth mentioning took place in the month of June when summer was at its peak. My grandmother, who was crippled after the birth of my third uncle, used to have a *Kangri*, an earthen pot covered with willow, in which live charcoal was placed and used as a personal heater, generally in extreme cold weather of Kashmir. I remember her using the *Kangri* in summer as well, mainly to light the *Jajeer*, a piped *hookah* that she smoked.

During this time I had noticed my father and uncles smoking and throwing the cigarette butts around. I started collecting these stubs with the intention of smoking them secretly. Going a step further, one day, I purchased a pack of 'Charminar' cigarettes from the neighbourhood shopkeeper. Failing to locate a matchbox in the kitchen (to light the cigarette), I went to my grandmother, and asked for her *Kangri*. She asked me why I wanted it. I told her that I was feeling cold. She lent me the *Kangri* but doubted my intentions for, very obviously, there was no reason to feel cold during the peak of summer. After secretly lighting the cigarette in the corridor, I quickly returned her the *Kangri* and rushed back to complete smoking the cigarette.

I guess she might have noticed some traces of smoke, from my breath because it appears she shared this incident with my father. My father, in his own wisdom, didn't react immediately. He beckoned me after nearly two days and said, "It appears that some boy was smoking in the corridor a few days back, just find out who the boy is and let me know." I was overwhelmed with guilt and practically started sweating. My father never asked me the details, which bothered me a lot. The impact of his actions was that I left smoking there and then. The important point to note is that had my father beaten me up, chances are I would have become a chain smoker and might have been smoking even today.

## The Entry to the Middle School

I am from a family of teachers. My father, Late Sh. Nand Lal Koul, was a well reputed teacher of Sopore. He was very popular amongst teachers, students and their parents alike. He was known for both his taste in Urdu literature as well as his humour. He would play the harmonium with great ease and sing Urdu *ghazals* very well. He had great aptitude to teach English and mathematics and was well known for that not only in the school but also in the whole town.

As a child, I always felt very proud of being his son, mainly because of the respect and reputation that he commanded as a professional as well as for being a noble human. He had a cluster of meaningful friends from all communities. It was a pleasure to see his Hindu and Muslim colleagues, well-reputed teachers, flocking around him, even after school hours. He always had a smile on his face.

He was posted at the Government Middle School, Babayusuf, where my grandfather had worked as a headmaster in his days. I always wondered why he didn't admit me in his school. Finally, in the fourth standard, on my mother's persuasion, he arranged my transfer to his school. I was very happy since the school was very well known, throughout the district, for its quality of academics. Over the years it has produced quality engineers, doctors, teachers and various other professionals.

It was a huge school, located adjacent to 'Sopore Bandipora Road' opposite a small lake called 'Bugh Jheel'. The school was excellent in everything except for the building, which was very weak and appeared to have lived its life. I remember when we would climb from one story to the other; the stairs would make creaking sounds as if they cried out in pain.

On many occasions, we overheard the teachers' express concern and worry, probably fearing a catastrophe, if ever the school building gave way. They had been persuading concerned officers for assistance but then Government procedures were known to take time. I studied in the same school and in the same building until my eighth standard. Luckily, neither the staircases nor the foundation gave way, during my stay.

Discipline, in this school, was paramount mainly because the teachers were very competent. There was something about this school that made it different from others. As I see now, maybe it was the teamwork, the dedication to the profession and the mutual respect of the teachers for each other that set it apart. As a result, students would get substantial care especially those who were good in their studies.

I am deliberately penning down the details because the formative years, particularly the years one spends in school, play a big role in the development of the personality and the characteristics of an individual, which finally, in one way or the other, remain with him lifelong. For success of any individual, I would give full credit to the teachers who must have laid strong foundations during their formative years. To illustrate this point, I shall narrate some examples where teachers made substantial difference to the lives of some financially deprived students.

The day at the school would begin with a prayer, led or rather sung by a team of three or four students. I remember one of them was a good flute player. His name was Kundan. I was lucky to be part of the team. The other three were Tej, Khaliq and Rasool.

We would sing three well-known poems, one of which, I remember was of Dr. Iqbal, the famous Urdu poet of *Saray Jahan Se Achha . . .* fame. The tune of the prayer was composed by my father. Kundan punctuated the songs with his flute, which was mesmerizing. Years later God was unkind; I learnt that in the early 90's militants had killed 'Kundan', in his house, while his wife went missing since. I remember him as being a very bright student who had done very well in his career as an Agricultural Engineer.

The prayer would be followed by a moral lecture, given generally by Mohamad Ramzan Sahib. He was a strict disciplinarian and gave exhaustive elaborations on the values of life, which, I am sure, would have influenced the personalities of a number of students, the lucky ones. Thereafter, the students would read out the national news, which they would compile from the newspapers, since very few middle class families could afford radio sets those days, we didn't have one at our home either.

As mentioned, Mohamad Ramzan Sahib was the custodian of discipline in the school with his strict nature and thus could never be taken for granted. Incidentally, he was given the President of India award for being the best teacher in the state of Jammu and Kashmir. He would teach many subjects but was especially good at mathematics. He was a great friend of my father, for whom, I remember he used to have a lot of love and respect. He taught mathematics to our class and was strict and sincere to the core. I fondly remember him as being a man of many great qualities.

I remember one particular day when he got stuck while solving a complex question on the black board. After a few trials he instructed us to call Nand Lal Ji, my father, who was teaching in the adjacent classroom. This was testament to his regard for my father's command over mathematics.

My father entered our class; both of them discussed and solved the problem right there, in front of the students. I distinctly remember both of them laughing, shaking hands and then my father leaving for his class. I am sure he must have left with enhanced respect for Mohd. Ramzan Sahib, for having the courage to ask when in doubt.

This was an example of the teamwork, which was prevalent in the school at the time. The teachers shared, updated their knowledge and lived like a family. Students and the teachers would also live in utmost harmony irrespective of the faith or religion that they followed. Probably instances like this provided the initial exposures of *Kashmiriyat* to me as an innocent child.

Going on school picnics or excursions was yet another experience. Generally, the school arranged one-day outings during which we would travel by buses and we would carry our own food. An omelette with rice, enriched with the fragrance of my mother's blessing, used to be the special dish, which I would look forward to and cherish during these outings. There were times when it would be an overnight stay and on such occasions school authorities would make arrangements for food and lodging. The excursions were very educative because the teachers would conduct activities in a very different style and take utmost care of the students.

I remember once Pt. Jawaharlal Nehru, the then Prime Minister of India, visited a place called 'Doabgah', a village about 5 kilometers from Sopore, to inaugurate a 'Drudging Project' on the river Jhelum. Our school team was selected to recite and sing the prayer songs over a raised makeshift platform, in honour of the distinguished guest. It goes without saying that we were thrilled at the prospect. That was the day I saw Pt. Nehru for the first time. He was dressed to kill and looked glorious in the white *Achkan*, embellished with a pink rose and a Gandhi cap. One could see bliss radiate from his smiling face.

I would like to mention here a practice undertaken at the school called, *Safaie Ka Hafta,* 'The Week of Cleanliness'. No studies were conducted in the school during this week. The students would clean the whole school themselves under the constant and strict guidance of the teachers. The jute mats, on which we used to sit in the class rooms, would be brought down and cleaned thoroughly on the bank of 'Bugh'. In those days our school didn't have stools and desks. This one week was sufficient to clean the entire school thoroughly. It served as a great lesson about keeping our environment clean, something which over the years was drilled into me.

I shall subsequently narrate some experiences as a hostler, while I was a Cadet in the Military Academy and as a member of 'Indian Scientific Expedition to Antarctica' where I could address certain situations with ease because the mind had been trained at a young age due to activities such as *Safaie ka Hafta* and many more. While in service, I never had any inhibitions in ensuring a clean office environment. I have been very particular and demanding about such things and it had fruitful results both in the civil and military environment, wherever I worked.

Back then we had to face an examination of the Jammu and Kashmir board at the end of Class VIII. It used to be a serious examination since for the first time question papers were set and corrected externally and not by the school. I passed the examination with a first division and was amongst the privileged group of few who achieved this distinction in our town but I must mention here that some of them had performed much better. I remember the neighbouring women visiting us in groups to congratulate my mother. This was a tradition and one of the occasions when people would share moments of happiness together. My mother played a gracious hostess by serving *Kahwa,* the famous local tea and *Kulcha,* the local bread.

Our teachers, who would otherwise keep quiet, congratulated and patted us on our success. Our school had classes only up to the eighth standard. The day we took our transfer certificates, they advised us to do well in the higher classes. May be that was their last valuable, though informal, moral lecture and the only one without the ritual prayer as a prelude.

Having spent some valuable years in this school, I left with a heavy heart; it was like leaving one's own home. I could feel myself moving away from the warmth of my *Gurus/Ustads,* something I had grown used to over the years.

In this context, I reproduce the following befitting lines from a book 'The Courtesan of Lucknow' by Khushwant Singh:

'Like a pet singing bird let out of its cage,
My bonds are loosened when I love the bondage'.

## Entry to the Higher Secondary School

After leaving school I had to take admission in M. L. Higher Secondary School, the only Higher Secondary School in the town. The school had beautiful single-storey, well spread out buildings, made of bluish stones with red tin sloping roofs. It had a very scenic ambience—a magnificent gate with a metallic road, huge flowerbeds on either side, leading to the Principal's office and the lecture rooms. It had European looks with a huge playground, consisting of separate hockey and football fields. There were a number of extracurricular activities for such students who wanted to take part in them, depending upon their interest.

Physical training was a daily activity and would be supervised by professional instructors. Our physical instructor, Mr. Mohammad Sultan Sahib, was a product of the famous Physical Training College, Madras (Chennai). He was young, very handsome, well built, and physically tough. He had made his presence in the town felt so much that crowds of people would come to see him in the evenings at the playground.

Incidentally the time he joined the school coincided with the release of Raj Kapoor's film 'Nazrana', in the local theatre known as 'Samad Talkies'. In the introductory scene, of the movie, Raj Kapoor and Mr. Sultan are shown taking part in a 'Shot Put' competition, along with other college students. Raj Kapoor stands first while Mr. Sultan followed in second position. In reality, Sultan Sahib was the 'Shot Put Champion' of the Physical Training College, Chennai where the film was shot and the scene was obviously scripted to show Raj Kapoor, the hero of the film, winning the championship.

I was closely associated with Sultan Sahib after I joined the NCC in the school while he was the NCC teacher, as well as an honorary Lieutenant. Under his guidance I attended an NCC camp, passed the Junior Certificate 'A' of the NCC and was made a Sergeant. As a Sergeant, I led the NCC team of the school and took part in school debates. These experiences were new and enriching.

As regards academics, the school had very well qualified staff in all the faculties. It was one of the best Higher Secondary Schools in the valley and boasted of well-equipped science laboratories.

Sh. T. N. Ticku, one of the famous personalities in the Jammu and Kashmir Education Department, was a teacher in the same school. He also happened to be my maternal uncle. Today, he is about ninety-two years old and lives in Jammu. In later years, he retired as the principal of the same school. Honest to the core, he commanded a great reputation as a teacher, a strict disciplinarian and an able administrator.

It was a pleasant sight to see him walk through the Sopore market. The road stretched for about two kilometers, with shops on either side. As he crossed, the shopkeepers would rise one by one on either side. When one shopkeeper sat, the other would rise as a wave, on either side of the road, would set in. I haven't, in my lifetime this far, seen any person who commanded such respect. Such were the teachers of the school both in science and humanities streams.

Products of the school have in time risen to very senior levels, which include a number of chief engineers, super specialist doctors, educationists and senior administrative officers.

I passed the Higher Secondary final examination with a first division and was amongst the four first division holders in the District of Baramulla.

# Days in the Degree College

I had to wait for about a year before getting admission in the engineering college. During this period, I took admission in 'Sherwani Degree College'. The college was named after 'Mohammad Maqbool Sherwani', the famous valiant soul who had put up a brave front to the invaders from Pakistan in 1947, when they invaded Kashmir. He was later brutally killed by them using nails which were driven into his forehead, only because he had fought to save his Hindu brethren and kept the flag of *Kashmiriyat* flying high.

As mentioned, my stay in the degree college was a waiting period until I got admission to an engineering college. However, I gained some valuable experiences during this stay. It was a huge college adjacent to the Higher Secondary School with a common playground. The principal of the college, Mr. Salam Dar, was well known throughout the state for being a strict disciplinarian.

He would ensure that the college campus was kept spick and span, to the extent that at times he even inspected the standard of the cleanliness in the washrooms of the college, personally. He would conduct surprise checks and sit in the class rooms to see how the lecturers taught. He was known to travel by bus daily, to and from Srinagar which was about 40 kilometers away and as expected was never late to the college. The drivers of these buses never dared to overload the bus, in which he travelled, which otherwise was a common practice, since he never tolerated people breaking rules. This extended even beyond the college.

In those days one particular instance became the talk of the town. Once he boarded a bus in which the local session judge was also travelling. On seeing that the bus was overloaded, Mr. Salam told the judge, "You should feel ashamed that the driver has dared to overload the bus in your presence and you are silent!" They say that on seeing Mr. Salam the driver immediately swung into action and offloaded a few passengers. These were the characteristics of a good citizen. Am sure his strong character would have influenced many students and others as well. As a public figure he became an example for the locals.

As a co-ed college, with an appreciable strength of students, he had ensured that all measures were taken to guarantee the safety of girl students. The college prides itself for creating many meritorious students. Mr. Saifudin Soze, the former Central Cabinet Minister was a lecturer in the same college those days.

Debates would be held in the college on Fridays and he was the lecturer in charge of the activity. I remember an instance when all the students had gathered and the debate was about to commence. Mr. Soze pointed to me and asked me to stand up and speak. I told him that I had not given my name to participate in the debate but he didn't listen and made me speak extempore, my first such speech. In later years, this event gave me the much needed confidence, as I grew in service.

# PART II

## Kashmiriyat

# Chapter 3

# SOME GLIMPSES

We lived in a dense area in Sopore called 'Sangrampora'. I have some fleeting images of our old single storey house complete with a thatched roof. I also hazily recollect scenes of the construction activity when my grandfather added two more storeys to the house, leaving the upper storey vacant and in a skeleton form, perhaps due to financial constraints.

The society we lived in was well-knit with a cluster of Muslim neighbours on one side and Hindus on the other. Our immediate Muslim neighbours were very fond of me. The lady of the house was called 'Mokha'. I remember that whenever she went out of town, she would bring back some sweets and biscuits for me. Her daughters were very affectionate as well and loved us like brothers. Similarly, other Muslim and Hindu neighbours lived cordially and shared moments of joy and sorrow together.

My parents told me that when I was about two years, I had developed a skin disorder on my right leg and would often cry out in pain. The Muslim woman would take me to her home, look after me and make me sleep on her bed. This continued for over a month. They also mention that she took me to some *Hakim* and rubbed the locally made ointments given by him daily until it was cured. My parents probably reiterated this so that I remember it throughout my life. I should say, and say it with pride, that they have succeeded.

'Mokha's' husband, generally referred to as 'Ame Seitch,' was a tailor and worked from home. Very often he would remain awake late into the nights. I remember he was very fond of Hindi film songs and the only one in our locality who had a radio set. He would play the radio at a high volume and this, for us, was a blessing in disguise.

The university results were declared on the radio and only the roll numbers of successful candidates were announced. Parents in the neighbourhood along with their children would approach him on every such occasion. He would oblige readily and turn on the radio at high volume, as usual. His radio, on such occasions, brought smiles to many and anguish to others.

I remember, my grandmother was particular that I drink a cup of pure milk every day. However, the milk available was, more often than not, diluted. One of our Muslim neighbours called 'Doshabas', who lived about two rows across the street, somehow learnt about this. They had a cow that gave very little milk which hardly sufficed their own requirement. The elder woman of their house called upon us one day and told my grandmother that someone from our house should collect two cups of milk from their house, every morning for me.

My mother and grandmother were taken by surprise and thanked the woman for the gesture. Thereafter, my mother would collect the milk herself, each morning. The husband of the Muslim woman was an old noble man and a staunch Muslim with a thick and long beard. One day my mother got busy and sent me to fetch the milk in the morning. On entering their house, I saw the woman and her husband in their room. The woman had already milked the cow and kept the milk for us aside, in a small metallic pot. As I handed over my pot to her, she poured the milk into it. Thereafter she put a few drops of water in her empty pot, rinsed it thoroughly and put it in my pot. She did this probably to ensure that even the last few droplets of milk, stuck to her pot, were also given to us.

However, I was stunned when suddenly her husband yelled at her for mixing drops of water with the milk, which was meant for me. I could see irritation on his face, though he knew that the poor woman had only rinsed the pot to ensure that we got even the last droplets. He warned her that in future, not even a trace of water was to be added to the milk which 'Kaka Ji' was to drink. I was fondly called 'Kaka ji' at home.

When I came home, I narrated the incident to my mother and grandmother. Today, while writing about this incident, I look up towards the sky with utmost regard for the old man, the real Muslim, with his long grey beard, for this vivid example of '*Kashmiriyat*', the culture, of which we were proud! May the old man's soul rest in peace!

We would return from the playground, in the evenings, nearing dusk. That generally was the time when the young neighbouring Muslim girls would gather, stand in two rows facing each other, put their hands on each other's shoulders and sing 'Kashmiri Folk Songs', swinging back and forth in rhythm. The atmosphere would be filled with bewitching melodious songs, called *Roh,* which continued until the last glimpse of light. What a way to bid farewell to the day and welcome the night! I, at times, crave for those moments but alas . . .

While I write about this, the *Roh* folk songs echo deep in my mind and take me back on a journey to my childhood, through the dense streets of Sopore.

My grandmother and parents often narrated bitter stories of the agony they faced when the invaders from Pakistan attacked Kashmir in 1947. They say the invaders came in waves, armed with weapons and spread their wild tentacles on the peace-loving Kashmiri people. Their ire would often be directed towards Non-Muslims and those Muslims who tried to save their Non-Muslim brethren.

When they were about to reach Baramulla District including Sopore, the Sikhs and Hindus left their hearths and fled from their homes. They hid in jungles and other safe places without food for days together. Many families were separated. It appears that my parents, along with my grandparents, hid in the jungles adjacent to the 'Wular Lake'. My grandmother, as mentioned earlier, was crippled after the birth of my youngest uncle, about a decade before this incident. She narrated that my father would carry her on his shoulders, walk and at times run for miles and miles in the jungles for fear of their lives. Many of their close relatives, who were caught off guard, were shot dead.

The invaders, for some reason, were known to be more brutal towards the Sikhs. My parents narrated that on many occasions they had witnessed many elders of Sikh families lining up their women folk, on the bank of the 'Wular Lake', beheading them with swords, as a last resort to save their honour. They would then kill themselves after immersing the bodies, of the women, in the lake. It appears that brutality was at its zenith, during such periods and one wonders where *Baghwan* alias *Allah* lived those days.

My parents would often return to their house expecting the calamity to be over, but to their misfortune some of the invaders would return repeatedly. On one occasion my father was caught and was asked at gunpoint what he did. He posed as a Muslim and told them that he cooked for rich people. He was lucky to be spared while many others were not. One of my aunts was made to board a truck to be taken along with them, leaving her

three-month-old baby in my uncle's lap. When the truck
started, my uncle ran behind it, like a mad man and
begged them, if nothing else, then to take the baby as
well. By God's grace better sense prevailed and one of
the invaders made her jump out of the truck to join her
husband and the child. Such gestures, they say, were
very rare.

It was at such times that our Muslim neighbours gave
shelter to the Hindu women folk, at the cost of their
own lives. My grandmother and parents say that these
Muslim women even loaned their clothes helping them
camouflage as Muslims. The invaders mistook them
for Muslims, as they had completely merged with the
Muslim families, with whom they ate and lived until the
crisis ended and thus they were spared from the clutches
of the demons. My mother and grandmother were given
shelter by 'Doshabas', the same family which gave us
the milk.

We owe the lives of our parents to those Muslim families
who saved them in 1947 else, we would have not been
around to tell the tale today. This was *Kashmiriyat* at
its prime, the culture whose seeds were sown by our
ancestors. Thereafter, the culture of *Kashmiriyat* was
nourished by the sacrifices and the hard work of Hindus
and Muslims, together, over the ages.

*Kashmiriyat* was woven with the delicate threads, spun out
of such sacrifices, hard work, love for each other, mutual
respect and the regard that bound Hindu and Muslim
communities, which had withstood the test of time, those
days. Our parents and their relatives had experienced

*Kashmiriyat* at close quarters. As a result, they had no communal feelings and passed on these traits to us.

I recall an instance when I was a student of about eight to nine years old. It was peak winter and extremely cold, the temperature that year had dropped to about minus seven degrees centigrade. We had winter vacations and I needed a notebook for my homework. My father gave me some money to buy it from the stationery shop. He asked me to put on my shoes but I wore nylon slippers and walked for a distance of about one and a half kilometers over a road covered with frozen ice.

On the way, I slipped many times and my feet turned numb by the time I reached the shop. I paid the shopkeeper and by mistake, he returned more money than what he owed me. I kept quiet, returned home richer, and was happy about it.

On reaching home, I told my father about the incident thinking this would make him happy too. On the contrary, he expressed his dissatisfaction and advised me to go back to the stationery shop immediately to return the excess money to the shopkeeper. I remember he didn't bother to ask me to put on my shoes, this time round. I went again, in my slippers, with numb feet and told the bookseller that he had returned more money than what I had paid him. He was very happy to hear it and said. "That is like Nand Lal Ji's son". He blessed me and told me to keep it up. I returned home and told my father that the bookseller had given me his blessings. He was happy and so was I. This incident, as I realised later, had a lot of impact on my personality.

As a child of about eight years old, I once accompanied my maternal uncle to board a bus at 'Batamaloon Bus stand', located in Srinagar. While boarding the bus he saw a Muslim woman, easily about forty to fifty meters away, carrying a heavy bag in one hand and her child in the other. She was to board one of the other buses. My uncle told me to run and help the woman carry the bag, seat her comfortably in the bus and then return, quickly. I obeyed faithfully. After boarding the bus, the woman patted me and showered her blessings. On my return, I had a strange feeling of satisfaction. The memory has stayed on. It was an exposure to one of the valuable facets of *Kashmiriyat*: the chivalrous nature of the men in the valley. Later, when I grew up I realized that such an outlook might have been the primary reason why women, in those days, were not spotted standing in buses, irrespective of whether they were Muslims or Hindus.

My twin brothers, Shadi Lal and Chand Ji, were classmates and quite bright in studies. They also studied in the Government Middle School Babayousuf, the same school that I described in the initial chapters. They had a Muslim classmate named Ali Mohammad. My father, a teacher of their class found that Ali was also good at his studies but came from a humble background and that none from his family had studied beyond the primary classes.

On further investigation my father found out that Ali's father was a truck driver by profession and there was a high possibility that Ali wouldn't be able to continue his studies beyond a few classes. My father called Ali's father to inform him that he would take special interest and care of his son, as he was good at studies. This was only because he wanted to ensure that Ali didn't drop out. This encouraged the young boy. On Ali's father's request, my father went on to tutor him even beyond school hours, at our home along with my twin brothers. Ali mingled with us and became like a family member. I remember we were all very fond of him.

His parents started visiting our house out of gratitude and shared their moments of joy and sorrow with us. Ali, later, became a doctor and then a reputed pediatrician. My mother tells me that he married a Hindu girl of the same profession and brought her to my mother to receive her blessings. They gifted a beautiful sari to her, which she still preserves and wears on special occasions and refers to it with pride as Ali Mohammad's sari. Recently, she got to know that he went to the Middle East and finally settled down in the United States of America.

Such memories of the town and its people are in plenty. I also remember that a famous Muslim, 'Khawaja Samad Pandit', was the richest man of our town. His family possessed a fleet of cars those days and a Tonga, which would be decorated like a bride. He also owned the local cinema Hall, known as 'Samad Talkies', the only theatre in the town. In my childhood, I saw most of the movies in this theatre. My father was also fond of watching movies, probably, this being the only source of entertainment available in the town those days. He was also fond of reading film literature and passed on these traits to me to such an extent that I have invited and encountered several adventures, in my student days, only to watch a movie.

Coming back to 'Khawaja Samad Pandit', I always wondered how the surname of the richest man in town was 'Pandit' though he was a Muslim. Similarly, there were some Muslims in various parts of Kashmir with surnames such as 'Rainas', 'Bhats' and 'Kouls' as well. I learnt later that it was because of the fact that generally the Kashmiri Muslims were converts who had converted from Hinduism to Islam under some rulers and thus the commonality in surnames.

# Chapter 4

# FESTIVALS THAT NOURISHED 'KASHMIRIYAT'

Here my aim is not to get into the genesis of the festivals or to make a commentary on them but to highlight how the two communities would celebrate their major festivals and the impact it had on us as children. The major religious festivals that we Kashmiris celebrated with full verve in Sopore were 'Shivratri' and 'Eid'. 'Shivratri' was celebrated by Hindus and 'Eid' by Muslims.

The celebration of 'Shivratri' festival was spread over a three-day period in the peak winter season. Generally, thick snow would engulf everything like a white blanket and the freezing nights were bitter cold, which turned roads into skiing tracks. The main *Puja* would be observed during the night, which preludes the day of 'Shivratri'. The marriage of 'Parvati Ji' and 'Lord Shiva' used to be solemnized in every Hindu home on this day. A set of earthen pots would be decorated as deities of Shiva, Parvati and other gods. The pots would be filled with pure water, high quality walnuts and sugar cones were then immersed into them and the stage would be set for the main *Puja*.

In our house, a number of delicious vegetarian dishes would be on the menu that night, but dinner was served only after performance of *Puja* by our *Guru Ji*, the family *Brahmin*. Needless to say, he was in great demand on this night and would generally get delayed because of his lengthy client list. We, as children, would run out of patience primarily because our mouths would water while we waited to eat the yummy preparations. To have dinner at the earliest was all we longed for. At times, we would fall asleep only to be woken up by our parents on the *Brahmin*'s arrival.

In later years this issue was solved by a simple approach. We, five brothers, would spread out in five different streets, with the aim of catching hold of the *Brahmin* at the earliest and persuade him to come to our house first. This worked well over the years. During the main *Puja*, the *Brahmin Ji* would make everyone immerse a sugar cone and in case of the absence of some family member, the same would be done in proxy to ensure the involvement of all the family members in the auspicious activity.

The second day's *Puja* would be performed by the elder of the house, both in the morning and evening. We children would eagerly wait for this day called 'Salam' because firstly, the elders, including our relatives, would visit our house and give the children pocket money, which we spent in any manner we wished. Secondly, on this day, we were free to eat non-vegetarian food and a number of Kashmiri non-vegetarian dishes would be prepared in our house. I remember, being impatient we would occasionally make an intermittent visit to the kitchen to check on the progress of preparation of these delicacies.

My father kept denominations of currency handy on this day because a number of people such as the postmen, carpenters, electricians, plumbers, helpers, folk dancers and many others visited our home to wish us 'Happy Shivratri' and in turn were given tips.

This was the day when my father would especially await the arrival of his close Muslim friends. After entering our house his friends would hug my father and wish us all 'Happy Shivratri'. My father was a good host, and served them heavy tea with delicacies such as *Kebabs* and other non-vegetarian Kashmiri dishes. My father would thank them for their visit and see them off personally. Although the festival was celebrated by Hindus but the happiness was shared by our Muslim brethren as well.

I remember my father was also very close to a Muslim family called 'Khandeys,' who were the second richest family in Sopore. It so happened that they had requested my father to tutor their children, which he did with the dedication for which he was known. The tradition of teaching their children continued from one generation to the other. He became like their family member. Incidentally, their younger son, Mr. Mohidin Khandy, and I were classmates and very thick pals. I would eat and dine with him and his sisters who treated me like their brother. My father would treat him like a son, and he in turn had a lot of respect for my father to the extent that, even now, whenever he remembers my late father his eyes become moist. He would be amongst the first visitors to wish us on 'Shivratri'. This ritual has continued over the years and even today, he is always amongst the first callers to wish me on 'Shivratri'.

Coming back, on the third day the *Puja* would be carried out in the later part of the afternoon to symbolize bidding farewell to the newlywed couple, 'Lord Shiva' and 'Parvati Ji'. The women would immerse the contents of the pots in the river 'Jhelum'. This would be followed by the ritual of sending the soaked walnuts to relatives as *Prasad*. My mother would go a step further and send some of these wet walnuts to all our Muslim neighbours and some close Muslim friends as well.

As regards 'Eid', the Muslims would celebrate this with pomp and show. First, they would go for prayers to the 'Eid-gah' and, on their return, the elders would give *Edgi*, pocket money, to children and the full celebrations would start. We would join our Muslim friends and wish them 'Happy Eid' or rather 'Eid Mubarak'. On this day, a hit movie would be scheduled for release in the local cinema hall, a trend which has spread across the country and is even today a much awaited occasion. As expected there would be an acute rush for tickets. More often, we children would buy the tickets in black, paying three to four times the actual cost of the ticket.

The Muslim families would visit each other's houses and the sounds of 'Eid Mubarak' would resonate all around. My father visited 'Khandeys' and all his Muslim friends on this day to wish them 'Eid Mubarak' and they awaited his arrival with eagerness. The harmony with which the festivals were celebrated exuded the shades of the culture of *Kashmiriyat* in full.

# PART III

## *Mud Splashes*

## Chapter 5

# UNCARED SPARKS TO A DEADLY FIRE

The fine threads of *Kashmiriyat*, which I have elaborated before, were woven by our Hindu and Muslim ancestors, with their selfless sacrifices to ensure unity between the communities. The essence of *Kashmiriyat*, remained alive for years to come. As mentioned before, *Kashmiriyat* was embedded in our DNA and our elders, through examples had taught us how to nourish and keep it going.

This culture of *Kashmiriyat* has often been threatened. In the middle 18th century, during the decades that the valley was under Afghan rule, its very concept was buried deep underground. During this period Kashmiri

Hindus were subjected to unthinkable atrocities, widely depicted by the nineteenth century British Historian Sir Walter R. Lawrence, Tyndale Bisco[1] and various others in their writings. Their description of such atrocities is beyond human imagination, which, one can understand, must have been the primary reason for many Kashmiri Hindus leaving the valley from time to time, often for good.

Over the years the roots of *Kashmiriyat* grew deep and strong, so much so that when invaders attacked the valley in 1947 many Kashmiri Muslims went all out to save their Hindu brethren, even at the cost of their lives. Many such instances have been narrated by our parents and grandparents who owed their lives to some of these noble Muslim neighbours and friends.

The great Mohamed Maqbool Sherwani, the soldier of the gospel of *Kashmiriyat* and many other daredevils came to the rescue of the culture of *Kashmiriyat* during this invasion, keeping it alive against all odds. Credit, in this endeavour, goes to both Muslims and Hindus alike.

In the late 70's, when my parents moved to their new house, we once again had immediate Hindu and Muslim neighbours. The adjacent house belonged to a Muslim family. They showered lots of love and affection on us and so did my parents who treated their children like their own. I remember when I would come home with my family on annual leave, we used to meet the Muslim

---

[1]     *Kashmir, Wail of Valley, Atrocity and Terror*, 1999—M L Koul

lady 'Dedha' first, take her blessings and only after that, we would see our mother and other family members. If ever, by mistake, we happened to open our door first, my mother would ask us to meet 'Dedha'. This was not for show and goes a long way to demonstrate the strong bonds in diversity, shared back then. I remember a day would be fixed when we would go over to their house for a meal and would feast over the delicacies prepared by them.

Towards the latter half of the 1980's, the veins of *Kashmiriyat* were bitten by some hardcore militant activity, aimed at destabilizing Hindus and their peaceful coexistence in the valley. The administration seemed to be in deep slumber and couldn't identify the sparks that threatened the delicate petals of the flowers of *Kashmiriyat*. The first casualty of this uprising was of 'Smt. Prabhawati' from Nowgaon village of District Chadoora in March 1989. She was killed because of the bomb explosion, which took place in Hari Singh High Street in the city of Srinagar. The noble lady was the mother of Dr. Inder Bhat who had been my course mate and room partner in the engineering college, about whom I have spoken before. I had been so close to the family that when I would go for days together to their house the lady fed me with her own hands just as a mother feeds her son. May her soul rest in peace!

The uncared sparks kept swelling to the extent that auspicious religious places became platforms to propagate filthy slogans asking Hindus, clearly and crisply, to exit the valley leaving their women folk behind. In the days and months ahead many Hindus were killed.

This was against the ethos of *Kashmiriyat*. When the administration finally woke up, the sparks had turned into a deadly fire and from there on the situation went from bad to worse. Even today the situation continues to burn, sometimes with flames and sometimes without.

My aim is not to go into the depth of this 'Cancer' because it may involve volumes of work and more importantly is beyond the context of this book. The fact however remains that this deadly fire has engulfed and spread its poisonous flames all over the valley and is probably not an easy proposition to handle, for mere cosmetics will not help. When treated at one place the sparks simmer and echo in another. In consequence, the face of our beautiful Kashmir has been splashed with mud all over, to the extent that she today looks frustrated with pain and anguish.

My family was also a victim of the happenings of the time. My youngest brother, Ravi, who worked in 'Kupwara' was on his way home to Sopore one day and while waiting for the bus decided to purchase a watch, for a friend, from the local Army Canteen. After doing so and while en-route to Sopore the bus was stopped by a contingent of the Paramilitary Force and one of the passengers, a Muslim, was apprehended under suspicions of being a militant. Following this, all fellow passengers, mostly from the Muslim community, having noticed my brothers' visit to the Army canteen before boarding the bus, suspected it of having something to do with the detention, of the fellow passenger. Under the prevailing circumstance one wouldn't blame them for suspecting my brother of being an informer. Within hours word of the incident spread through the neighbouring localities and my relatives, having heard of the same, came and advised my parents, brothers and others in the family to leave immediately, fearing the worst.

The whole family left hearth and house in utter hurry that night. Most believe that had they not done so, that very night, they would have been brutally killed. My mother did not even inform 'Dedha', our Muslim neighbour, due to the prevailing circumstances. Putting a simple lock on the door they fled in a truck to Jammu.

My brother-in-law, Sh. A.K.Raina, Deputy Director, Food and Civil Supplies—Government of Jammu and Kashmir, was killed by terrorists a few days later. In fact, he had been the only such person to be killed in office. They say that the condition of the office furniture testifies that he had not been an easy prey. He had given the demons a tough fight until a bullet, from the terrorist's gun, silenced him. That was the time when the real exodus of the Hindus started and the rest as they say is history.

'Dhedha', as expected, felt very bad about the whole event, especially because my mother had left without informing her. However, under the prevailing circumstances one was rightly overcautious regarding information due to the apprehension of inviting unnecessary attention of miscreants.

Many days later, another brother of mine had gone back to the house. Understanding 'Dedha's' disappointment he called on her, took her to our house and together they opened the door. Right there lay a pressure cooker, full of half-cooked rice along with some cooked vegetables, in the vegetable bowls, the *Thalis* (plates) lay spread out on the sheet in a manner ready for dinner to be served. The scene depicted the harshness of that evening when taking note of the seriousness of the situation and the impending danger, my mother decided not to serve dinner to the family, though it was ready, choosing instead to make a heated escape from what now appears to be a rather narrow one. Was the end so near? No one would ever know . . .

The situation worsened and thousands of Hindu families fled the Kashmir valley for good. There is a Kashmiri saying that there came a time, under the rule of some barbaric rulers, when only 'Eleven Kashmiri Hindu families were left in Kashmir'. I could never believe it, but the turmoil from 1989 onwards convinced me that it must have been a fact. The eleven families must have flourished over the centuries to face yet another exodus now.

Even today, whenever I have childhood dreams, I wander through the streets of Sopore only to wake up with an acute hangover. The pangs of separation of my birthplace are so intense in my subconscious mind that I am convinced they must have affected my brain, in some way, slowly but steadily.

One can only hope that the broken threads of *Kashmiriyat* are picked up again and by some magic, woven together and blended skillfully to what it once was. I do not expect this to happen in my lifetime. Nevertheless, if only it happens, it will be worth the time. Future generations will then relish the taste and essence of *Kashmiriyat*, which otherwise they are devoid of today. Only then would the mud that is splashed over the beautiful face of my Kashmir be wiped off and its original luster restored. Amen!

# PART IV

# In The Vicinity Of The 'Dal'

## Chapter 6

# INITIAL EXCITEMENT

Right from my childhood I have always wanted to be an engineer. As mentioned earlier, I enrolled at the local degree college where I literally prayed and waited to get admission at the engineering college. I filled up the admission form but was unsure of being selected, as in those days there was only one engineering college in the state of Jammu & Kashmir. Being a Regional Engineering College, fifty percent of the seats were reserved for students from other states, as was the norm for all Regional Engineering Colleges in the country.

Admission to this particular college was very important because it would automatically entitle me to the loan scholarship from the Government of Jammu & Kashmir.

I didn't apply in other engineering colleges outside the State, as I knew it would have been difficult for my father to afford the fee given the large family he had to support along with other responsibilities, including the education of my four younger brothers.

Finally, the call came. I was asked to present myself before the interview board, Regional Engineering College, Srinagar, on the specified day and time. This was indicative of the fact that I had cleared the first iteration of the selection procedures.

On the D day, I boarded a bus to Srinagar and thereafter took a city bus for 'Naseem Bagh' where the College was located. It was next to the 'Hazratbal Shrine', famous all over the world as it houses the pious relic of Prophet Mohammad. On reaching the college campus, I was mesmerized by the scenic surroundings. The college was situated on the bank of the famous 'Dal Lake' and the campus had a thick cover of 'Chinar' trees, probably planted during the 'Mughal Empire' or even before.

The Principal's office was in a separate single-storey building amidst the beautiful surroundings. The environs themselves were reason enough for me to pray for my admission in the college. However, that being said, I was pretty apprehensive and rightly so because acing the qualifying examination with a first division was probably not sufficient for an entry unless one did very well in the interview.

The interview was spread over a number of days and groups of students were called in for the interview each day. Those who were part of the interview that day, including myself, waited nearby under the soothing shade of the 'Chinar' trees. One could not have asked for more on an anxious day as this.

Lo and behold, my name was called and I was made to sit in the waiting room by a staff officer who asked me to pull out three cards, one each from a separate stack. Each card had a set of questions, which pertained to different subjects including General Knowledge. He told me that I would mostly be asked the questions listed in the cards. The 'Selection Committee' interviewed the students in the adjacent room. I went through the questions listed in my cards. In the meantime, a student came out and I was asked to go in.

I answered all the questions and felt satisfied but in the interim, the Chairman posed a few more questions. The Chairman was the Principal of the Engineering College, Dr. Munish Raza, the famous geographer, who later, went on to become the Vice Chancellor of the Delhi University. He asked me to name my hometown. On hearing that I was from Sopore, he asked me to elucidate about the town's background and the origin of its name. I replied with confidence on the same lines that I have detailed in the first chapter of the book.

He posed a series of other questions; one of them was about 'Bhabashukurdin Shrine' located on a hilltop adjacent to the 'Wular Lake'. I was impressed by his knowledge of Kashmir, more so, because he was not a Kashmiri. My grandmother had told me the story about the shrine when I was a child. Generally, she would tranquilise me with such stories each night, while putting me to sleep. I narrated it with utter confidence. By now, I felt comfortable and had no difficulty in responding to his other questions. I left the interview room extremely satisfied but I was told to keep my fingers crossed, which I did, knowing fairly well that there could possibly be better students in the pipeline.

I remember the day the postman knocked at our door and handed over a telegram. It brought the anticipated news of my selection. I was allotted 'Chemical Engineering'. My parents were very happy while I was on top of the world for; it was an important step forward of realizing my dream to become an engineer. The fee, in those days, amounted to about three thousand rupees.

My father was probably short of money. I remember overhearing a conversation he had with my mother on the aspect. He asked my mother to help him in case she had some money. My mother opened the tin box, in which she would store her expensive clothes and savings, something she rarely did. She readily handed over the cash of about two thousand rupees to him. I recall that this left her with practically no savings in spite of which, she was happy and contented. My father was very relieved and happy, as he had overcome the first hurdle of paying my initial college fee. This was only the beginning.

I had to be a hostler so my parents purchased new bedding, clothes, an expensive shaving kit, college uniform as specified and various other costly items. Finally, the day arrived when I left for Srinagar with bag and baggage. Many of my close relatives, along with my father, came to see me off at the bus stand. I was extremely excited and proud at the prospect of making my entry to a professional college.

On reaching the college, I paid the fee along with other students. We were told by the Registrar that all the faculties would have a common syllabus for the first half of the course and thereafter we would branch into our respective specialties.

I was allotted a room in the Hostel located on the bank of the 'Dal Lake', undoubtedly one of the most scenic hostels one could ever imagine. I had two other roommates, one of them very delicate and innocent looking. He was from Srinagar itself. I set my belongings in the room and from then on senior students started coming in groups to rag us. The college was known for its fierce ragging and the seniors used to be rough and merciless.

One evening, after classes, while we three were in our room, I saw the parents of Ashok, the innocent looking roommate, approach our room to meet their only son. At the same instance I noticed a group of seniors approaching our room. I feared we were in for intense ragging and so I quickly invited the parents of my roommate for a cup of tea and was about to head for the canteen, when they entered. I pretended to be busy with the guests so as to avoid the wrath of the seniors, who thankfully mistook them as my parents and thus didn't disturb me. Sadly, they instead ragged Ashok mercilessly, in front of his parents. While leaving our room the seniors told me to look after my guests. The mother of my roommate cried while his father, who appeared to be a senior officer, felt helpless and highly annoyed.

The mother asserted that she would not leave her son back at the hostel, where students were discourteous and had the audacity to rag the boy so cruelly and that too in front of his parents. She rolled up his bedding, packed his belongings and told her husband that they should take their son home that very night and make him a 'Day Scholar'.

By the time this entire episode wrapped up it was dark. I along with my other roommate helped carry Ashok's belongings to their car. While they drove off I felt guilty since I was, in more ways than one, responsible for the entire episode.

That is how I lost my first roommate and the college, a hostler. Whenever I met Ashok, over the next five years, the scene always replayed within me. The ragging in the college continued for the next three to four months and towards the end, its intensity lessened by the day. The ragging made me very tough mentally. As time passed, we developed good relations with the seniors, some of whom were particularly helpful.

I finally settled down to hostel life and would visit my hometown generally once in a month. On my first visit home, my friends received me well, as did all the relatives, which generated a feeling of pride in me. My mother would prepare my favourite dishes and finally

I would leave by the morning bus to reach college on time.

Our college had a semester system and each semester lasted for six months. It had two huge campuses, one called the 'Old Campus' and the other, as expected, the 'New Campus', both situated on the bank of the 'Dal Lake'. The two were separated by the Kashmir University campus.

The old campus was located in 'Naseem Bagh', densely populated with thick 'Chinar' trees, complimented by the 'Dal Lake'. The combination was breath taking, to say the least. We were privileged to see many 'Bollywood' movies being shot around this area, for obvious reasons.

The New Campus had beautiful modern buildings, which housed our hostel, library, uniquely-designed lecture halls and staff quarters. The whole campus exuded tasteful architecture, which was a treat to the eyes. The two big wooden jetties adjacent to our hostel, projecting into the 'Dal Lake', added to the charm. It was an apt place to sit and watch the moods of 'Dal', for long hours. I noticed that the 'Dal' looked very 'dull' whenever the wind went to sleep, which was generally rare.

The 'Dal' was a faithful companion. When we woke up in the mornings, we would see the 'Dal'; we would sleep after seeing the 'Dal' and at times in our sleep, we dreamt of the 'Dal'. In other words, during those years, the 'Dal' was here, there and everywhere.

Chapter 7

# Honeymoon Ends

With the commencement of lectures, the initial honeymoon and the excitement started dwindling day by day. The load of tutorials, mainly the drawing assignments started to take its toll. We, the students, realised that the pattern of studies in the engineering college was very different from what we were used to and accordingly some of us tried to review our own technique.

We shuttled between the old and new campuses, with half a day of classes in either of the campuses mainly because the main laboratories and the workshop were located in the old campus. The mechanical engineering department was the only to be fully set up in the new campus.

We had a galaxy of teachers in various faculties; some of them were renowned not only in India but had a reputation internationally as well. During the first three years the initial foundation in various subjects was laid by several competent teachers such as Dr. Syed Ali, a reputed professor and Head of the Department (HOD), Physics. The concepts of third dimension taught by him are still fresh in my mind.

Mathematics was taught by Dr. Izhar Hussain, HOD of Mathematics faculty, who was known as the third great mathematician in the country in those days. He was unassuming and I remember the ease with which he would teach. Dr. Jeerath, expert in 'Material Science' was HOD, Chemistry. It was said that he was a visiting faculty of some foreign universities as well.

The Humanities faculty, headed by Ms. Basaria, was rich and boasted of highly qualified teachers who taught us English literature, Political Science, Civics, Economics and many other subjects from the humanities stream.

Dr. Labroo who taught us English had done his doctorate in 'Phonetics' from Oxford University. He was a great teacher. I remember very well that he broke down one day while teaching us the culminating chapter of the novel, Tess of D'uberville by Thomas Hardy.

As was common in his class, the students got appreciably charged while he narrated the tragedy of the main character 'Tess'. His description of the tragedy was phenomenal. He was so talented that during his lessons the events would play out in front of our eyes.

On this occasion he himself became so emotional that he broke down and couldn't proceed. Incidentally, Dr. Labroo had selected my poem 'Down the Hill of Udhampur' for publication in the college magazine 'Sabzar' in 1970. As mentioned earlier, he had advised me to pursue the hobby.

The poem was translated into Hindi by a Hindi translator, Ms. Saroj of Chandigarh and the Hindi version was published in a journal in 2007, after a span of about thirty-seven years.

The other teaching staff were also good and taught us with the same dedication and sincerity. The tutorials and the tests kept us very busy and initially I found it difficult to cope up with the speed that the semester system dictated. Finally, I adopted the mantra—be attentive in class and solve the tutorial problems or understand their solution if solved by any other student. This process worked comfortably for me.

During the initial months I would keep account of my daily expenditure and show it to my father. My father insisted that I do not show him the details as he had full faith in me. This made me much more responsible and I tried my level best not to be extravagant, being fully conscious of his responsibilities and faith in me.

Looking back, I strongly feel that his belief in me made me what I am today. I am deliberately including this experience for, this event made me very responsible not only as a student but also during my subsequent years in service and as a parent as well.

After passing my second semester examination, I was happy to learn that I was entitled to the merit scholarship of Rupees seventy-five per month. This was a reasonable amount in those days when the mess bills would generally not exceed one hundred fifty rupees. My parents, as was expected, were very happy and proud when they learnt about it.

This added another dimension of responsibility to me because firstly, for continuation of the merit scholarship it was necessary that the scholarship holder pass every semester examination with a minimum of sixty percent marks. Secondly, in the event of having to reappear in any subject, which used to be very common in engineering, the scholarship would cease.

I was conscious of these conditions and by Gods grace continued to avail the scholarship throughout my tenure as a student in the college. This was one of the primary factors, which made me confident in whatever I did then and since.

During the course of our second winter break, while I was at home, a misfortune befell on us. It was a chilly night in the month of January. Everything was covered in a thick blanket of snow. Just before dawn, asleep on the first floor of our house, we were awoken by the sound of desperate cries. My father opened the window and I remember the scene when we saw our neighbour's house in flames. All of us rushed out and tried to take out whatever little was possible before the spreading flames engulfed our house as well and reduced it to ashes. The three families, consisting of my two uncles and ours, were left without anything including a roof over our head, in a matter of minutes. My father's circle of friendship was so intense that within an hour a friend of his sheltered us in his spacious house. We continued to live in that house, very comfortably, for a number of years, until I completed my engineering.

The experience of having been a hostler had contributed a lot to the development of my personality. One such notable aspect was the development of the characteristic to face the 'fear of the unknown', whenever the situation arose. I also applaud the way my father moulded my psyche, as a child, illustrated earlier in Part I. He succeeded to an appreciable extent in driving away the initial vestiges of fear in me.

I recall that during the summers there used to be an exhibition in Srinagar, called the 'Industrial Exhibition'. This was organized by the J&K Govt. and would be conducted on a very wide canvas. People, from every nook and corner of Kashmir, would come to visit it. There would be plenty of music and various other items/exhibits of interest. One item, which everybody waited for, was that of the 'Fireman'. It was conducted towards the closing every day. The fireman would climb a tall metallic pole that was permanently positioned next to a wide pond, full of water. After climbing the pole, he would throw down some pieces of paper to see the direction of the wind and to judge its intensity. Once ready he would, to the amazement of onlookers, set himself on fire. The pond below would be simultaneously lit. He would then jump like a fireball and fall into the pond with a bang. There would be a lot of gasps from the crowd followed by a thunderous applause. This stunt was further made famous in the film 'Haathi Mere Sathi' by the superstar Rajesh Khanna.

Coming back, one day after college, my two roommates and I boarded a city bus to the exhibition, in the heart of the city, about twelve kilometers from the hostel. After reaching the exhibition ground the three of us pooled in our money and gave it to Vijay, one of us, to keep in his custody. We were short of money and had just enough to afford our return tickets, by bus, to the hostel. Vijay, now the custodian of our money, started playing hide and seek to make us aware of his importance, at least, at that time. Though I tried to stick to him there was a lot of rush and it so happened that I was separated from the other two and despite my frantic attempts, failed to locate them. Soon it was almost midnight and I was left with neither a penny in my pocket nor anywhere to go—a very unique yet frightening situation. With no other option in sight I decided to walk back to my hostel, fully aware of the fact that the journey would take me through lonely and deserted surroundings during that dark night. I recalled my experience as a child, mentioned deliberately in the preceding chapter, when my father had largely succeeded in removing the fear of darkness from my mind. The extent of his success was on test that night. I started walking back towards the hostel and after covering a distance of a couple of kilometers, the road took me to one end of the 'Dal Lake'. I walked alone until I was about to reach the 'Nagin Bridge', situated over the confluence of 'Dal' and 'Nagin' lakes. It is the same bridge, which had figured in many 'Bollywood' movies until the mid-eighties. It used to be a favourite location for most directors.

The faint image of the bridge over the lake seemed engulfed by an envelope of darkness. I was in no mood to appreciate one of the most beautiful spots in the world, especially at that hour, for obvious reasons. To add to the already eerie setting, something strange happened when I stepped onto the bridge. With darkness all around, I could see the faint profile of a tall man crossing the bridge. Soon I could hear him shouting at what appeared to be the sky. "Oh! My Lord, where is my son? He hasn't returned after the war and no one has seen him dead. Allah! Give me my flesh and blood. Today, I have come to demand that, don't send me back disappointed", he kept repeating.

This continued even as I walked a few steps behind him. As I got closer I realised that he was praying with folded hands, in the direction of the 'Hazratbal Mosque', locally known as *Dargah*, which was situated very near to our hostel. The *Dargah* is world famous and houses the holy relic of Prophet Mohammad, as mentioned earlier. The man didn't realise or acknowledge my presence, though I walked almost next to him. I guess the pangs of separation from his son made him focus all attention on the holy *Dargah*.

I was taken aback by his high-pitched cries, which were fraught with pain. He gave me company, though inadvertently, until my hostel gate from where I slipped inside the hostel campus. He continued ahead probably to the *Dargah*. His cries still ring in my ears with a hope that God would have, someday, reunited the forlorn father with his son. Amen!

Vijay the custodian of our money that night and I grew very close during our college days. He subsequently married my cousin. A few years back he passed away after a prolonged fight with cancer. May his soul rest in peace!

We three roommates kept our room spick and span, as compared with other students. On one occasion, the final year students got a message that the Provost was making a sudden visit to the hostel, to discuss some important issues. The students came hurriedly to our room to inform us that the meeting would take place in our room, for obvious reasons. Needless to say, the Provost appreciated our well-maintained room, while leaving after his discussions.

As I progressed from one semester to the other, the syllabus and the subjects started becoming broader and more complex. All the faculties had common classes until fifth semester and by that time; all of us were introduced to mechanical drawing, physics, chemistry, architecture engineering, topographic surveys, electrical engineering, civil engineering, mathematics, etc. Subjects related to humanities, which mainly included English Literature, Economics, Civics, Political Science and sociology, were also covered by the end of the fifth semester. Machine Drawing and Electrical Engineering were considered comparatively tougher than the others.

I remember, I was excited after writing the electrical engineering paper to my satisfaction, in the fourth semester. We had a day's break before the next paper. I had a fascination for movies, and this was excuse enough to indulge. I decided to watch a movie that evening, in the city and freshen up for the next paper. The cinema halls were generally located in the city and were quite far. I decided to see Dilip Kumar's 'Dastan', which had been newly released in a theatre called 'Firdous'.

I enjoyed the movie which ended around 11P.M. I had planned to board a city bus to come back to the hostel. To my utter surprise I was told that on the route, from 'Firdous' to our hostel, buses don't run that late because the area in between, known as 'Lal Bazar', was not considered particularly safe. There were a number of taxis but they also refused for the same reason.

It had been almost a year since I walked back to my hostel from the exhibition, as detailed in the previous paragraphs. On this fateful night, after waiting a long time, until everybody including the cinema staff left, I, once again left with no option, decided to walk back through lonely streets, with no habitation over long stretches and through the infamous 'Lal Bazar', to get back to my hostel. To add to this predicament, I was not even sure about the route. Mustering all my courage I took the first step forward and very confidently too.

I started my journey, on foot, through the lonely roads, with habitation beginning to thin with each step. At every corner I was received by dogs, barking and dutifully following me until the end of their respective territories. I had heard somewhere that when the street dogs bark and run behind a person, one should not run else they may attack and bite. I followed this logic, had a few stones handy and over the course realised that it worked.

This orchestra, of barking dogs, continued behind me. By the time one group stopped, at the termination of the territory, the other group would start. I was literally kept on my toes more so because I was aware that the area was not considered safe. In the midst of deserted streets, barking dogs and the darkness of the night I didn't realise when I crossed 'Lal Bazar'. I grew so used to the company of the barking dogs that whenever they stopped, I felt uneasy. Just when I started getting a feeling that my destination was nearing, to my horror, I found that the street suddenly terminated after a couple of houses. There was no sign of existence beyond a few meters. I continued to walk ahead only to be greeted by a huge lake, which literally started where the pathway ended. By that time I think it must have been around 1:00 or 1:30 A.M. if not later.

As my anguish began to dawn the tension began to grow. I saw a few boats anchored on the bank of the lake and realised that it must be the 'Nagin Lake'. My destination was thus, on the opposite side of the lake and there was no other option but to cross it by boat. I went back and forth around the houses, where obviously the fishermen or boatmen resided, with the hope of finding someone who would ferry me across.

Mustering courage, I knocked at the doors of a few houses. "What is wrong with you at this time of the night?", was the angry response from one. I requested if someone could take me across to the other side of the lake and added that I was on my way to the engineering college hostel. I was told that two to three houses ahead I should knock and call for 'Zoona', who could possibly help. This should have brought me some relief except I realised that 'Zoona' was a 'female' Kashmiri name and the idea of calling out the name at that awkward hour was not very encouraging. I feared being beaten blue and black by the locals. Contemplating the fact that I was anyways being beaten black and blue from within, though not very apparent, I decided to call.

Initially, I called out to 'Zoona' slowly but then got louder until yet again there was again a crude response from a male voice, "Why the hell are you calling a lady, so loudly and at such a time of the night? Have some shame." I apologized profusely, stated the facts and added that the name was given to me by one of his neighbours and in good faith. The man was nice enough to offer his help readily and took me in his boat to the opposite bank of the lake, which as I had guessed was the 'Nagin Lake'. I was dropped off just adjacent to the world famous 'Nagin Club' which is located on one of the best spots in the world. Foreign tourists from all over the world generally came to this club, as it was a favourite sailing haunt. I thanked the boatman from the bottom of my heart and found him to be very noble and helpful. He extended his help at a time when he could have easily avoided it.

As I started crossing the 'Nagin Club', I remembered that a few months back, we had seen 'Dev Anand' and 'Hema Malini', shooting on the jetty, for a couple of hours, for the movie 'Sharif Badmash'. Like on the previous occasion, I was not in the frame of mind to appreciate the beauty of the spot, though I otherwise loved it.

My room was still about one and a half kilometers ahead and my only aim was to reach it as soon as possible. I walked on the lonely road with huge apple gardens, laden with apples called *Hazratbal* on my left. When I reached the room, my roommates were fast asleep, probably tired of waiting for me. I didn't waste any time and jumped into the bed.

It may be worthwhile to mention another incident in connection with another movie in 'Srinagar' since I believe that these incidents eventually had a strong impact on my personality.

I was with my younger brother who was to appear for the first profession of his M.B.B.S. examination. Due to the temporary closure of the medical college hostel I joined him for some time and we lived in a rented room, on the second floor of a house, located in the 'Karannagar' area of 'Srinagar'. One late evening I arrived from my college and my elder cousin arrived from 'Sopore', almost at the same time. He, like me, was also fond of movies. We decided to go for a late night movie in order to not disturb my brother, while he prepared for the examination. The landlady was strict and didn't expect us to come late to the house. We told our younger brother that we would be back by mid night. He planned to stay up and study through the night and thus asked us to give a gentle knock at the main gate so he that he could come and open the gate.

After watching the movie, we walked back home for about four kilometers. To our surprise he didn't respond to the gentle knock, and thereafter not even to the loud ones. We were convinced that he had fallen asleep. After making a dozen loud calls we decided to leave the place to avoid facing the landlady's fury. We walked back to 'Lal Chowk' where we tried a few hotels unsuccessfully, it being around 2:00 A.M. by then. Being winter; we started shivering due to the biting cold even though we had several layers of clothing on, including flannel shirts, thick sweaters and woolen coats.

Finally, with no hope in sight, we decided to go to the city bus stand and sleep in a bus. Some of the city buses, in those days, generally had no doors and both of us occupied three seats each and lay down to sleep. The bitter cold prevented us from getting good night's sleep; however, we did manage to grab a few winks. I was awakened by the sound of a few donkeys braying while they came close to the bus, rather our bedroom. It was around dawn, I woke my cousin, informing him that we had some more friends waiting for us. He got up and we laughed aloud. On our way back we shared the experience of seeing a movie under such trying circumstances. My cousin is now no more, may his soul rest in peace!

My passion for movies often turned a simple visit to a cinema hall into a memorable adventure. I remember my father would tell me any incident, good or bad, is always an experience and cultivation of any experience, good or bad, is always good.

Such experiences of hostel life must have unconsciously helped me imbibe fearlessness into my personality during those years. Maybe such incidents also helped me develop a fearless approach in later life as well, where on occasions I had to march daringly during dark nights through thick jungles of inhospitable areas in 'Mon' and 'Tuensang' districts of 'Nagaland', or climb the snow-clad mountains of 'Arunachal Pradesh' right up to the 'McMahon line,' or pierce through the dense jungles of 'Assam' in areas infested with wild elephants.

Life as an engineering student continued and there came a time when I realised that I was not cut out for 'Chemical Engineering'. This was mainly because I had the germ of joining the Defence Forces and there was no entry for chemical engineers. I spoke to my father about wanting to switch over to 'Mechanical Engineering'. As was his nature, he had no objection and left the decision to me.

In our college the Mechanical Engineering faculty was considered very strict and tough and some of my friends warned me about this. Many of them who were in Mechanical Engineering switched over to 'Civil Engineering', which was considered comparatively easier. I applied for the change and received approval from the academic council. I finally landed in the Mechanical Engineering faculty, which was the start of yet another phase of my life as a student.

By the time I finished my eighth semester, a Board of Naval Officers landed in our college to select the students from the Mechanical and Electrical Engineering faculties, for commission in the Indian Navy. Many students applied and so did I. The board conducted broad interviews during the preliminary selection and the final selection was to be conducted by the Service Selection Board after we passed our tenth semester. All the students who would finally be selected, after tenth semester, were to be paid the salary of a sub lieutenant for the duration of final year.

All the students who had volunteered were interviewed and only two students were selected. One of them was from Electrical Engineering branch and I was the proud second, selected from Mechanical Engineering branch. I, however, was not sure of joining as I had learned that after marriage there was substantial separation of the officers from their families, unless they were posted on the shore. I put this specific question to one of the board members and he replied in a lighter vein that it was fine because every time one returns from the ship to the shore, it's a fresh honeymoon.

Meanwhile, I progressed from one semester to the other. Our HOD of Mechanical Engineering, Dr. T. V. Balasubramanium, was both a great academician and a very good human being. We were told that he was also on the visiting faculty of some foreign Universities. He was an authority on Machine Design and taught us the subject for a couple of years. Once we decided to miss a lecture, ensuring that it was not one of Dr. Balasubramanium's. Such an activity was termed as *Let Us*.

The next day, to our surprise, he came to the class after the matter had been reported to him, in his capacity as HOD. He said something that was to leave an impact on most of us, "Yesterday you have wasted the efforts and the hard-earned money of your parents by missing a lecture. Believe me, as of today I can't afford to admit my son in a college like this since the cost of education is expensive and beyond the means of an average person like me. You will realise this the day you become a parent". Probably it was the last time we attempted any *Let Us*.

In the final year, we were allotted project work, by the HOD himself. This was part of and an important activity in the degree course in engineering. To my utter surprise I was given a project on solar energy on—'The Design and Fabrication of a Solar Vegetable Drier'. It was one of the latest topics those days and there was not much material available, neither in our college nor in the university libraries. Dr. Balasubramanium had realised this and told me to work harder since it was not a straightforward project. Mr. Nomani, Assistant Professor, was nominated as my guide since he was an expert on 'Heat Transfer'. He was known to be serious and hardly smiled. When I met him, after the project was allotted, he told me, very frankly, that he had no knowledge about the subject and would not readily know where to source materials on solar energy. He assured me that he would provide me complete moral support and I was fully convinced of the same.

There were some models of solar energy on display in the thermodynamics lab, placed on the initiative of one of our Asst. Professors, who had done some initial work on the subject. When I went to the lab, to my utter horror I found the models had been removed, as was the related literature from our library. I approached the Professor, who feigned ignorance. I ignored him and felt that he might have had some personality clash with my guide who generally would mind his business and was not too social by nature. I requested my HOD to change the subject of my project but he refused stating that he had a lot of confidence that I could do it.

I then met all the professors and Head of the Departments of the five branches of engineering of our college. As luck would have it, the new HOD of Chemical Engineering had just returned after completing his tenure in one of the Universities in America. He told me that there was a Professor, who was the HOD of Mechanical Engineering of an Engineering College in West Indies, who had done some work on the application of solar energy in the USA. He gave me his address in the West Indies. I bought an *aerogram* and wrote a simple request knowing fairly well that the chances of this working were slim. The letter might have reflected my innocence and haplessness.

One day, to my great surprise the postman delivered a huge parcel covered with brown paper. It came from some university in the West Indies. On opening the packet, I found vast material on the applications of solar energy. What a man and what a gesture! I thanked God and realised that there were still some good people in the world, which is what kept it going.

I perused through the material day and night and started work with zeal and confidence. My guide was very happy and encouraged me a lot, as did my HOD who called me home, vetted the design aspect of my project and gave his valuable suggestions. Finally I designed and fabricated the 'Solar Vegetable Drier'. Even the workshop staff were quite excited about the project. One day I, along with the workshop staff, lined up the fabricated equipment below the faculty building to verify the working of the model, for the first time. My guide was watching us from the first floor of the faculty block. On observing the black smoke gushing out of the exhaust with an appreciable speed he got excited and was literally about to jump. He came down and noted the increase of about 60 degrees between the temperature of the air at the inlet and that at the outlet. I saw a huge smile on his face. The notion, that he never smiled, fell flat that very instance.

We appeared in our tenth semester examination and in the interim I responded to an advertisement calling for applicants for 'Permanent Commission' in the Armed Forces. It mentioned that the candidates appearing in the final year engineering examination were also eligible to apply. I applied and received an acknowledgement from the Adjutant General's Branch with intimation of the date, duration and location of the 'Service Selection Board', abbreviated as S. S. B.

Subsequently, we were also intimated about the tentative date for our project viva voce, in accordance with the availability of the external examiner from the Patiala Engineering College. To my dismay I found that both the dates clashed. I checked with Dr. Balasubramanium, the HOD, if the date for examination of the 'Project Work' could be changed, as otherwise I wouldn't be able to appear for the S.S.B. I was frank in telling him that it was difficult to qualify for the S.S.B but I still wanted to avail the chance. I remember his words even today, "Don't worry, I would not like to come in the way of a good career." He contacted the external examiner, discussed my case and got the date changed. What a great man!

Our examiner from Patiala Engineering College arrived on the specified date. I was given the maximum marks by him for the project work. He applauded me, during the viva voce, in the presence of my HOD and guide. Dr. Balasubramanium, made a special mention regarding the 'Project Work' and the 'Merit Scholarship' in my Character Certificate, which I hold very close to my heart even today.

With regard to the SSB, I have covered it in detail, in Chapter 10 of this book.

# Chapter 8

# BEYOND ACADEMICS

With both the lush green campuses of the college located on the bank of the world famous 'Dal Lake', the ambience of the college was mesmerising, to say the least. 'Teen Chinari', the famous tourist spot, was visible from our hostel and at times tempted us to row the boats of our 'College Boating Club' right up to it. It was a small but delightful island in the middle of the 'Dal Lake' guarded by three well spread magnificent Chinar trees and attractively fenced all around. We had seen many 'Bollywood' movies being shot at this spot. There was another 'Char Chinari' located near 'Nehru Park'.

As mentioned earlier, the old campus was densely populated with huge 'Chinar' trees, so much so that the sun rays had to force their way down by piercing through the branches. Even then, they hardly succeeded in altering the seamless shade, woven by the overlapping branches, clothed with broad palm shaped 'Chinar' leaves. In autumn, it was a remarkable sight when the Chinar leaves would turn fire brown, wither and fall on the ground. These leaves covered the ground seamlessly and the whole area, in totality, seemed to be on fire. Such breath taking scenes have been captured intelligently by some renowned 'Bollywood' film directors, in their famous movies as well as by some photographers of great repute. The overall ambience of the college made it, what I called, 'God's Own Institution'.

The college encouraged its students to take part in creative work. As a result of this there were many clubs, which enabled genuine students to participate. In fact some of the clubs nurtured a few students to become professional in accordance with their aptitude and keen interest.

I remember the first activity that I witnessed, after joining the college, was the get together of students and staff on the eve of 'Janamashtami'. The event was organised in a huge hall known as 'Common Room'. The Principal Dr. Munis Raza addressed the gathering. Many, including myself, were left spellbound hearing him speak about 'Lord Krishna' and the importance of 'Janamashtami'. This was not only because of the content of his speech but also on account of his impressive style and communication skill.

Similarly, on the eve of 'Guru Nanak Ji's' birthday a memorable function was organized in the college. Two famous Punjabi singers of the time, Sh. Asa Singh Mastan and Smt. Surinder Kaur, had been invited to grace the celebration. Sh. Bagwan Sahay, the then Honorable Governor of Jammu and Kashmir was the chief guest. The two singers arrived a little late and Sh. Asa Singh apologised saying they were delayed as a tyre of their car, on the side on which Smt. Surinder Kaur sat, burst on the way. There was a burst of laughter, which condoned their delay and set the ball rolling. The atmosphere, for the rest of the evening, was full of melodious tunes and they kept the audience spellbound by punctuating the songs with some anecdotes and jokes.

A series of lectures on 'Guru Nanak Ji' followed as well as the address by the Governor. However, the person who stole the show that evening was Mr. Phun Sung, a lecturer from our Mechanical Engineering Department. He was an alumnus of our college and was known to have been a brilliant student. His background was interesting, in its own way. He was from a very backward area of the Ladakh province, in the state of Jammu & Kashmir. His hard work added merit and value to his personality. He had an impressive command over spoken English. On being asked by the students about his exceptional spoken English skills, he said that he would listen to the 'Voice of America' very often to set his pronunciation right and thereafter he practiced extensively to perfect his Spoken English. He cleared the Indian Administrative Services examination with flying colours and held very important appointments including one in the PMO (Prime Minister's Office), Secretary Education and later Chief Secretary for the state of Jammu & Kashmir.

His first appointment was as SDM, Sopore, my hometown. I remember an instance when I was about to join Indian Military Academy, Dehradun. I had visited his office to get some certificates attested and found him busy in his chamber, which uniquely had the layout of a courtroom. He was hearing the arguments of a case regarding an old lady. While waiting, I couldn't help think that the college had lost a very popular and brilliant teacher while the engineering community a good Mechanical Engineer.

I entered his chamber, conveyed my regards and told him about my selection to the Indian Armed Forces and the purpose of my visit. Welcoming him to my hometown I, on a lighter note, mentioned that he had come a long way beyond his core subject of Mechanical Engineering. He laughed and replied that in the years to come even he would like to see how much of Mechanical Engineering I would be doing in the Army. At this we both had a hearty laugh. He congratulated and wished me a good career in the Armed Forces. He advised me to work hard since it was not very easy for one to rise beyond a 'Major' in the Army unless they did exceptionally well. In later years I was to realise how correct he was.

Returning back to where we left, as part of the extracurricular activities in our college, we had a 'Music club', which would conduct a grand annual function every year. Sh. Rajendhar Kachru, the famous *ghazal* singer was the Secretary of the club and had made the club well known in the entire university. He was my senior by a few years. Later on, he became a popular *ghazal* singer and was often seen on 'Doordarshan', the national TV Channel.

A day before one such Annual event, Sh. Kachru told another student Sh. M. P. Singh and myself to join him to present a 'Group Song'. The event was to be held in the famous 'Tagore Hall', Srinagar. Sh. M. P. Singh was a good singer, while I was not a singer by any means. However, I didn't refuse the offer, as I was confident that their talent would camouflage my limitations. The song was a huge hit on the day and some people started to congratulate me as well, I guess they had not heard me sing alone. To keep up this false reputation I never attempted it again.

In addition to the 'Music Club' we also had a 'Band Club'. It was fully equipped with all western instruments that one could usually only see in professional orchestras. The coach, Sh. Ghambir Singh, had retired from the Army Band and was a master of all the western instruments. I tried learning the 'Cornet', which is a smaller version of 'Trumpet'. In the fifth semester I was made the captain of the club. This, I must warn you, was not because of my proficiency in any western musical instruments but because of the administrative skills I exhibited in running the club.

I proposed to change the name of the club to 'The Orchestra Club', which was approved by the Professor-in-charge, Sh. B. L. Ticku. He was a Professor in the Electrical Engineering Department. I succeeded in organizing a program on Radio Kashmir, Srinagar where our western tunes were recorded and played as part of the 'Youth Program'. One morning, by chance, my parents turned on the radio; they were thrilled to hear my name and the tunes that followed. We soaked in every ounce of the publicity the program gave us. Each of us was given a certificate and fifty rupees by the producer of the program.

The college had a 'Boating Club', which carried out many activities and the celebration of their annual event used to be very professional. This club was by far the best amongst the rest. Their annual function was generally organized on the 'Nagin Lake'. A few houseboats would be hired for the occasion. During one such event our 'Orchestra Club' was invited to perform an array of western tunes. Dressed to kill, in our college blazers and lead by the coach, we were gracefully and prominently perched on the roof of a 'House Boat'.

We punctuated other events such as diving, boating, surfing etc. with our melodious tunes. This added charm and colour to the function so much so that the chief guest, The Honorable Governor of Jammu &Kashmir asked our principal to accompany him to the rooftop of the houseboat where we were positioned. He came up to applaud us and mentioned that initially he had mistaken us for a professional orchestra hired for the event. He congratulated and advised us to keep up the good work.

Our 'Common Room' was huge and housed a number of Chess Boards, Carom Boards, Cards Tables, a very huge HMV Gramophone, almost the size of a piano apart from other items for entertainment. The front wall of the room was fully glazed and one could view the delightful ambience of the college while sitting here, including the magnificent 'Dal Lake'. There were entertainment corners; each manned by the concerned Secretary of the particular activity. I happened to be the Secretary of the 'Quiz Board'.

The Common Room was so impressive that on one occasion Sh. Ajit Wadekar, the then Captain of Indian Cricket team, on a visit to our college mentioned that he had yet to see a 'Common' or rather 'Entertainment' room like that in any institution.

## Chapter 9

# BITTER PUNCTUATIONS

The academics and extracurricular activities went hand in hand, complimenting each other. However there were times when some bitter instances threatened to mar the great culture of the institution. One such incident happened during the second year of my stay in the college. A small scuffle between students turned ugly, ultimately leading to a fight between two communities. The college authorities closed the college for an indefinite period and hostlers were instructed to vacate the hostel with immediate effect. Buses were arranged and we, with our luggage, left the hostel for our respective homes. Three months later, we were called back, after losing about a semester each.

A similar incident took place a few years later and we met a similar fate. Once again, we were asked to vacate the hostel, head home, only to return when the college opened after a few months. In the bargain, we ended up losing about a year and this hurt every student dearly. Such bitter events make up for some bad memories but then, as they say, all's well that ends well. I am sure that the students who were the genesis of these undesirable events would have matured enough and may have repented for the damage they had caused to many careers.

I remember, during one such forced vacation, I was on the lookout for an opportunity to teach in any school, against a leave vacancy of a regular teacher. In the meantime, one of the richest men of Sopore approached my uncle to teach his three children science and mathematics. My uncle suggested me to teach these children. The children studied in well-reputed residential schools in Himachal Pradesh and had come home, for a few months, during the school vacation. I accepted the offer readily wanting to keep myself usefully busy.

The first day when I went to teach the children, a huge gate led me to the magnificent house with stunning European looks. The house reflected the amalgamation of two cultures, which was apparent as their father was a Muslim and the mother a well-cultured Christian. The personality of the children exuded the essence of western culture. I found them very intelligent, receptive and affectionate. Over time I developed a lot of affection for these children. Their mother later told me that they looked forward to my arrival each day.

After completing a month I was paid my fee. This incidentally was the first earning of my life. Their mother was pleased with the manner in which I taught the children. She felt that I was doing a social service by teaching the children to their satisfaction. Finally, the day came when I had to depart. The separation was very tough and touching. The children gifted me a pair of cufflinks, which I still hold dear to my heart. I don't really know where they are, today, but am sure that they must have done well for themselves. May God bless them!

# PART V

## The Transition

# Chapter 10

# STUDENT TO A GENTLEMAN CADET

My roommate, Inder Bhat, and I were both from the same faculty of Mechanical Engineering and lived in the same room within the hostel for a long time. We had great understanding and regard for each other and shared a very healthy competition all along and generally celebrated, when one of us scored better than the other, in class or university tests. In my personal view, he was a better student. Both of us wanted to do a post-graduation in 'Industrial Engineering' and accordingly opted for the elective subjects. At the back of my mind and through my growing up years, I had always harboured a fascination for the Army. After completing the final semester examinations, we packed our bags, vacated the hostel and left for our respective homes. Dr. Inder Bhat, as he is now known, finally did his doctorate in 'Robotics' from IIT Kanpur and, at present, is a Director at one of the National Institutes of Technology. He enjoys a great reputation at the national level, both as an academician and as an administrator.

I had responded to the advertisement for a Permanent Commission in the Indian Army after the final semester examination. Dr. Balasubramanium, our HOD, had been gracious enough to respond to my request to advance the date for the examination of my project work, thus enabling me to attend the Service Selection Board (SSB) at Bhopal. My parents encouraged me even though I told them that there was hardly any chance of my selection but I still wanted to see where I stood.

My father got a number of rigs stitched as specified in the Ministry of Defence 'Call Letter'. In my heart of hearts, I felt that it was a wasteful expenditure for the chances of my selection were very feeble since I had not prepared for SSB at all. The fare and the lodging, for the duration of the SSB, were borne by the Army and hence I considered it a paid vacation.

I left for Bhopal and while changing the train at New Delhi Railway Station I came across one of my course mates from Electrical Engineering who was also on his way to the SSB at Allahabad. I found him engrossed in a book, which contained the details about SSB interviews and as it appeared that he seemed to have thoroughly prepared for it. I was as unprepared as one could be and didn't know a thing about the SSB tests. I wished him luck, bid farewell and caught the train to Bhopal. I reached Bhopal a day early and decided to watch the famous movie 'Sholay', which had released a few days earlier. Apart from the heroes, I remember that the audience whistled and danced, in the cinema hall, on the appearance of comedian 'Jagdeep', on screen as 'Surma Bhopali'.

The following day I reported to the office of SSB Bhopal. I was shown the barrack where our batch had to stay for the duration of the SSB and met some of the batch mates who had already arrived. Our activities started the next day. To begin with, we were told to write the 'Intelligence Test', which more or less filtered the candidates. I thought I did reasonably well in the test.

Subsequently, other tests followed which included 'Group Tasks', 'Individual Tasks', 'Obstacle Courses', 'Debates', 'Group Discussion' etc, over the remaining four days. The 'Obstacle Courses', was a time-bound test and probably I was not up to it since I had not attempted any such exercise before. Keeping this in mind, I chose to attempt such obstacles, which carried more marks even though they appeared comparatively difficult. Knowing that it was either now or never I gave my one hundred percent to complete as many obstacles as I could. In the bargain, I got injured and was left with a number of 'tattoos' spread all over my body, in the form of bruises.

On the third day I faced the main interview. Colonel Daniels, the President of the 'Service Selection Board' was in the chair. He enquired into my family background and asked me how many brothers and sisters I had. I hesitatingly replied that we were five brothers, as though he would impose a fine on me. He understood my state of mind, smiled and said that he had seven brothers and a few sisters as well. Making me feel comfortable he then enquired about my hobbies and extracurricular activities. I mentioned my achievements in school, NCC, debates, and the Orchestra Club. He also asked me some pertinent questions about the 'Cornet', the instrument I played, including the difference between the 'Trumpet' and the 'Cornet'. I ensured that I didn't bluff during the interview and was honest whenever I didn't know a particular answer. The interview was very elaborate and lasted for about an hour. At the end of it I felt that I had done reasonably well. Colonel Daniels also seemed satisfied with my answers.

During this period I remembered how, as a boy I would envy one Major Pushkar Das, whom I had known closely as he belonged to our area and was related to one of my uncles. I remembered that whenever he would come home on leave, we kids would observe him very keenly and hope to grow up to be an Army officer like him, someday. He later rose to the rank of Lieutenant Colonel. Incidentally, he is the father of Ms. Sunanda Pushkar who is now married to Dr. Shashi Tharoor, Minister in the Central Government.

There were many more tests and during these four days of elaborate tests and evaluations, the members of the SSB Board would have definitely left no stone unturned to analyse us completely. They would have got to know, in-depth, our strength and weaknesses. We learnt that about three to four batches of the candidates, who had reported earlier, were completely rejected and not a single candidate had been selected. This made each one of us very conscious, particularly those who had toiled hard even undergoing elaborate coaching. Frankly, by now, I began to look at this experience as being more than a 'paid holiday', as I had thought earlier.

Finally, we were called for, what was termed the 'Conference.' This was the last event of SSB wherein candidates would individually face the entire Service Selection Board, with a lady psychologist in attendance. Each candidate was made to stand and members shot their specific questions. It may be noted that at this juncture results of all the tests were at the disposal of the members of the board. The President of the SSB asked me if I had attended coaching classes to which I replied by mentioning that I had not even read a single article on the SSB; forget attending coaching classes. I added that this was because I had been busy with my final semester examination and the project work, mentioned earlier.

I was also asked to guess who would be selected from my batch. I mentioned three names, which included mine. From the body language of the Board members, I started to get a positive feel about my inclusion. I felt it was a blessing in disguise that I had reported as a raw and fresh candidate else may be I would have tried to be somebody I was not.

When the 'Conference Session' of all the batch mates was over, we were called in a hall for the declaration of the results. There was pin drop silence, broken only by the announcement of the names of the successful candidates. I was thrilled when my name was called. Surprisingly the two other names I had suggested earlier were also called. The three of us were asked to stay back for our medicals while the rest were encouraged to try again. On top of the world, I was very impatient to convey the news to my parents.

The three of us were asked to shift to a different barrack until the completion of our medical tests, to be conducted by the Medical Board in Military Hospital (MH), Bhopal. Like the selection process, the medicals also involved elaborate tests that continued for a couple of days. I was temporarily rejected and asked to undergo a minor surgery for removal of the DNS (Deviated Nasal Symptom), while the other two were declared fit. I had to report to the Medical Board at Bhopal MH after undergoing the surgery within the specified time.

I rushed home. My maternal uncle, SH. T. N. Ticku, about whom I have mentioned before, knew the doctors in Srinagar Hospital very well and got Dr. Abdul Ahad, one of the best ENT specialists of Srinagar Medical College, to perform my operation. I guess it was because of my uncle's reputation that many renowned doctors came to enquire about my welfare in the hospital, which included Dr. Guru who later rose to become a Minister in J&K Cabinet but was subsequently killed by the militants in Srinagar. I was also looked up by many medical college students who were my younger brother's course mates in the same medical college.

After a few days, I left for Bhopal and reported to Colonel Hamid Ali, the Commandant of Bhopal MH, and the President of the Medical Board. He immediately placed me as I had innocently mailed him a letter informing him about my surgery and a little delay in reporting to MH Bhopal. He directed me to the concerned surgeon. To my utter shock the specialist announced that he was not satisfied with the operation and wrote a remark to the effect.

Colonel Hamid Ali called me and I could sense that he was upset. From his talks, I gauged that he had a soft corner for me. He told me, "Sunny, the fact is that the operation has not been done to the satisfaction of our specialist and I think it will not be possible for you to join the Indian Military Academy. Don't lose heart, try next time."

He read the evident disappointment in my eyes. I couldn't help think that I was now being thrown out after getting so close to my destination. Colonel Ali pondered for a while and said what was then music to my ears, "I will declare you 'Provisionally Fit' and give you a chance to report to IMA, Dehradun. However, you will have to face the Medical Board in IMA". While saying so he opined that the chances of my clearing the Medical Board were slim. Although a half chance, I more than readily accepted. Understanding the rarity of the offer, I couldn't help but appreciated his positive approach and thanked him sincerely.

On my return from Bhopal, I was asked to come to the newly built house, which my father had constructed, in the new colony of my hometown Sopore. My parents moved to their own house after a span of about five years since the fire engulfed our house, as mentioned before. We remain ever grateful to my father's friend who had sheltered us in his house, since that fateful day when the fire had left us hapless and helpless on mother earth, covered by thick snow and without any protection overhead.

On hearing of my arrival, my uncle came and took me to Dr. Abdul Ahad, the surgeon who had operated upon me, and told him the entire story. He rechecked and said that he felt the operation had been perfect. He fiddled with my nose with a few more pricks resulting in a few drops of blood, advised me to report to IMA and wished me good luck.

I went back home and after a couple of days I received an intimation from the Adjutant General's Branch to report to 'Alamein Company', IMA Dehradun, with immediate effect since the training of the batch had already started. My parents and other relatives were very happy, but extremely apprehensive because of the rider that I may have to face the medical board again. I moved to Dehradun immediately though half-heartedly because of the fear of rejection by the medical board.

# Chapter 11

# ESSENCE OF THE INDIAN MILITARY ACADEMY

I reached the IMA on 26th January but the Academy was closed on account of it being Republic Day. I was thus asked to report to the SUO (Senior Under Officer) of the 'Alamein Company', who was a cadet from the senior batch. I kept my luggage somewhere in the corner and reported to him. I saw a number of cadets all around, some carrying a bicycle on their shoulders and some crawling over rubbles with bruises all around. They were probably my batch mates and were being punished, rather ragged, by the senior cadets, as a matter of routine.

On reporting, the SUO looked at me from top to bottom. I thought that I was smartly dressed in a double-breasted coat, bell-bottom trousers, shining black shoes, slightly long hair with reluctant natural curls on either side. He came out of his cabin from where he had a full view of his Company. He showed me the plight of my batch mates and said that these were some methods to make the cadets physically tough and there was nothing to feel bad about as they and their seniors had gone through this phase as well. I was getting mentally prepared to join the not-so-fortunate batch mates in the prevailing activity.

He further told me that our course had commenced a few weeks back and I was a late entrant. He then asked me about my hobbies. I told him that I play the 'mouth organ' and 'cornet'. He was very happy and asked if I had the mouth organ with me. I had one and he called all the seniors and his batch mates, and I entertained them. They were happy and asked some of my batch mates to take me to my room and help in carry my luggage.

I was allotted Platoon III of 'Alamein Company' by the SUO, who asked me to report to the Administrative Office of the Academy next morning. I was not disturbed the first day, thanks to the mouth organ. I made some friends and one of my immediate neighbours was Gentleman Cadet Pradeep Tambay, who is incidentally the younger brother of Flight Lieutenant Vijay Vasant Tambay, the Fighter Pilot whose aircraft, Sukhoi-7, was shot down at Shokot, Pakistan in the 1971 Indo Pak War. His wife, Ms. Damayanti Tambay, claims that Flt Lt Tambay was captured by the Pakistani Army in 1971 after the crash and is alive. He told me that his brother had married just six months before the occurrence of the unfortunate incident in 1971.

We see Ms. Damyanti Tambay very often on various TV channels whenever issues related to POWs captured by Pakistan are discussed. I faintly remember, though I am not very sure, that he once mentioned that she has been an 'Arjun Award' winner and a lawn tennis champion. I take this opportunity to applaud her steel strong patience for she has been fighting the pangs of separation so bravely for nearly forty-three years now. Tambay and I became very good friends. Though he wore the anguish of his brother's absence in his heart, he was always proud of his sacrifice.

The next day I went to the 'Administrative Office' and presented all my papers and original testimonials. I was admitted after completion of all the formalities, followed by a short medical examination. To my relief, the Academy had no issues as regards my medical fitness. I was told that I would be treated as a Second Lieutenant on paper for all matters relating to my pay and allowances, which would only be paid after I earned the commission. For all practical purposes I was a 'Gentleman Cadet (GC)' and would continue to be so until I passed out of the Academy. This meant that I had to obey all the instructors, which included Non-commissioned and Junior Commissioned officials (NCOs and JCOs), in accordance with the rules.

I was provided the guidance of an NCO in collecting clothes, muftis, curtains, bed sheets, innumerable sets of various uniforms including a few sets of dinner jackets, to be worn on different occasions and a 'bicycle' which was a lifeline since no other vehicle was authorized to the cadets till they passed out. I was directed to the

'Academy Barber Shop' where my long tresses were shorn off, announcing the commencement of my transition from a 'Student' to a 'Gentleman Cadet'.

The Academy tailor fitted everything in record time. The schedule of classes was displayed on the notice board and from that very moment the rut started—where one was not expected to ask why or expect any mercy, where instructors wore hearts of steel, where emotions had no place, where one carried out things which would otherwise be termed 'impossible', where it was drummed into the mind that the human body never tires and human endurance has no limits.

The next day started as early as 4:30 A.M., by which time one was expected to be ready in all respects and dressed for the physical training in (PT) rig or overalls. We reported to the designated Appointment Cadet, from the senior term for the 'Pre-muster'. He checked our turn out ensuring, under a torch, that we were cleanly shaven and after sometime, we peddled off on our cycles for the first period, which generally used to be rigorous PT, drill or swimming. We then cycled to our magnificent dining halls where we were served lavish food just as if we were princes. The first day I could not eat a full breakfast, for this very reason, it was too elaborate, lavish and rich. The senior student, who sat next to me on the dining table, told me that after a few days, I would feel the quantity deficient because of the appreciable physical exertion I would have to endure. I realised later that he was right.

After breakfast, we rushed to our rooms to put on the requisite uniform in accordance with the type of class/

lecture/demonstration. The very first day I found the cadets rushing, catching hold of their cycles and moving to the classes in squads, fighting against time since the distance between two consecutive classes was generally a few kilometers.

Cadets were restricted to cycle in squads of four or six else, they had to dismount the cycle and run with it to the destination while ensuring they report to the class on time. Thus, the cadets always joined the squads at the very first opportunity. Likewise, I joined a squad to go to one of the outdoor stands. On the way, I saw the cadets forming a single file to cycle down a hill. I cycled down the hill like the others but unfortunately skidded and rolled down cycle in tow, sometimes over me, sometimes under. I was bruised but there was no time to pay any attention to the wounds. I jumped back onto the cycle, without delay, just to make sure that I didn't miss the squad. I joined one of the squads and reached the outdoor stand on time.

The routine continued until lunch followed by punishments from senior appointments and under officers, on some pretext or the other. We were then lined up for games, horse riding and other club activities. In the evening, dressed in our working attire we sat for the study period during which silence was strictly maintained as it was common for our senior appointments and instructors to pay surprise visits. This tight routine continued and got tougher each day, to the extent that a few cadets decided to quit as they couldn't withstand such demanding physical and mental levels of toughness.

I continued to advance because of my determination though I was weak in physical aspects. I, however, didn't clear my drill test in time, which otherwise entitled a cadet to get a 'Liberty Pass' to visit the town on Sundays, dressed strictly in Academy Muftis since civil clothing was not allowed. Surprise checks were carried out in the town and defaulters were adequately punished.

One day, two cadet friends and myself decided to go to town in civil clothes, since we were not eligible for the 'Liberty Pass'. I put on a dashing printed shirt while they were in white shirts. As we reached the Dehradun clock tower, one of the instructors, who was riding a scooter with his wife, spotted us. This sure was a bad start to our adventure.

Cadets were only authorized to visit certain specified markets, restaurants and cinema halls in the town while other areas were out of bounds. While we sat for lunch in one such specified restaurant, we were shocked yet again by the presence of another instructor, who was with his family, seated a few tables away from us. We finished the lunch in haste and headed to a cinema hall to watch the movie 'Kabhi Kabhi'. During the interval, we realised that there was another instructor watching the movie with his family but fortunately, he occupied the row ahead of us and hence didn't see us, like the others did. We left the cinema hall a few minutes before the movie ended, picked up our cycles and rushed to the Academy, not knowing what lay in store for us. Punishments for committing such actions used to be harsh and one could easily ruin a week or two, if not more, completing the punishments specified during various times of the day while others would be relaxing in their rooms.

The next day, after breakfast, the instructor, a captain, who had seen us near the clock tower, sent for both my colleagues, through a cadet. They reported to him and as expected, came back with a sullen faces since they had received a week's punishment. Thankfully, when asked they feigned ignorance about the third person, which was me. I guess the instructor didn't recognize me because of the coloured printed shirt I had worn. To my surprise I was asked to report to the captain, who was still in the dining hall after probably reviewing the quality of food and service, being the assigned duty officer. I suspected that most probably my friends had snitched on me, but they completely negated the thought. When I met him, he asked, "Koul, how are you? How is the food?" Surprisingly after telling him that everything was fine, I was asked to leave. My friends, who were waiting for me, outside the dining hall, couldn't help having a hearty laugh.

In the meantime, we passed the drill test and didn't ever venture to repeat such an adventure in future. I must admit, I was one of the rare cadets who was never punished, more so since I seemed to have luck in my favour rather than on account of my discipline. As a result, my dossier, in which such punishments were recorded, was spotless.

Days passed and before we had realized, we had finished our second term. By this time, I had qualified all my physical and academic tests. We went home for the term break and returned refreshed to face the next phase with more vigour and strength for, the term was considered much tougher in all respects: academics, outdoor camps, physical tests and some commando exercises.

In academics, cadets were expected to be very specific and objective in their answers and there was no scope to beat around the bush. One had to do well in all respects to avoid relegation, which meant a loss of six months. This was something I could hardly afford. The only positive streak was the fact that we, now in the final term, had no seniors to make our lives miserable.

The sixteen kilometer run was an endurance test like few others. Completely decked out in battle rig, armed with a filled-up water bottle, from which we were not allowed to drink and a self-loading rifle, we were made to run literally against time, which was specified. To fight ones thirst, while a bottle filled with water hangs behind, needed some resolve and determination. Other tests were equally demanding.

It was during this period that I met Mr. P.N. Koul, the former Indian Chief Council in Lhasa and Chairman of Indian Co-operation Mission Nepal. He invited me home for lunch at Vasant Vihar, a posh locality in Dehradun. I was showered with a lot of affection and became a regular visitor to his house. His son Abhilash, probably in his ninth standard those days, would generally come on his scooter and look me up in the Academy every Sunday morning.

Mr. P.N. Koul was the younger brother of Mr. T.N. Koul, the former ambassador to the then USSR and USA. I had the opportunity of having lunch with him when he visited Dehradun after his term, as ambassador in the USA. This was in the year 1976. I remember I was highly impressed by his towering personality. We had a very long, informal chat during which he asked me why I had joined the Army. Mr. P.N. Koul immediately responded saying, "Come on brother don't interview him. Don't you know why I had joined the Army?" Mr. P.N. Koul had been a 'Gunner' and left the Army as a Lieutenant Colonel. Subsequently, he joined the civil services and received an Honorary IAS. He held many prestigious appointments during his service and settled in Vasant Vihar, Dehradun after his superannuation. His younger brother was Lieutenant General Hariday Koul from Armoured Corps who had done well in 1971 operations.

Days passed and the cadets began 'reverse counting' the days left for our scheduled 'Passing out Parade' (POP). That year, the POP was to be a special parade, during which The President of India was to present the colours to the Indian Military Academy, an event which had occured after about 13 years. The whole show was expected to be extraordinarily long and more complex when compared with the normal duration of POPs. Practice for the parade started about five months ahead of the day. Each day a few cadets would fall down during the drill, infuriating the Academy Adjutant, Major Narang.

Riding on a magnificent white horse, he would yell, "Don't fall like a coward, have some determination. You would not like to fall in front of the President of India, our Supreme Commander". There would be men ready with stretchers to clear off such cadets so that the proceedings continued without any disturbance. It was akin to a situation in the battlefield when a soldier falls to an enemy's bullet, the body is cleared from the scene and the battle goes on undisturbed. I remember one day a Senior Under Officer (SUO), with a sword in his hand, fell down without slouching. The Adjutant mounted on his horse said loudly, "That is how a soldier should fall, if at all he has to".

# Chapter 12

# THE TALLEST DAY

As the day approached, I learnt that invitations to the parents of cadets had been sent, from the Commandant's office, requesting them to attend the 'Passing out Parade'. It was clearly emphasised that they would be treated as the Commandant's guests and lodged within the Academy premises, unless they preferred their own arrangements.

My parents arrived a day prior to the POP along with my aunt, wife of Sh. T.N. Ticku, about whom I have mentioned a few times before. They were accommodated in the room next to mine and a junior cadet was assigned to look after them right from their arrival until their departure, as I would be unavailable to do so due to our busy schedule and rehearsals. The dinners, were also rehearsed since it was being hosted in honour of the President of India and thus had to be perfect. Parents of all the Gentlemen Cadets, who were passing out, were accorded the same courtesy. Gentleman Cadet (G C) Rajaraman, was responsible for taking care of my parents and aunt, whom I was able to meet only briefly the evening before the 'big' day.

15th December'1976, the 'D' Day dawned bright and cheerful. The lush green campus of the Academy was decorated like a bride for the occasion; birds winked at the sky and declared the day with their sweet chirps; the hustle and bustle commenced with the arrival of the mess boy with a huge steel thermos of tea followed by another who carried biscuits. This was how we normally ushered our day in the IMA, but today seemed special. This was to be a momentous occasion in my life that marked the transition from a 'Gentleman Cadet' to an 'Officer'. A day that would be the watershed between the two important phases of my life in the Indian Armed Forces.

My day had dawned much earlier as I had to prepare for the tallest day, in my career this far and attend to a number of things. I dressed up in accordance with the dress code; went to my parents' room, took their blessings and reported to the officials in the 'Drill Squad', along with my other course mates. We were dressed in blue patrols with a white 'web belt', dark blue 'peak caps' and sparkling black 'ammunition boots'. This was punctuated by the 'Self Loading Rifle (SLR)', with a shining butt.

Our drill instructors received us with amicable smiles, probably for the first time. We were made to fall in as per laid out procedures, which were already rehearsed enough. In the distance I could see all parents and guests being seated at their designated places, by the junior cadets and the staff on duty. The essence of our secular threads was on display with the presence of a *Pandit Ji, Granthi Ji, Moulvi Sahib* and a *Priest,* who were there to recite prayers to the colours, which were to be presented to the Academy by the President of India.

The Academy Adjutant came galloping on his white horse like a powerful current of fresh air, like a warrior landing from the sky after a victorious battle, dressed in his blue patrols, embellished with shinning ceremonial medals, thick line yards and a sparkling sword in his right hand.

He addressed us all on the horse back and said, "Gentlemen Cadets, I congratulate you today for, in a short while from now you shall be declared officers. I am proud of being associated with all of you throughout your stay in the Academy. I have dealt with you strictly and may be very harshly for reasons that are quite understandable. The Indian Military Academy is one of the best Military Academies in the world and produces equally good Army officers. I wish that all of you advance in your careers. I shall be the happiest person if you do well but mind you, shall even a thorn ever pierce your foot I will feel the pain. Good luck, but remember that no cadet will fall down today during the parade". For a man with a reputation of having a heart of stone this was the first time that we had a glimpse of his emotional side.

VVIPs arrived in accordance with the protocol, starting from the Academy Deputy Commandant, Academy Commandant and the Chief of Army Staff General T.N. Raina. Pin drop silence prevailed only to be broken by a fleet of pilot motorcycles leading the President's Guards, riding on well-built horses, followed by the President's magnificent horse carriage itself. And thus arrived the President of India Hon'ble Sh. Fakhruddin Ali Ahmed who, like all Presidents, was also the Supreme Commander of the Armed Forces. The drill squad in front of 'Chatwode Building' looked fabulous with the presence of the cadets, complimented with the Academy Band in attendance. The parade was conducted with a excellence, the Academy Adjutant on his white horse, making his presence felt with a visible sense of confidence. On a lighter note, I am sure that he would have won over the hearts of many a woman, that day.

While marching on and saluting the President I spotted my parents along with Mr. P.N. Kaul, about whom I have mentioned a little earlier. After the salutation, we entered the 'Chetwode Building' in 'Slow March'. We entered from one end as Cadets and left the building, from the other end, as Officers. While marching out of the 'Chetwode Building' one couldn't miss the important message, engraved in big golden letters:

**"Safety Honour and Welfare of Your Country Comes First Always and Every Time.**

**Honour Welfare and Comfort of the Men You Command Come Next.**

**Your own Ease, Comfort and Safety Come Last, Always and Every Time."**

This message leaves an everlasting impression on the officers' mind and is behind their everyday success. We were received by our physical training and drill instructors. Our drill instructor, who was otherwise famous for making our lives miserable, was very emotional that day and I could see tears in his eyes. Together they were our *Gurus* and had toiled a lot to help us see that day.

My father had also come to receive me. He hugged and congratulated me, shook hands and said, "From now onwards we are friends."

At this stage I would like to share, with you, something personal. While shaking hands with him, that day, I took a silent pledge that whenever I return home after the day's work, I shall look straight into the eyes of the person who opens the door in case I had done some positive work, else I shall enter the home with my eyes down. Having said this, I must admit that I have not always entered my home and looked straight into the eyes of the person who opened the door, whether it was my helper, parents, wife or children. However, this practice made me accountable to myself at the end of each working day.

Let me also share that I had always taken upon myself the initiative to be very frank and honest with my father throughout his life. To say that he was a good friend would be an understatement. A frown on his face would disturb me a lot. It was always my conscious endeavour to iron out any differences that ever cropped up between the two of us, however minor. Looking back my only regret is that I did not contribute financially to the extent desired as I lived away from my family . . .

After the POP, all the cadets were asked to move for the oath taking to be followed by the 'Piping Ceremony', the event that we all had waited for eagerly. During the ceremony, my parents and my aunt were with me, along with G C Rajaraman. My parents put the 'Pip' on one shoulder and my aunt, supported by Rajaraman, on the other. We threw the peak caps up in the air, danced and rejoiced for having earned the commission for which we had toiled day and night. I could sense the pride my parents felt as they wished me the best.

Despite my best efforts I am aware that I have not been able to express in words, the emotions felt and experienced that day. I had never seen so much happiness on the faces of my parents ever before in my life. The radiance of bliss probably let away their hidden sense of achievement. Suddenly the scene, when my mother had opened her tin box, about six years ago, to take out her savings, to the last penny, handing it over to my father to enable him pay the first installment of my fee, at the time of admission in the engineering college, flashed clearly before my eyes. I guess this was the reason I didn't take a single penny from my parents, during my one year stay at the Academy, even though we were not paid during the period. I arranged my pocket expenditure through alternate means and cleared it after earning my commission when we were paid arrears of our salary, as a Second Lieutenant, for the training period. Am sure my parents had no clue about this else they would have ensured otherwise.

After seeking clearance from the Academy, I took my parents to Haridwar and Rishikesh and two days later went to Saharanpur to board the train for Jammu en-route to Kashmir and my hometown, Sopore.

At Saharanpur railway station I met 'Tej Hali', a fellow cadet from Kashmir, who had been commissioned the same day. I introduced him to my parents and we travelled together till Jammu. This was to be a well deserved break of three weeks.

Along with my parents, I reached my hometown Sopore. Being the month of December, winter was at its peak. My parents had moved to the new house about a month ago. I was welcomed by the snow, which spread out like a blanket and painted the surroundings white, even hiding the uneven surface of Mother Earth. My friends and relatives were thrilled and congratulated me on becoming a commissioned officer. They invited me to fabulous lunches and dinners replete with delicious 'Kashmiri cuisine', especially the non-vegetarian items.

Two years later, I learnt that 'Tej Hali' was killed in an unfortunate accident during one of the military exercises in Assam. May his soul rest in peace!

The author (2$^{nd}$ from right) with his parents (3$^{rd}$ & 4$^{th}$ from right), Smt. T.N. Ticku (Aunt, 1$^{st}$ from right) and Gentleman Cadet Rajaraman (1$^{st}$ from left) at the Indian Military Academy, Dehradun, after the Passing Out Parade

# PART VI

# Beyond The Academy

## Chapter 13

# BOMBAY SAPPERS
# HEADQUARTERS

Three weeks after passing out of the Indian Military Academy, at the end of my leave, I left my home town, Sopore, to report to 'Bombay Sappers Headquarters', Pune. I was joined by five other young officers who had been my course mates in the Indian Military Academy. We were instructed to stay with the men in a barrack to understand and experience their way of living and problems they faced. Even though, we went to the Officers' Mess on and off, we practically lived and ate with men in the barracks, an experience which was pretty educative, to say the least.

The officers' mess at the Headquarters was magnificent in all respects and well known, in the defence circles, for its splendid get up. During this time there used to be an important event called 'VC Day', observed by the 'Bombay Sappers Group' in honour of General Bhaghat, a staunch 'Bombay Sapper' who had been awarded the 'Victoria Cross (VC)' for exhibiting bravery of the highest order during the Second World War.

Here I met Lt Col Raj Kapoor who was posted in our centre. He had many friends in the film industry and was pretty close to 'Vinod Khanna', the famous actor, probably because of his association with the 'Osho' commune. Vinod Khanna would sometimes visit the officers' mess, along with the Colonel, who later quit the Army. Years later the same Colonel Raj Kapoor made the famous serial 'Fauji' and gave 'Shahrukh Khan', the well-known actor and superstar, his first break in the acting world. The Colonel also worked in some movies which included Feroze Khan's 'Qurbani'. Coming back, we young officers worked day and night for a couple of days leading up to the event, which went fantastically well.

After about a month and a half stay at the Headquarters we were asked to report to the 'College of Military Engineering (CME)', Pune for the Young Officers course in 'Combat Engineering'. It is at this place that I was introduced to and made to handle live mines, of all types, for the first time. I recollect that if there was any time in my life when I have mustered up full concentration, with all faculties of the brain in attendance, it was here while handling the live mines. One was very conscious of the fact that there was hardly any scope for error during such handling. The course also took us to Mumbai for a week's exposure to the exercises at sea.

# Chapter 14

# REGIMENTAL LIFE

After undergoing the exhaustive course in the College of Military Engineering, I landed in my Regiment. The experience at the Regiment was fabulous for it was knit like a family. The seniors meant business in the office and they never shied away from enforcing it, whenever the situation demanded. However, beyond the office, I was treated like a brother officer by the same seniors, both in the mess and at their homes whenever I was invited or forced myself on them. The regimental life provided a lot of learning not only about 'mines' and 'explosives' but also about the social fabrics with which the families of officers and their men were woven together during times of peace and war.

The Regiment had 'Maratha' and 'Khalsa' troops, the great warriors. As a lieutenant, I was fortunate to be posted to a Field Company called the 'PVC (Param Vir Chakra)' Company, as Platoon Commander. I was instructed to take over as the 'Field Company Commander', in the officiating capacity, due to an acute paucity of officers. There was an 'Honours' board in my office which displayed the names of the brave officers of the Company with Major RR Rane's name right at the top, with the mention of the 'Param Vir Chakra (PVC)' against his name, followed by the names of five to six other officers of the Company who were decorated with the 'Vir Chakra'.

The 'Param Vir Chakra (PVC)' is <u>India</u>'s highest <u>military honour,</u> awarded for the highest degree of bravery and self-sacrifice exhibited by a soldier while fighting the enemy in the 'Theatre of War'. It can and often has been awarded posthumously. Major Rane belonged to the same Company and was the only surviving 'Param Vir Chakra' awardee at that point in time. Each year, ever after his superannuation, he was given the honour of being carried in a special vehicle, during the 'Republic Day Parade', in Delhi, drawing well-deserved attention from the announcers and audience.

The PVC Company was one of the most decorated Field Companies of the time, not only within our Regiment but amongst the whole Corps of Engineers. Any young officer posted to our Regiment was always asked to spend a few days in the PVC Company before joining their own. Needless to mention, the experience was extremely educative. I was fortunate to be posted to this Company and equally proud of having commanded it for about a year, though in an officiating capacity being a Lieutenant.

I had a close friend, Captain Vinod Tiwari, who was my senior. We would generally be seen together beyond office hours so much so that if someone asked for me, he was advised to look up where Captain Tiwari was and vice versa. The two of us would go fishing every Sunday to 'Silised Lake', about fourteen kilometers from our mess. The routine was to have breakfast, collect bait which consisted of a tin filled with earthworms and leave with a packed lunch. He had a beautiful Japanese telescopic fishing rod and I made an improvised one out of a good bamboo and nylon thread, embellished with a nice cute float. On lucky days, we would get a good catch which was then handed over to the mess boy to prepare snacks or a fish curry. To my good luck, Captain Tiwari did not eat fish and so I would relish the preparations all by myself but for another Bengali officer, who otherwise had no patience to go out fishing.

On one such occasion we caught what according to the Captain was a fish but to my astonishment looked more like a snake. Contradictions followed but I must admit he was more confident of his claim. To settle the question we both decided to go to the house of the Commanding Officer, known for his knowledge about fish. On entering his house, Captain Tiwari narrated the story about our disagreement. He had a look and called out to his wife asking her to come and see the 'Ill' fish, which we had caught and was supposed to be a delicacy. The fish was cleaned, fried and served. We all enjoyed it together and the CO thanked us for the disagreement that brought us to his doorstep.

Alwar, I must mention, had beautiful picnic spots—a few beautiful lakes, with a lot of exemplary architecture, constructed by the Rajasthani Kings. The 'Silised Lake' had intermittent huge pillars with wide plain tops, spread all along the boundary of the lake. It seems in olden days female dancers would dance during nights, one each on these huge pillars, well spread around the lake, to entertain the kings who watched the performance from a central platform.

There were many beautiful palaces in the vicinity, some ill maintained. In one such palace, I found a caretaker's child jumping on a beautiful, aesthetically made billiards table, which was otherwise allotted to him, by his father, for doing his homework. The palace was practically deserted and uncared for, with only the caretaker and his family being its occupants.

There were a few interesting experiences of regimental life that I would like to share with you. After reporting to the Regiment, an evening was fixed for my formal 'Dining In' in the Officers Mess. On this occasion, all the officers, along with their families, join to formally receive a new officer as he becomes a part of the family. Generally, it is a lavish cocktail party, followed by dinner, finally culminating in the young officer being carried to his room.

The event started and I was introduced to the officers and their wives. I asked for a soft drink to which they obliged initially. After some time the officers offered me an alcoholic beverage. I thanked them and told them that I was comfortable with what I had been having. When they insisted further I admitted that I don't drink. On hearing this one of the senior officers became a little adamant and insisted that I have the drink. This was not unusual, and generally young officers didn't talk much on such occasions. Nevertheless, I mustered some courage and told him, in the presence of other officers, "Sir today is my day and I would like to have the drink I prefer." Though I was unaware, the Commanding Officer, standing nearby overhearing the conversation instructed the Mess Secretary to offer me whatever I wanted. The particular senior officer obviously didn't appreciate my reply at the time but we went on to become good friends. I always adored him for his professional competence through which we youngsters always learnt a thing or two. However, after this incident, no officer ever took me for granted.

On another occasion, as already mentioned, I was asked by the Commanding Officer to take charge as the Commander of the PVC Company. While doing so he clearly mentioned that this is the most decorated field Company in the Regiment and for that matter probably in the whole Corps of Engineers. He instructed the Adjutant to give me a thorough briefing.

The Adjutant gave an exhaustive briefing for two primary reasons—because I was inexperienced and also because men of this particular unit were proud to belong to the PVC Field Company. During this briefing he cautioned me about a particular Sapper (Jawan), even asking me to note down his name. He advised me to refrain from issuing this Sapper an outstation pass, as he was highly indisciplined and was known to overstay his leave. After the briefing, I went to the Company office and took over as Company Commander.

The next day being Saturday was the day of the 'Arzi Report'. On this day each Sapper would put in his request, including the request for an 'Outstation Pass', formally with the 'Company JCO' in attendance. During this process, the Company JCO informed me that he would now march the Sapper, about whom the Adjutant had mentioned. Like the Adjutant he also recommended that I deny the Sapper's request.

The Sapper was marched in and he put in his request. I told him that he had a very poor record and that there was a standing instruction not to grant him leave or an 'Outstation Pass'. Having said that I asked him to be frank and tell me his problem. He was almost in tears when he told me that he had a grave problem at home and was compelled by the circumstances to behave in the manner that he did. He added that the problem in question had now become even more complex because of the fact that he had not been granted the 'Outstation Pass' for quite some time. After hearing his plea I was convinced that his problem was genuine and it was in everyone's interest to send him home. I informed him that I was approving his 'Outstation Pass', for the week end, at my own risk and it would be very bad for me if he disobeyed by not turning up on Monday morning.

My Company JCO was taken aback and advised me not to do it since it would bring a bad name to the Company, but I stood firm on my decision and signed the pass and left for the mess in high spirits, as the next day was Sunday.

Come Monday I was at the office and the Company JCO gave me the 'Morning Report' with the status "All well Sir, except that the particular Sapper had not returned back". From the body language of the JCO, I understood that he felt vindicated. With a feeling of having been let down I instructed him to report to me after every half an hour until 10:30 A.M., by which time all absentees were expected to be reported to the Regiment Headquarter. The JCO reported to me thrice with the news that the Sapper had not turned up.

Deciding to report the matter to the Adjutant, without any further delay, I got up, put on my cap, pulled my forlorn and with a final look in the long mirror went to the Adjutant to break the news. I saluted and entered his chamber. Returning the salute he asked how my first day as Company Commander had been. I replied that it was fine except for the absence of the particular Sapper, about whom he had warned me earlier. On hearing that, he enquired if the Sapper had absconded to which came my reply that it was I who had sent him on an 'Outstation Pass'. The Adjutant expressed shock that I had done so in spite of his specific instructions to the contrary. I apologised for not following his advice, accepting that we now had to deal with the situation since the incident had already occurred. He expressed his disapproval after which I saluted and returned to my office. To mention that I was not in a good mood, for on the very first day I had probably blundered, would be an understatement.

A few hours later, as I sipped on a cup of tea, the Company JCO rushed in to report that the Sapper had turned up and wanted to meet me. I called for him and on his arrival scolded him for not turning up on time. He explained that he had come back in spite of the grave problem at home only and only because of me and my concern for him. He told me that after finishing his work, he had traveled day and night to keep his word and my prestige but unfortunately missed the bus due to which he was delayed by a few hours. I patted him and looked into the eyes of my Company JCO who tried to shy away. Once again I put on my cap, looked into the mirror, probably with a little more confidence this time round and went to the Adjutant's chamber. As I saluted him, he looked up at me and said, "Yes, any more flaps?" I replied, "There is no further flap, Sir; this is to inform you that the Sapper has come back and reported to the Company." Am sure he was pleasantly surprised but pretended otherwise. From his body language, I could sense that in his heart of hearts he appreciated my decision.

In consequence, the Company JCO also didn't take me for granted thereafter. I have mentioned this incident in detail mainly to emphasise the fact that some of our men do have complex problems at home and at times, an officer has to come up with an out-of-box solution to address such situations. The officers, at times, through their wives, associate, with such families, through welfare activities and thus assist them to overcome such difficulties. Such initiatives do make a difference, in the long run. I later learnt that the incident had become a *Langar Talk* (gossip in the mess over a meal) and the men, in general, felt that I as a new young officer had shown courage in the interest of the welfare of the Sapper.

On one occasion, a 'Board of Officers' was detailed to oversee the sale of some furniture items in the Officers Mess. An auction was organized to sell the items and I presided as the Chairman of the board. Before commencement of the auction, I asked the Sappers who were present there to find out who was genuinely interested in purchasing the main items. This was to ensure that no purchase was made in proxy for the 'Unit Baniya'.

One Sapper wanted to have the sofa since he had just got married and was allotted the married accommodation. Another Sapper wanted to buy the carpet. These were like small dream items for the Sappers, as they could not afford such things, in the open market, those days. I recollect that we finally sold the sofa set for about two hundred rupees and the carpet, which was in excellent condition, for about two hundred fifty rupees. All items were sold at affordable rates and I intimated our Regiment Headquarters about the sale along with the relevant documents.

The next morning, I was called by the Adjutant who was surprised at the fact that we had sold the furniture items for literally peanuts. He was annoyed and had already reported the matter to the Commanding Officer (CO) and was asked to meet him. On entering the Commanding Officer's chamber, he asked me the reason behind selling the items for such small amounts. I told him that the furniture was sold to our own boys who could otherwise never afford such items. I also expressed my apprehension that the items would have been bought by the *Unit Baniya* through proxy and in turn sold back to our boys for hefty amounts.

He appreciated the thought and expressed his happiness. He further informed the Adjutant to make me the officiating Mess Secretary due to the paucity of Majors in the Regiment who would otherwise generally fill this position. As a result of this my reputation within the Regiment started to build slowly and steadily. The Adjutant, a pretty senior and experienced Captain and I went on to become good friends.

During my tenure, I would often go along with my men on different assignments, all along the Rajasthan border. I loved the area, the sand and the whistling sand dunes where we would live in tents during peak summer. The local people lived in far-flung villages called 'Dhani's' and expressed great love for the Army. They would stop our vehicles forcibly and compel us to have a cup of tea. I remember talking to them informally and during such conversations learnt that they were very happy with the 'Pokhran Atomic Explosion (Pokhran-1)' which they called *Dhamaka*. The reason behind this was their assumption that the immediate rains that followed the explosion happened because of it. As a result of these showers their area saw a rich harvest after many decades. Here, every hut had a catchment area and water was very scarce. For many families, the main job of the day was to fetch water, on camel carts, from distant areas, for which they left home in the morning and returned only at sunset. I hope and guess that things might be different now.

After spending a few months in the naked desert in various areas such as, but not limited to, Barmer, Jaisalmer and Pokhran, I was called back to the Regimental Headquarters at Alwar. I was pleasantly surprised when asked to take over as the Adjutant of the Regiment though I was still a Lieutenant, while generally the Adjutant used to be of a Captain rank. The Second-in-Command, had taken over as the officiating Commanding Officer. He was an outdoor person and a swimmer at the 'Command Level'. After the morning PT with the men the general routine involved us going to the firing range, practicing throwing a few live hand grenades and then returning to the office for work. Working with him was always a pleasure.

During this period I went on my annual leave and left for my hometown, Sopore where in a few days I was to be married. I reached home on 6th August 1978 and the marriage ceremony was held three days later, on 9th. One day I found many Army convoys moving around, with hidden 'Tactical' signs. There were strong rumours that an operation was to take place. The movement of regular Army convoys, well camouflaged with no apparent 'Tactical' signs, only added strength to these rumours. I didn't mention this to anyone except my newly wedded wife, Kunti, that if the rumours were to be believed, chances were that I could be called back at anytime and that she should be mentally prepared for it. Fortunately the rumours stayed as rumours and I reported to my Regiment only at the end of my sanctioned leave.

On my return to the Regiment, I met another officiating Adjutant, the then Captain Manjgaonkar who went on to retire as Brigadier Manjgaonkar, President of the Bhopal Service Selection Board. He then informed me that a signal had been received from Army Headquarters that I had to be relieved immediately to proceed on a two years, Post Graduate Level course, on Survey Engineering, to the then 'Survey Training Institute', presently 'Indian Institute of Surveying and Mapping', Hyderabad.

The Commanding Officer called me to his chamber and advised me to make the best of this opportunity since there was a saturation of officers in the corps at the time. As per instruction from Army Headquarters, I had to be relieved immediately and so the date of 'Dining Out' from the 'Officers Mess' was fixed, as was the 'Bara Khana', the farewell dinner, by the men. I was intimated of the same, accordingly.

By now, I had become a part of the regimental family and I started to miss the Company of the officers, whom I regarded, mainly because of the love and affection that they had showered on me. They and their families expressed similar feelings.

My men hosted a fabulous 'Bara Khana', punctuated by colourful events viz; 'Sardars Bangra' and 'Marathas Folk Dance'. They compelled me to play my favourite tune on the 'mouth organ', for they had heard me before. I agreed and soon they bid me farewell which was very emotional and touching.

Thereafter, the evening of the 'Dining Out' arrived, with all the officers and their families in attendance.

I remember that I consumed about thirty peg measures of lime cordial that evening. While the party was on, I found the Commanding Officer, the Second-in-Command, and the Adjutant discussing some matter in a room and as I tried to enter. The CO hinted to me to leave them alone, probably in view of the discussion. I turned back, though in my heart of hearts I felt bad because it was my 'Dining Out' and I felt they could have discussed, whatever matter was being discussed, later. Soon the CO with the other officers came out of the room and joined me.

The officers and the families collectively asked me to sing a *ghazal*. I was not a singer by any standard. I had recited *ghazals* on a number of occasions and reluctantly sung a few sometimes as well. This evening I heeded to their request subject to the assurance that they would not leave me deserted, after hearing my crude voice.

I sung the following *ghazal*:

> *'Jeenay ka raaz mein nay muhabat mein pa liya,*
> *Jiska bhi gam mila usay apna bana liya . . .'*
> *(I found the secret of life in 'love'*
> *I adopted the grief passed on by others . . .)*

The officers were so drawn into the mood of the ghazal that they turned off the lights. Later, on a lighter note I did mention that I was afraid they all might have left away under the cover of darkness. The evening drew to a close after the Commanding Officer gave a wonderful speech, followed by mine. I was then presented with a memento and I remember entering my name as Lt P.N. Koul in the 'Officers Mess Visitors Book'. I also added a remark which I fail to remember now. I was then carried on a decorated chair by the officers signing the famous song, "He's a jolly good fellow'.

The next day I met the officers in their offices. I was taken to the Alwar railway station to be seen off by both the officers and men. I was to witness a strange activity, on the railway station platform, with even the stationmaster in attendance. I saw the Adjutant giving instructions to some of the men, while a table was being laid on the platform, covered with a clean tablecloth. He then poured beer in a huge beer mug hurriedly while another officer held the Captain's applets in his hand. I was then taken to one side of the platform. The officers stood in front while the JCOs and men watched the happenings from a distance. I was clueless and began to get a little confused. At this juncture, there was some murmur and the Commanding Officer, of the Regiment, arrived.

I saluted the CO as he came closer. He patted me on the shoulder and informed me that he had decided to make me a Captain and that too at that very moment, on the railway station, as it was either now or never. I recall that the Regiment had no vacancy of a Captain, at that time. Nevertheless, the applets were dipped in the beer mug and the CO personally did my 'Piping Ceremony'. He whispered to me silently saying, "You should not mind, under the given circumstances, if you are required to remove one pip later, though we shall try our level best and ensure that such a situation does not arise".

He then said, "Pran, this is what we were discussing in the mess last night when I asked you not to enter the room". This was something that to my knowledge had never been done before, or since, in the Regimental history—'A Piping Ceremony' at a railway station and after having been dinned out as a 'Lieutenant', the night before. I was humbled by this gesture on the part of the CO and the Second-in-Command, who it seems was the man behind the suggestion. Great people, great family!

The train arrived and I was garlanded by the officers and men. A sense of regret dawned on me that I would never get to serve with them again as after the successful completion of the course I would be required to converge towards the specialized field of 'Surveying and Mapping'. With a final whistle, the train took me away from my Regiment, never to return.

# PART VII

# The Combination

# Chapter 15

# SAPPER AND SURVEYOR

Taking me away from the Regiment, the train brought me to New Delhi the same day. From here I boarded the 'Dakhshin Express' since it was the fastest train from Delhi to Hyderabad those days. I got down at Secunderabad railway station and took a cab to Uppal, located about fourteen kilometers away. The 'Indian Institute of Surveying and Mapping (IISM)', the then 'Survey Training Institute (STI)', is located here along with other national scientific organizations of repute.

The driver stopped the cab at the gate and I was greeted by the huge aesthetically designed signboard which read 'Survey Training Institute, Survey of India'. Having reached my destination, I was guided to No. 15 Party of the Survey Training Institute, by the receptionist, where I reported to the course officer. During our brief conversation, he informed me that the institute had a number of training units, each called a 'Party' and the No. 15 Party imparted training to the officers. He also informed me that eleven Army Officers had been detailed for the two years course by the Ministry of Defence and some officers had already arrived from various corners of the country. He directed me to go to the Officers' Hostel where I was allotted a single room.

The institute had an impressive campus, huge and magnificent. It had beautiful buildings, two trainee hostels, a nice guesthouse, a huge auditorium and an array of sport fields. Volleyball ball seemed to be a favourite game, mainly because it was field oriented. The institute was self-sufficient with a bank and post office located within its premises and exclusively meant for it. It had a reasonably good dining hall where we had our meals. In addition to the 'Survey Training Institute', there were three more Directorates located within the campus. These Directorates had twin roles which meant that apart from their assigned role, they had the added responsibility to support the practical aspects of the training. They were complimentary to the academics of the institute and thus intentionally placed next to it, in accordance with the guidance of experts. I was reminded of the Medical College Srinagar, which had a huge 'State Hospital' attached to it to make the training practical oriented.

There was a huge residential colony, lavishly laid out, not more than a kilometer away from the institute, which housed the officers, instructors and other institute staff. An officer, however, needed a substantial number of years, in service, to enjoy the privilege. There were two huge central schools, one in the institute area and the other next to the residential colony. This gave a strong sense that the concerned authorities had taken adequate welfare measures right at the very inception of the institute. Both the central schools had a good reputation and a number of their students were already studying in various IITs and other institutions of repute.

The Institute was set up in the early seventies under the aegis of the United Nations Development Program (UNDP), with the full support of International Training Centre (ITC), Holland. At its inception, it was staffed by Indian and foreign experts of high repute, which also included Mr. Konesney who is known internationally as the 'Guru' of 'Photogrammetry and Remote Sensing'. In those days, the main thrust had been on 'Photogrammetry', one of the specialized subjects in the science of 'Surveying and Mapping'.

This was the only place in India where one could see huge and expensive Photogrammetric machines imported from 'Wild' Switzerland, installed in air-conditioned buildings, built for the purpose. The officers and men from Survey of India, with many from the Army as well, had been trained in this institute and had undergone 'Advanced Courses' in 'Photogrammetry', 'Cartography', 'Geodetic Science' and various related subjects. It was, in more ways than one, a unique training centre on our side of the world. Trainees would be deputed from Sri Lanka, the then Burma, the Middle East and African countries.

The institute had been set up, by the United Nations, to strengthen the application of Photogrammetry, Geodetic Science and other relevant faculties, aimed at modernizing the Cartographic products in India as well as to help adjacent underdeveloped countries.

The institute, over the years, has revolutionised mapping in our country. Survey of India, the National Mapping Agency, under the Ministry of Science and Technology, to which the institute belongs, commands a great reputation all over the world. Survey of India (SOI) has always been abreast of the latest technology making sure it was equipped with whatever was current at the time. It is one of the oldest Government organisations in India and carries forward its legacy right from the days of Colonel Sir George Everest, an officer from 'The Royal Sappers', who was the Surveyor General of India about two hundred twenty years ago and in whose name the highest mountain peak of the world is named.

The two-year course on 'Survey Engineering' started on 13th November, 1978. The first officer whom I met in the dining hall while having my lunch on 12th of November was Major B. Nagarajan. We exchanged pleasantries and realised that he had been one term senior to me in the Indian Military Academy. I guess we had not met because he was from a different Company. The following day, after breakfast, we reported together to the course officer. Other officers came in one by one and we were made to sit in the designated classroom, which was huge and had the luxury of a partitioned enclosure, where we spent some private moments during the short breaks.

The course officer and his team of instructors were professionally very thorough in their respective subjects and clearly meant business. They commenced their respective responsibilities after taking a brief introduction from all the officers. We were told to pair up with an officer of our choice and the pair would remain partners for the duration of two years and work together while carrying out the field observations, practical assignments and other activities that were assigned from time to time.

Captain Nagarajan and I paired up as partners and so did the remaining officers. Luckily, the two of us shared a good understanding and our partnership became exemplary not only through the course but also beyond. In fact, we became good family friends and remain so till today. Incidentally, in later years he, at the level of a Major General, took over as the Additional Surveyor General of the institute. He received the doctorate degree in 'Geodetic Science' from Ohio University (USA), and is today considered an authority on 'Global Positioning Systems' in the country.

The course started with a bang. We were informed by the course officer that there were more or less four semesters, each of six months, of which two had to be conducted in the institute campus. The other two, being purely field oriented, would be conducted in the field where we would stay in tents. Each academic session, of six months, was to be to be followed by fieldwork, of the same duration. In a way this was good for, by the time you were fed up with one, the other would start.

At the end of the two years, we had not only to qualify the examination of the 'Survey Training Institute' but also of the 'The Institution of Surveyors'. The later would entitle us to their membership. We had heard that the examination conducted by the Institution of Surveyors was very difficult and warranted regular and exhaustive studies. There was a condition that if the examination of the 'Institution of Surveyors' was not cleared, within three attempts, the concerned officer would then be returned to his unit. There had been a few such instances before and none of us wanted to return with this stigma.

I was newly married while some of my other course mates took short leaves and got married one after the other. In a few weeks, the field season started, scheduled for the next six months.

After expiry of the first term, we moved to our first camp at 'Ghatkeshwar' village for field training, a few kilometers away from the main road. We were told by the Course Officer, known in the field as Camp Officer, to report on a particular day from the institute. After carrying out a few formalities in the institute office, we were transported to the campsite. We were pleasantly surprised to see the nice white tents pitched beautifully with an aesthetic sense. We were well placed in these tents, which were furnished adequately with a study chair, a study table, a kerosene lantern, a fresh *Durry* spread on the floor and a camp cot. The tents had attached washrooms as well.

The Camp Officer's tent stood magnificent, set up next to the camp entrance, which was manned by a security guard. The Camp Office, the class tent, the mess and the kitchen tent were suitably signposted and thick white limed round stones clearly demarcated the walking tracks which lead to every tent in the 'U Shaped' camp lay out. The two firefighting points, placed at the two extreme corners of the camp, with baskets and shovels painted freshly with red paint, broke the monotony of the predominant white colour, which added to the charm. An optimum use had been made of the resources available in this barren land.

To be precise, the camp wore the look of a beautiful village girl robed in her whites, with beautiful red earrings hanging from her two ear lobes, taking every care to make the most of the resources available around.

Each group of two were authorized a cook called 'Camp Khalasi' (CK). As a result, the group of six officer trainees, were authorized three CK's. They took care of the cooking, washing of clothes and cleanliness of our residential tents. These three comfortably took care of us and our complex menus, which was decided by one of us designated as the Mess Secretary. This was done on a rotation basis, between the six of us. We had two local officers who were from Hyderabad. They were of great help in identifying the right three CKs. Narsimha, one of the three CKs, knew only 'Telugu' and did not understand even a word of Hindi.

In the meantime, I started picking up a few frequently used 'Telugu' words and a couple of sentences. The very first day I got up early, pushed the table and the chair outside the tent and laid out the shaving kit. I saw

Narsimha and told him, while showing my shaving mug, *neelu tiskara*-fetch me water. He did it fast and by that time I started humming loudly the latest sentence I had picked up a night before *neelu tiskapo*—take away the water. Narsimha came running from the kitchen tent and took away the mug of water. I told him not to do so but he didn't listen. I called the Telugu speaking friend and told him to call Narsimha with my mug of water and ask him why he took it. He called Narsimha and the poor chap said that the Sahib only had told him to take away the water. I then realised that he had not understood that I was humming for my entertainment. By now all the officer trainees had come out of their tents and laughed at this humorous situation. Whenever Nagarajan and I meet, we talk of this incident and laugh aloud.

Fieldwork would generally get over during the day unless we had some field exercises at night that involved observations of some specific stars. The time of these astronomical observations would be dictated by the 'Astronomical Tables and Charts' and most often the timings would be inconvenient. The field training took us to various campsites. We were like gypsies shifting our camps from one site to the other; with a difference, that we lived in nice tents and had staff to look after us.

After completion of the fieldwork, we got marching orders to proceed to Hyderabad. Oh, what a relief! I fixed a suitable house in the nearby vicinity of 'Tarnaka' which was adjacent to the then Chief Minister Dr. Channa Reddy's house owing to which we never experienced a power failure during our entire stay of three years.

I was accompanied by Nagarajan when I went to occupy the house and hardly had any luggage—the IMA specified a black tin box with my name 'Gentleman Cadet P.N. Koul' painted on it, a kit bag and an army style camp cot rolled up in another small kit bag. We found that the landlord, Mr. Thomas John and his wife were not at home. My belongings were so little that I put them in a small corner under the staircase outside the house and decided to go and watch a movie. We returned, found the belongings intact and occupied the house in the evening. On a lighter note, Capt Nagarajan told me that I might not need a house as I hardly had anything with me. Both of us laughed and in a few days, I started setting up the house, since my wife was to join me soon. A dining table set and some basic furniture, were the first additions. Nagarajan and I purchased similar scooters before my wife joined me and thus I was partially ready to face the initial challenges of married life.

My wife joined me and we started our household in that house. When she prepared the first meal Nagarajan was with us. The food was served in *Thalis* and three steel bowls since we didn't possess, rather couldn't afford any crockery or luxurious items at that juncture. By that time, Nagarajan and I had developed a good understanding. I found him to be a very sincere friend, a typical product of a joint family, a sincere son, and a dedicated brother but above all a good friend. I told him frankly that we had to build everything from scratch mainly because I was seriously against the 'Dowry System'. I had conveyed the same to my brother-in-law, who was the eldest male member in my wife's family, since my father-in-law was no more, but he had not taken it seriously.

On the day of our marriage when we were about to depart for my home along with the bride, I observed a truck had been loaded with Dowry items including, but not limited to, expensive furniture, crockery and what not. I told my father that it was not acceptable. He agreed and solemnly conveyed it to the elders on the girl's side but I found them taking it lightly. I told everybody present that I would not recognize the marriage if the truck is not unloaded and detached from our convoy, comprising of a few cars. It was then that the seriousness of my statement was realised and it became amply clear that dowry items would not find their way into my house. At once, the truck was detached and unloaded.

They, however, impressed upon me to take two small tin boxes. One contained a few steel utensils like *Thalis*, a jug, 3 bowls, a few *katoris* and spoons since it had a religious association. These utensils were worshipped during the proceedings of the marriage ceremony. Traditionally, parents presented these items to their daughter on the day of marriage, at the time she stepped towards the boy's place after the ceremony. The other box contained dry fruits. I agreed readily since I found it convincing and we left for our place. Incidentally, there was also a lot of property, comprising of farmland and apple orchards, which my father-in-law had legally bequeathed to my wife when he was alive but

I persuaded her that we would not accept it as well. I thanked my parents and my wife for their co-operation and the encouragement.

I told Nagarajan that we were being served the first meal in the same *Thalis*, the same vegetable bowls, with water from the same jug and in the same tumblers. Even today when I recollect the scene, I strongly feel that there can't be any better tribute that a girl can pay to her parents than serving her first meal after marriage in a few simple utensils gifted to her by them, at the time of her departure from their place. I was told by my wife that those *Thalis* had been bought by her father long before for this purpose, when he was alive. I requested my wife to serve me food in one of these *Thalis*, always, which she does even today. Sometimes, I am the odd man out on the dining table since I eat in a traditional *Thali*, while others eat in smaller ones.

The routine of going to classes for the day and returning in the evening continued. We started taking outings during the weekends. Hyderabad had beautiful sparkling cinema halls and we saw a number of movies whenever possible. I saw a few good movies for a second time because of my wife. Movies were also screened at the Institute Auditorium once a week.

We also began visiting the 'National Geophysical Research Institute (NGRI)' as we had become friends with some young scientists who persuaded us to visit the NGRI because their film club arranged a regular movie show, once a week, in their open air theatre.

I remember that on one such weekend evening they showed the film 'Mera Naam Joker'. Unfortunately it started to rain heavily. Most of the people left, as the rain showed no signs of stopping. Two couples, one being my wife and myself, decided to stay on and under the protection of our rain caps we continued to enjoy the movie uninterrupted. We thanked the organizers for the uninterrupted entertainment, despite the rain.

At the beginning of the course, all the course mates decided to visit 'Hussain Sagar Lake' along with their families. The lake was about seventy kilometers from our institute. Most of us had purchased new scooters and were not very confident about riding. One officer who was a local volunteered to arrange an old 'Austin Car' from his brother-in-law to accommodate our wives so that they could have a comfortable journey. When we started our journey, he was overjoyed since he was the only person with a car, albeit a borrowed one. As we were reaching the lake there was a gust of wind and from a distance, we saw the bonnet of his car get unhinged from the clamps and crash against the windscreen. He lost visibility and stopped all of a sudden. By then we had all reached, the women having alighted from the car were laughing uproariously and so did we. The officer felt embarrassed and there must have been minor damages but no one talked about it.

The next day the officer was furious in class and expressed his displeasure as all of us had laughed when he was in a thick soup and none of us had the courtesy to ask if there had been any damages. Everybody kept quite sheepishly hiding a smile. Meanwhile, the second session of six months in the institute campus was about to get over and the second field season about to start. My wife planned to visit my hometown since I had to live in the camp for the next six months, initially at a place called 'Bhongir'. I, however, took permission to live in a guesthouse, for a couple of days, which was adjacent to our camp. During this period we would put the pressure cooker and a few kitchen related essentials in a haversack and tying it to the spare tyre of the scooter would ride the 'Mobile Kitchenette' to our house in Hyderabad. We would do this over the weekends, because we had only one pressure cooker and a few utensils as part of our limited possessions. The mobile kitchen was brought back, late on Sunday, when we returned to the guesthouse.

We would generally start back from Hyderabad very late in the evening. I remember an incident when on one such occasion, we started around 11:00 P.M. on our scooter. On the way it started to pour. I kept riding and was very conscious that my wife was with me as the ride took us through villages and isolated roads. My wife cooperated, gave me courage and we reached the guesthouse at mid night completely drenched. To our horror, there was no accommodation since there had been a murder nearby and the police had occupied the entire guesthouse.

Left with no option, at this hour, I decided to disturb the Assistant Engineer who controlled the allotment of the Guest House. He noticed that my wife and I were drenched and called his staff who carved out a little space, in his office, to accommodate a small bed that he brought from his house. Thus we spent the night comfortably and thanked him for the gesture. His wife was further gracious in inviting my wife for lunch when she learnt that I was to go out on fieldwork and that evening we moved to the Guest House.

My wife was to leave for Kashmir after two days. That very night we were scheduled to go for night observation of the 'Polar Star' but my friends, including my partner, didn't allow me to come for the observations and forcibly sent me back. They said they would take care and I should be with my wife. They made us buy two tickets for a 'Telugu' movie starring N.T. Rama Rao. It was on the lines of the famous Hindi film producer Sh. V Shantaram's *Do Ankhey Barah Haath*. We enjoyed the movie accompanied by delicious *Mirchi Pakorey* and later returned to the Guest House.

The next day I entered the huge class tent and found all the officers busy doing computations. We wished each other and the course officer enquired about how the night observation had been. Guilty and hoping against hope that he was unaware of my absence, I replied that it was fine. In the interim, my partner told me that everything was fine as none, other than them, were aware of my absence. To be honest, I felt miserable during those few minutes of suspense since I had never done anything like this, in my career before.

After a few days, I accompanied my wife to Delhi by train from where she was scheduled to fly to Srinagar. Flying from Hyderabad to Srinagar was an expensive affair those days. After seeing her off in the afternoon,

I was to return to Hyderabad the same evening by 'Dakhshin Express'. On reaching the airport, we learnt that the flight, which my wife had to take, was cancelled due to bad weather. However, there was another flight scheduled with only a few seats left resulting in a huge rush. I was tense and went to the airport duty officer since our plan had gone for a 'six'. I then learnt that there was only one seat available and the duty officer was inclined to accommodate my wife however, a travel agent pleaded with the duty officer to accommodate his foreign client. I chastised him severely leading to an avoidable scene at the airport, which finally culminated in the allotment of the coveted seat to my wife. I heaved a sigh of relief after sending her off and proceeded straight to the railway station to catch the 'Dakhshin Express'.

The two years passed very fast since we were generally busy with our studies and field training punctuated by socializing events that were conducted in the officers' mess or in one of the officers' houses. I was lucky to get a membership of the prestigious 'Secunderabad Club' which we used extensively even though it was about fourteen kilometers from our location. We cleared the 'Survey Training Institute examination' and the examination conducted by the 'Institution of Surveyors' and then awaited our posting orders. I was lucky to be posted as an instructor to the same institute but to a different unit called the No. 39 Party (Survey Training Institute) where the officials of supervisory level were being trained. Their training was akin to the officers' except for the minor difference in syllabus. They also had two sessions in the institute campus and two on the field. I was designated as course/camp officer for a batch of about a dozen officials.

In the meantime, my wife had again left for our hometown, Kashmir, while she was carrying our first child. During this period, she had a tough time and was indisposed for about eight months with strict instructions of restricted movements, due to certain medical conditions. My parents looked after her in my absence. By then, I had set up a camp in 'Ibrahempatnam'. The batch of trainee officials and the team of instructors also joined and the fieldwork commenced.

I would study at night to keep myself abreast with the Survey Technology and be in tune with whatever I had just learnt from the professionally competent instructors, who taught and trained us at the Institute. I was very strict with the instructors and the staff and also looked after their welfare as and when required. Nevertheless, I came across as a serious person, which was very well taken. The trainee officers were experienced officials from 'Survey of India' and were nominated for the course after qualifying a tough competition test. A few of them were postgraduates.

I suggested to the trainees that we could try and finish their theory portion, as well, if I conducted classes after dinner, instead of them wasting time in their tents or just loitering. All of them agreed and the team of instructors encouraged them. Except Saturdays and Sundays, a lecture class was held every day in the huge office tent and all of us enjoyed the class mainly because they were dedicated students.

One day, when I entered the class I realised that nobody had turned up. After waiting for five minutes I went back to my tent. After a few minutes, I could detect some activity and the security guard informed me that everybody had assembled in the class and were awaiting me. I, however, did not go. The trainees felt that I had been annoyed and thus sent the senior-most instructor to request me to come. He explained that the trainees regretted coming late to the class by few minutes and were apologetic. I, however, did not budge and the class was not conducted that day. The next day, the routine continued and since then they never delayed any class. This was the main reason why we were able to complete the theory syllabus, of the entire two years, during the night classes. This was something that was normally not to be done in the field, which helped the young officials perform better when they returned to the institute.

My wife, now in Kashmir was expecting our first child in the beginning of April. On the bright day of 2nd April, 1981 I got a telegram from my father that I had been blessed with a son on 1st of April but my father chose not to inform me that very day because I might have taken it as a April Fool's day prank. My leave was not approved since our camp was going to be closed in a few days. After the closure of the camp, I took a month's leave and went home. I was thrilled to see everybody and meet Navin, the new arrival. When he was about three weeks old, we went to Pahalgham. I remember during this trip he cried a lot when we entered a restaurant. On seeing us the owner played some music and Navin suddenly turned quiet. I guess he probably started enjoying the music. I then told my wife that he would develop a keen interest in music as he grows up. This turned out to be true to the extent that in his later years he would not be able to concentrate on his studies unless there was some light music being played in the background.

I shall never forget the scene of my father weeping bitterly after we took Navin from his lap at the airport, to return to Hyderabad. It was as if we had snatched the most precious possession of his life. My mother says that he refused to eat anything that evening.

As I resumed my duties in the Institute, I received the posting order from the office of the Surveyor General of India and I stood transferred to 29 Party (North Eastern Region) with its headquarters at Shillong. As was the practice, I was given a sendoff from the office and a 'Dining Out Party' at the Officers' Mess.

# PART VIII

*Frontier Callings*

# Chapter 16

# MEGHALAYA—
# INITIAL EXPERIENCES

Shillong was considered a hard posting in the Survey of India. This was mainly because of the tough field areas of Assam, Nagaland, Manipur, Mizoram, and Arunachal Pradesh, which at times even posed a risk to one's life. We, my wife and I, packed our belongings and dispatched them by road and left by train from Secunderabad railway station for Guwahati, which involved a change of train at Calcutta (Kolkata). At Calcutta we stayed overnight at the 'Nizam Palace'. All along, we were worried about our kid, Navin, who was only about three months old. The following day we boarded the train for Guwahati knowing pretty well that we were to face yet another change at 'New Bongaigoan' railway station, where there was a change from broad gauge to meter gauge. This involved a physical transfer of all the stuff to another train. My wife showed a lot of courage by holding the kid in one hand and extending help with other. It was no less than an adventure.

Finally, we reached Guwahati the next day and a friend received us at the railway station. He made us comfortable at his home and all the necessities of the kid were attended to. This was a welcome relief after a continuous train journey of three to four days. The care of the officer and his better half rejuvenated us again to face the last phase of our journey. After breakfast the following day, we took a bus to Shillong. While seeing us off at Guwahati bus stand my friend remarked, "Remember Pran, you are going from hell to heaven, and you will realise this when you reach Shillong".

After journeying for a few hours, we saw a breath taking view of a lake with clear blue water, guarded by lush green mountains on one side. Apparently, it was the 'Barapani Lake', a famous tourist spot. With such picturesque surroundings, Shillong unfolded to us, slowly but steadily. A vehicle was waiting for us, at the bus stop, to take us to the Shillong Officers' Mess where we rested for the night and planned to stay for some time until we fixed our accommodation. We had heard in Hyderabad that if one doesn't get Government accommodation in Shillong, the stay could become hell and naturally we hoped for better. The two big tin boxes that we had brought along was our support system, till the time our luggage reached. One my wife called the kitchen box, which could enable her to set up kitchen anytime, anywhere. The other contained our clothes, bedspreads and some emergent items. Thus, we could survive for some time until our luggage arrived.

The next morning I went to North Eastern Circle (NEC) of Survey of India, located at the famous 'Malki Point', the most envious location in Shillong. I reported to the office of Officer-in-Charge No. 29 Party (NEC) which was very impressive with aesthetically laid out, well-polished antique furniture. The Officer-in-Charge welcomed me to his unit and gave the initial briefing. He also informed me that on enquiry at the Estate Office it appeared that there was no residential quarter available. I thus started getting ready for 'The Hell', I had been warned about earlier.

He took me around the unit and fixed an appointment with the Director, the then Colonel S.M. Chadha, who became the Surveyor General of India in the late eighties. We entered the Director's office at the scheduled time. I was pleasantly greeted by a tall, well-built and handsome officer seated on the chair. His looks exuded tremendous confidence. I was impressed with his office which was spick and span with every item carefully placed. I found him to be very specific in his talks. Incidentally, he was the youngest Director, in the country, at that time. He was an alumnus of the 'Joint Services Wing', later named as 'National Defence Academy (NDA), Pune. General Rodrigues, Admiral L N Ramdas, and Air Chief Marshall N C Suri, the former Chiefs of Indian Army, Indian Navy and Indian Air Force, have been his course mates.

He briefed me on the 'do's and 'don'ts' of both Army and Survey life. I remember particularly one of the things that he said which was not to take any crucial decision in a hurry. He added that in such cases, unless the sky is falling over the earth, one could sleep over the decision till the next morning. He also spoke about the field area of the directorate, spread over seven states and the challenges it posed mainly because of the tough terrain and inhospitable activities prevalent in areas like Nagaland, Manipur and Mizoram. He emphasised that he was very particular that young officers should be made to carry out independent field work like any other field surveyor. This would make them wiser on the finer aspects of administration. This came as a strong hint that I shall depart from Shillong soon and probably for a substantial period of time. He offered us a cup of tea and thereafter we took his leave.

The Officer-in-Charge then introduced me to all the staff members in the unit. Amongst them were some strong, energetic and experienced young surveyors who had worked in some of the toughest terrains and inhospitable areas of the region. He identified a room and asked his staff to get some items vacated from there. They made space to put a table and chair along with a few visitors' chairs in front of the table. Pen stands, a glass top and other office accessories were also issued.

I was, however, told that I would mostly sit in the central hall, with the men and join them in carrying out field drawing, mockups and some fairdrawing originals (map publishing related materials), under an experienced section officer. I assumed charge, completed other formalities and left for the Officers' Mess, with a sense of satisfaction except for the accommodation part. I narrated the first day's experience to my wife and told her that the only concern was to arrange proper accommodation since she would soon be left alone with the little child.

Routine life started and in the evenings, we called on other officer families. We also started exploring Shillong and its markets. We found Shillong a very pretty and attractive city. One got the feel of being abroad mainly because the houses were not only nice but different, owing to their European architecture, predominantly made of wood. The ladies wore different dresses, some traditional and many western. The churches were grand and one could still see the city buses with huge vertical exhaust pipes fixed behind that emanated pungent smoke. Pretty lady constables still held the 'Stop' and 'Go' placard type luminous boards to control the traffic at various crossings. One generally got a feel that women were more dominating and worked much harder than men, while making time to groom themselves exquisitely. This was further emphasised by the fact that bridegrooms went to the bride's place and properties remained in the women's names in the revenue records even after marriage. This is a matriarchal society where the youngest daughter inherits the property.

I learnt a lot from the men in the central hall while competing with them at times. One day, we heard that Mr. Biswas, a reputed senior officer, who had worked in the toughest terrains of the North East in his younger days, had been instructed by the Surveyor General of

India to meet the Director NEC. He was assigned to write a brief compendium on 'Indo Burma Boundary', urgently required by the Government of India.

The 'Indo Burma Boundary' fell under the jurisdiction of No. 29 Party. Mr. Biswas was an authority on the same because in the capacity of the then Officer-in-Charge 29 Party (NEC), he along with his counterpart from Burma, had got the whole stretch demarcated by the 'Joint Field Survey Teams' of the two countries, using the latest Photogrammetric techniques, testament borne by the fact that he, on behalf of the Government of India, had signed the entire boundary strip maps. They say when the pillar on 'Mt.Saramati', the highest peak in Nagaland, along the Indo Burma Boundary ranges, located at a height of about 12,598 feet, was precisely laid, the message to that effect was immediately conveyed to the Prime Minister's Office (PMO) because Smt. Indira Gandhi's, the then Prime Minister of India, had desired so.

After meeting the Director, Mr. Biswas was directed to our unit as all the records were with No. 29 Party. Our Officer-in-Charge received him very warmly and I was told that he would be occupying my room. He expressed humbly that he was forcing me out of the room and I told him that I hardly sat there and generally worked with our men in the central hall. He was very happy to learn this and asked my Officer-in-Charge what was lined up for me. The Officer-in-Charge replied that I was about to be assigned some independent field tasks initially in Mairang, Meghalaya that would be followed by another task, yet to be identified. My

Officer-in-Charge told Mr. Biswas that he would be happy and satisfied if he could identify a suitable tough area for the youngster, which might put him wise on many aspects of the execution of the surveys in the North East region. Mr. Biswas asked for a couple of maps of the area around Indo Burma ranges. One could not but appreciate the fact that the contours of the area were on his fingertips. Ultimately, he marked an area with a soft pencil and sealed my fate. My Officer-in-Charge and I then left him alone. I found my room empty the next day and was told that he had been awake throughout the night and left after finishing his assignment. I asked myself, "Had God sent him here only to write my fate?"

One of my course mates, Maj. Vinod Mahindra, a bachelor, already posted to the same Directorate but in a different unit was lucky to get the last available quarter by the estate office. He had shifted from the mess a few weeks back and had taken possession of the quarter on a conditional basis, because it fell within the authorization of senior officers. Being a bachelor, recognizing my difficulty as a married man and understanding that he could comfortably get by living in the mess, he surrendered the quarter. This he did only after making certain that I was the next in line for occupation. Thanks to this generous gesture I was allotted the quarter, the next day.

This was done on a conditional basis that I would vacate it within a month in case an eligible officer was posted to any of the units, of the directorate, in Shillong. My friend asked me not to worry about the conditional allotment, as no senior officer would be posted there any time soon since most of them avoided postings to such difficult areas. I immediately broke the happy news to my wife. We soon shifted and found it to be a huge house with three bedrooms, a study, a huge dining hall, with a combination of wooden and concrete flooring and an attached servant's quarter. By then our luggage also arrived and we settled down.

## The Mairang Camp

A few days later I was ordered to move out to conduct an independent project work in Mairang, Meghalaya, about a three hour drive from Shillong. As per instructions, the job was to be completed within the next three months. I moved to the field area with the 'Khalasis' and porters assigned to carry our instruments and equipment on field. The 'Khalasis[2]' were trained permanent Government staff who were helpers and carried costly machines and instruments on their back. The senior-most 'khalasi' of my squad was Chander Singh, a highly dedicated Government servant.

We set up the camp and started the job enthusiastically. As a young officer I wanted to finish the job with lightning speed and set an example. Another incentive to finish early was that I could go back to Shillong and join my family. I had a good 'Camp Khalasi' who kept

---

[2]    Khalasis are the permanent Group 'D' staff members who in addition to various other jobs carry the survey instruments in the field

everything ready in time including a packed lunch, which Chander Singh would warm in the pressure cooker which he carried with him, to the field. I was always particular about eating hot lunch, even in the field.

It so happened that, after a few days work, some Khalasis and porters went to our Shillong office without my permission to complain to the Officer-in-Charge that I had been keeping them extraordinarily busy, much beyond the scheduled hours. In doing so they thought that my fieldwork would be paralyzed. Instead, I carried the instruments on my back while Chander Singh carried some other heavy stuff and we resumed and completed our days work in all respects. We returned late in the evening only to find all the people back, waiting in front of my tent with their heads bowed down. It appears that the Officer-in-Charge rebuked them that instead of helping a young officer, who believed in his hard work, they had left the area like cowards and thus ordered them to return. I later learnt that the news had spread through all the units of the directorate and thus my reputation started to build, right from the very beginning.

Thereafter, I got complete support of all the men for, in time they learnt that I looked after their welfare whenever they fell sick in the camp or had some minor day-to-day problems. During this period the one thing that I missed, all the time, was the company of my son. I finished the entire work within a month and informed my Officer-in-Charge through a courier. He asked me to hold on and await the Director's field inspection. Finally, one morning I saw the Director's sparkling staff car approach my camp location. I received the Director and my Officer-in-Charge. Their luggage was put in the Inspection Bungalow, which I had arranged for them.

The Director had a look at my records and charts and asked me to proceed to a point, which he indicated on the map. I took him to the correct location and he told me to go ahead with my observations and mark the position on the aerial photograph. My OC, extremely conscious, was happy when I did everything to the Director's satisfaction. Just when the two of us thought that it was over, the Director asked me to proceed to another far off location, indicated on the map. The whole procedure had to be repeated and I did it without any flaw. He then told me to leave while mentioning that he was happy with my work.

The next morning, after breakfast, the Director inspected the other administrative and technical records and wrote down his inspection remarks in his beautiful handwriting. My Officer-in-Charge was very happy and told me that the inspection remarks would be typed in the Director's office, forwarded to all units and displayed on all notice boards. After giving final touches to my work I headed out to Shillong. My wife was very happy to see me and proudly informed me that the news about my good work had spread and asked me to keep it up.

I resumed work in the office, and received compliments from the experienced and dashing surveyors for they had just read the 'Inspection Remarks' on the notice boards, promptly displayed by the Director's office.

# Chapter 17

# UNDER THE SHADOW OF THE BOUNDARY HILL RANGES

After a few days, I received the 'Technical and Administrative Instructions' from my Officer-in-Charge regarding my next assignment which was incidentally the 'hard' area marked by Sh. Biswas with his 'soft' pencil. The map depicted the last stretch of Indian soil, through the middle of which ran a dark ribbon-like thick line in North Southerly direction. This line represented the boundary between India and the then Burma.

I started collecting classified records, data related to various 'Ground Control Points' incident in the area, their accurate descriptions and other related information from volumes archived in the Directorate Library. It was interesting to read some references, as old as a century, related to fieldwork carried out by the British Army Officers, of Royal Engineers who, in those days, would be inducted to the field from London. It was a revelation to read that in many cases the officers had died enroute to India or in the Jungles of Assam due to Malaria, brain fever and other diseases.

I discussed the assignment with the experienced dare devils of our No. 29 Party who informed me that the area assigned was very difficult. Besides the terrain, there was substantial 'Naga Insurgency' predominant in the area and I was advised to be very careful. They also felt that probably one could not carry out work without intimating the Army, deployed along with the Assam Rifles, all along the boundary range. They were also responsible for the security of the people who carried out Government work in the area.

Additionally, I also learnt that my area of work was about a two day march from the road head. The vehicle would drop me, along with my authorized squad, of four to five Khalasis and porters, and return to Shillong leaving us on our own, for a couple of months, till such time we intimated our Headquarters after the completion of work. We would then be picked up from a place nearest to the exit point in the dense jungles.

I shared this news with my wife asking her to take care of herself and our son Navin, who was still a few months old. Finally, the day dawned when all the machines and instruments were loaded in a trailer, attached to a jeep and the Khalasis, led by Chander Singh, reported to me at my residence. My son was very sick and suffered from acute diarrhea. The intensity of his suffering was so severe that it could even warrant his admission in the hospital. My wife looked into my eyes and I requested her to take care. I left with a heavy heart, may be with a few tears hidden in my eyes aware that as I was leaving my wife, alone with the child in that plight.

The porters had already been asked to report to Tuensang. The office had issued them the request letter addressed to the administrative authorities for issue of their inner line passes. I planned to halt at Jorahat in Assam for the night, where my cousin, Wing Commander Rajendhar Nath was posted in the Indian Air Force. It started getting dark and suddenly I found huge sparks emanating from the left side of the running jeep over my left arm, which almost illuminated the profile of the jeep in the prevailing darkness. I got a shock, as did the driver. We were almost sure that the vehicle had caught fire. The driver applied the brakes and I tightened my grip over the instrument, which was placed between my legs, in accordance with the drill, to ensure its safety.

We inspected the vehicle and were surprised that the rear wheel had parted company and the sparks were a result of the friction between the metallic hub and the road. We were saved only because of the trailer which, on its weight, balanced the jeep. The driver informed me that we were very close to a place called 'Nowgong' but still short of a couple of hours from Jorahat.

The men along with the driver went searching for the missing tyre, which had rolled down the cutting that tapered down from the edge of the road. A hill tent was pitched for me next to the road while my camp Khalasi cooked a brief dinner. The next morning the driver took a lift in some vehicle, to the nearest town and got a mechanic who set the jeep right thus finally enabling us to reach Jorahat in the evening.

I spent the night with my cousin who made arrangements to accommodate my driver and others in the Airmen's Mess. The next morning we commenced our journey and reached 'Tuensang', the District Headquarters. I contacted the Assistant Commandant of the Assam Riffles, in whose Officer's Mess I stayed, informing him about my intention to march to 'Chingnu village', which was about eight hours uphill from the road head where our jeep would drop us. He mentioned that since it involved marching of Government officials and that too an Army officer, it had to be done tactically and under full security because the area was very sensitive and prone to the ambushes. He made arrangement for our march uphill the next day from an Assam Rifles post, located a few hours ahead of Tuensang, at the termination of the motorable track. The next morning, after breakfast, as we were about to move, it suddenly struck me to call on the District Commissioner (DC), even though it was a Sunday. I told my men to stay ready and instructed my driver to drive me to the DC's residence.

Reaching the huge gate I got down from the vehicle and sent a word across to the DC, Mr. Chetri, not sure whether he would oblige. Thankfully he did and his orderly ushered me into the drawing room and made me comfortable. I was soon joined by the DC to whom I introduced myself. He was curious to know what brought me to Tuensang. I explained my task and the area of my work on the map sheet. He was very nice and told me to be very careful because the area was infested with Naga undergrounds, operating from Burma, who were known to sneak into our territory, target the security forces and return. Mentioning that my area of work was beyond the last Indian Army Post called 'Chingnu', he noted that the setup of the 'undergrounds' was hardly a stone's throw away.

He cautioned me that as it was December, senior echelons of the self-styled 'Army of the Undergrounds' usually came across through secret routes, to the villages to which they actually belonged. Their purpose was twofold: to celebrate 'Christmas' with their families and to carry out the 'Forced Tax Collection' from villagers, often at gunpoint. He advised me to delay my departure for a day so that I could erase any mention of my rank 'Captain' from the papers and documents, under my possession. He was blunt and told me that though he had been very strict, some Naga villagers and even undergrounds had a soft corner for him because he had been trying to take care of some developmental activities in the district. He then took a piece of paper and penned down the following, "Mr. P.N. Koul is carrying out developmental surveys in the area of 'Mon' and 'Tuensang'. He should be provided all the possible help". He also scribbled something in 'Nagamese' which he said would help me in getting 'Naga

Interpreters' because at times their dialect changed from village to village. I carefully put the slip in one of the front-zipped pockets of the windcheater that I was wearing.

We drank a hot cup of tea and I thanked him sincerely. While parting he wished me all the best and rightly so because I was more than aware that I needed a lot of it. I immediately went to the Assam Rifles office and informed the officer that we would be marching up the next day, so that he could inform the concerned officials. As advised, I spent substantial time to erase my rank from the documents and official records. I also advised Chander Singh, the Khalasi, that in case anyone enquired about my profession, my rank and army background was never to be mentioned. Having worked for substantial years in such disturbed areas Chander understood the sensitivity. He assured me that he would take care and advise all the others, including the porters.

The next morning the jeep dropped us at the Assam Rifles post located at the termination of the motorable track, left us all 'footy footy' and drove off. I looked constantly at the jeep until it disappeared from my field of view and felt as if we were deprived off yet another lifeline.

I was received by the Post Commander who was an Asst. Commandant. He told me that everything was arranged. I saw a 'Section Strength' of his troops ready in their battle rigs, with their weapons and packed lunches, under the command of a Junior Commissioned Officer, awaiting marching orders from the Asst.

Commandant. I looked up towards the mountaintops that we had to climb. In the meantime, the marching orders were received by the Section Officer. I along with my full squad of porters and Khalasis joined and marched uphill tactically under full protection.

All through the climb I pitied the porters for they had a lot of heavy load, consisting of rations and instruments, on their shoulders. They were mostly Nepalese and thus physically pretty tough. After an uphill march of about seven hours we reached the village which was sparsely populated with a few 'Naga Murangs' rather huts. The area was habituated by the 'Konyak Naga' tribes, known as the headhunters of the North East and the most war loving tribe amongst the nine main Naga tribes. Both men and women were sparsely dressed. The men were mainly with bare chests and a small piece of cloth wrapped around their private parts. Some men also wore small brass miniature human heads. Women sparsely covered their chests and private parts, which reflected their primitive lifestyle.

We climbed uphill to reach the mountaintop where the last Indian Army Post at 'Chingnu' stood with pride, with one infantry Captain as the Post Commander (PC) who had been awaiting my arrival. He received me and after a hot cup of tea I was made to relax in a so-called room. The officer was very excited to see me because it was after a couple of months that he had seen any other officer.

At these lonely posts, one gets to see the same faces during daytime, in the evenings and again in the mornings. They remain cut off from the outer world, except for their radio conversations. In such circumstances one can only imagine their psychology when at times, coupled with the prevailing environment of loneliness, some of their companions get hurt or are killed by enemy ambushes or otherwise. Hats off to them!

That evening, I briefed the officer about my task and help required in enabling me to complete my task. He informed me that there was a curfew enforced in the area, most of the time, due to its sensitivity. The tracks that we had to take to reach 'Tsawlaw Top' were the same that the underground groups would use to sneak into our area. Thus, it remained mostly under fire, day and night, to prevent such incursions.

Promising his full cooperation to the extent possible, he informed me that I would have to move to the area of my work under full tactical protection, which could not be provided every day as it depended on his other commitments. His troops were mostly busy in conducting ambushes day and night. He advised me to chalk out my plan the next day so that we could discuss how best he could help and arrange the moves under tactical protection. I was happy, as he sounded very positive even in a place, which was no less than a war zone. The insecurity in the whole area, adjacent to the boundary range, was so alarming that the officers and men had strict instructions not to part with their personal weapon at any time, even during their sleep or whenever they would go to answer natures call. Their personal weapons had become a part of their body and one would see the weapons hanging from their shoulder all the time.

The next day we discussed my plan. The Post Commander required an advance notice of one night. He however cooperated to the extent of being informed about our destination only a few hours before our departure, for the first march. He felt that it was the best way to keep confidentiality about our movement. I briefed my squad to be ready early next morning to occupy a station, on a mountaintop located on the watershed of the international boundary range, above 'Tsawlaw', the Burmese village where the under grounds had their set up.

The Post Commander gave necessary orders to his men and warned everybody, including us, to keep our eyes and ears open during the long march of about seven hours, for as stated earlier we had to follow the track, which was frequently used by the undergrounds to sneak into our territory. The Post Commander shook my hand, wished me the best and thus we started off at about 5:00 am. I remembered the Deputy Commissioner of Tuensang who had adequately cautioned me about this place. We went down 'Chingnu' hill and thereafter climbed steadily upwards. While marching we heard the strange sounds of birds and beating of hollow tree trunks, akin to the beating of drums. I was surprised to hear all this for, I was aware that there were no birds or animals, not even dogs, left by the 'Konyak Nagas', in the area where they had hardly anything else to eat. The Patrol Commander explained that these were coded signals that the villagers gave to the underground groups indicating the march of security forces and their strength, on this particular track. If they didn't, they would face the consequences and most often be brutally killed by the underground.

Finally, around noon we reached our location. I had to start my observation from a circle and a dot inscribed on a plain big stone buried into and covered with the ground, in accordance with the detailed description given in my official records. I depended a lot on Chander Singh's intuition since he had worked extensively during the Indo-Burma boundary demarcation, with the joint survey teams of India and Burma.

We zeroed in on a stretch of area where we felt that the trees were a little spread out and not as huge. I ordered the minimum jungle clearance which required some trees to be cut, to ensure the inter invisibility between the stations. We then dug into the ground at many places and Chander Singh located a boundary pillar. After digging the area around the boundary pillar, we got another big flat stone, with a clean inscription on the top, which matched the office description. This was the point from where I carried out the first set of observations, lasting for about two hours.

After finishing the technical work we started our return journey without any delay, but from a different route through very thick jungles. At times, we had to make our way by cutting branches and shrubs with the 'Daw', a sharp edged mini sword like equipment. Following an alternate route was necessary because there was every possibility that the enemy may have planned an ambush if we returned from the same route.

I remember that we reached Chingnu village at mid night and climbed up the hill to our destination. The Post Commander received me and I persuaded him not to spoil the remaining part of his night. I drank a lot of warm water and retired after having dinner.

The next day, the officer told me that he had discussed my requirement with his Battalion Headquarters over the wireless. As Christmas was fast approaching, he had received word from the Intelligence that many underground groups had planned to sneak into the area. He therefore could provide me security only once a week, with great difficulty, since he had to plan and lay many ambushes; the first of which was conducted that very night. I completely understood his limitation but told him that it would result in an appreciable delay.

I recommended he speak to his Battalion Commander, over the wireless, stating that I was prepared to move and carry out my fieldwork without security cover and on my own responsibility. During my first march, I had realised that we had become very vulnerable by moving under the cover of security. In the evening, he discussed the same with his Headquarters who agreed subject to the condition that I gave it in writing, which I did without delay. I, however, requested the Post Commander to call the *Goan Buddah*, the village Head, and ask him to provide me a guide or interpreter in accordance with the DC's instruction. The village head came and agreed that a suitable tribal would accompany me until the next village where it would be the responsibility of the next 'Village Head' to provide his man to take me to the subsequent village and so on, until I finished the work.

I kept my base camp at 'Chingnu' post and planned to return, within a few days, after completion of my work.

The next day onwards I planned my tours to various places, each involving a march of about seven to ten hours. I was advised to halt at night, with the Village Heads in the *Goan Budah's* 'Murangs', as it would be safer.

One such move was to a village called 'Yimpang', again on the boundary hill range. The guide and the village head of 'Chingnu' village told me that nobody was allowed to enter 'Yimpang' owing to some devastating disease that had erupted in the village and which had already caused deaths. None of the neighbouring villagers had visited 'Yimpang' for a few months. Nevertheless, I told them that it was very important for us to go there and that we would camp in our hill tents outside the village, for a few nights.

We marched to 'Yimpang' but could not secure entry to the village. After discussions with the 'Village Head', the guide arranged a small hut adjacent to the Church. As we entered the hut, we heard the cries of some villagers. We later learnt that a villager had just succumbed to the 'mysterious' disease. We remained inconspicuous and left for our observations the next morning, returning late in the evening. That evening the village elders invited us to watch the proceedings in the Church. Here we saw some young Naga girls, lost in a trance, unaware of their surroundings, perform their religious dance, which lasted for a considerable time.

After visiting a few other places we finally returned to the base camp at 'Chingnu Post'. The next day I planned our move to a village called 'Pasoe', which was very far and involved a night halt at 'Yankhoe'.

The Post Commander at 'Pasoe' was intimated about my expected time of arrival at his post, located on the top of a mountain. The officer at 'Chingnu' said that he would himself arrange the guide who was a reformed Naga from the underground movement. I was told not to worry for the officer had a lot of confidence in him. He also told me that 'Yankhoe' was a notorious place because many from the underground, including some women members, hailed from the village. I became extremely conscious. The guide was called and asked to accompany me. While parting I jokingly told the officer not to be surprised if the man took me to 'Rangoon' instead of 'Pasoe' and we parted with a laugh.

On the way, I couldn't help but keep an eye on my guide, mainly due to his background and our destination for the day. A rigorous march of about five to six hours, which often involved rolling downhill, brought us to 'Yankhoe'. Our guide took us to the Village Head's 'Murang', a single room in the shape of a long hall, where we were told to halt

A few Naga men were sitting with the 'Village Head' and a few more joined to watch us curiously. The 'Village Head' was an old man with broad shoulders, bare chest, wearing a garland of miniature human brass heads and bluish tattoos, in the form of lines, on his face and forehead. I asked my guide to enquire about his age. The guide after asking him said the old man didn't remember his age but related his birth to some historical incident.

I also enquired about the significance of the human brass heads and the bluish tattoos on his face. I was told that the number of brass heads indicated the number of human heads that he had beheaded during the battle with their enemy tribes. I prayed that he shouldn't find reason to wear another brass head that night.

Showing the bluish lines on the face, he explained that these were heroic marks, which were chiseled with sharp needles, by the Naga women who received them after their victorious return from battles. During the long conversation, I learnt that a long time back there was intense rivalry between the Naga tribes, which resulted in a lot of bloodshed. This was the main reason that most Naga villages were strategically located on the mountaintops even though it involved considerable time and effort to fetch water from below or to reach their cultivation fields. The location of their villages on the mountaintops allowed them enough time to prepare for any attack from enemy tribes.

My camp Khalasi (CK) and Chander Singh opened my sleeping bag and instructed all to have their meals because we had to resume our march to 'Pasoe' at about 4:00 A.M., the next day. The big Murang accommodated the 'Village Head', his wife, my squad of eleven people who had slipped into their official olive green sleeping bags and me. Everybody was tired and slept like logs. Around midnight, while in deep slumber, I was suddenly woken up by Chander Singh. When I opened my eyes, to my utter surprise I felt a strange sensation in the room and saw a look of anguish on the faces of my men. I got a sense that everything was not alright. In the dark of the night I could see four to five well-built Nagas, sparsely dressed, two of them with red shawls, covering their chests, accompanied by a young man dressed in shirt and trousers.

Their leader was discussing something with the 'Village Head' while constantly watching me. He sent the young man to talk to me who, in fluent English asked me if I was from the Army or the Assam Rifles, since he saw us in olive green sleeping bags. I told him that I was not from either, adding that we were carrying out developmental surveys of the region, which would ultimately benefit the region.

He instructed me to open all my records and took his own time to read each line. Finally, he checked my chart that was mounted on a plain table. I could sense that he was still apprehensive. I then remembered the handwritten slip given to me by the Deputy Commissioner of Tuensang. I remembered readily that I had slipped it into one of the zipped front pockets of the windcheater, which I was wearing at that moment. I opened the zip of the pocket and handed him the chit, which he carefully read.

After a few tense moments he was convinced that I was not from the security forces which he went and whispered to his leader. He then summoned Chander Singh and other Khalasis and porters and quizzed them for a long time after which he suggested I relax and sleep. At that moment I couldn't help but think of the Deputy Commissioner, whose note ultimately saved us. I also admired and appreciated his popularity even amongst his enemies!

I had heard stories that these people at times sliced their own men with 'Daws' when they suspected them to be informers and therefore posed as though I had gone to sleep. After thorough discussions, the leader followed by his men left. That night I had a disturbed sleep before waking up, along with the others, at 4:00 A.M. to begin our scheduled march.

While getting ready and tightening the anklets over my trousers, stuffed in the hunting boots, I heard a commotion. We noticed a platoon strength of infantry soldiers, led by a Sikh Captain, raiding the Village Head's house. I, along with my men, was also caught. The soldiers sounded belligerent. I didn't reveal my identity, in front of the Village Head, but told them that I was a Survey Officer, carrying out the developmental surveys around the area and was about to march off, with my men, for the day's work. They then allowed us to proceed. While leaving I noticed them manhandling the Village Head and other villagers.

After marching the entire day, for about nine to ten hours with a small lunch break, we finally reached the 'Pasoe' hilltop in the evening. The security guard, at the gate of the post, stopped me and respectfully told me that the Post Commander had been waiting for me. After making the necessary entry I went in.

It was pitch dark and as I went ahead, I noticed the silhouettes of two men sitting on chairs next to a huge fire, probably beating the December cold together. On seeing me, one person got up and coming forward greeted me. He introduced himself as Major Joshi. I also met the other officer, a Sikh gentleman. We looked at each other in the light of the burning fire and realised that we had met that morning and him being the Army Officer who lead the raid on the Village Head's house, in 'Yankhoe', where we had halted for the night.

Major Joshi told me that he had been waiting for me very eagerly. The officer then asked me why I hadn't revealed my identity, which I explained. During our conversations I learnt that they had received intelligence reports, about a week back, that a self-styled 'Brigadier Khaloe' of the Naga Underground was planning to visit his village, to celebrate Christmas with his family and also to visit Yankhoe village, at a particular time, for the customary forced tax collection. The officer had arrived from Dimapur to execute the raid and catch the underground leader who was known, in the Army circles, to be very notorious. The raid, as was known by now, ended without much success.

I then narrated the incidents, of that night, to him revealing that some tribals wearing red shawls were at the Village Head's place for a long time but left well before the troops arrived. The officer told me that it must have been 'Khaloe' accompanied by his team. He told me that I should consider myself lucky for being left unharmed. He assured me that had they known my Army background, the consequence would have been brutal. He also discussed at length how the poor villagers were always faced with a catch 22 situation; if they revealed movements of the underground to the Army, the underground killed them and if they didn't their lives are made miserable by the Army. Due to this, village heads inform the Army about the movements, but usually give vague dates and in case correct dates are given then they provide wrong timings. Today's incident proved it and proved it far beyond a shadow of doubt.

The officer, along with his troops left the next morning and we continued to camp there. I fanned out all along the boundary hill range to complete my work. Major Joshi was great company. After finishing our work, we left with our baggage for another mountain top called 'Tri Junction Post', reaching there after an uphill march of about six hours. As the name implied, it was positioned partly in India, Bhutan and the then Burma. The post was commanded by an officer, Major Balhara, from Infantry. I found him very bright and learnt that he was a 'Sword of Honour' holder from the Indian Military Academy. I had to stay at his post for a couple of days to visit a number of locations over the international boundary.

During my stay, the officer looked after me like his younger brother. Generally, I would leave early morning and return around midnight, in the cold of December. He would have the helper fill one or two empty rum bottles with hot water and have it placed in my sleeping bag. To slip into the sleeping bag, on my return to the post, was a feeling enough to psyche me up for the next day's march. I remained thankful to him for his kindness.

I finally finished my work at the 'Tri Junction Post' and intimated my Headquarters, at Shillong, through a courier, to send transport to 'Tobu' village where I had planned to stay in the Officers' Mess. I instructed my men to be ready the next morning to march towards 'Tobu', which was perhaps five to six hours away. The Post Commander wanted me to stay another day, but I politely refused. The next day to my horror and despite my instructions, I didn't find my porters and other staff ready. Chander Singh told me that the Post Commander had warned all the porters against allowing me to leave that day because the rations were scheduled to be Para-dropped over the post along with meat on hoof. He then came to me and said that he had decided to hold me back, that day, under any circumstances.

After some time a chopper flew over and para-dropped the rations with some of them marked for the 'Survey of India Team', which included the meat on hoof. We had a gala dinner that night. The next day the officer saw us off and ensured that my porters were fully loaded with the 'surplus rations', most spared by the officer from his kitty. The porters carried the rations with them as a mark of gratitude on account of their hard and good work. I thanked the officer and his men for the sweet gesture and we headed out to 'Tobu'. Incidentally, I recently met the officer who has now superannuated from the Indian Army as a Major General and has been a decorated soldier.

The Infantry Battalion Commander, Colonel Tripathi, gave me a very warm reception at 'Tobu' and expressed his happiness for my volunteering to work on my own fearlessly. He also informed me that I had completed the scheduled work in record time. He requested me to put his 'Tactical Post' in order, which I did. He had to leave for a meeting scheduled at Jorahat and instructed his officers to arrange my send off a day before, thus allowing him to attend. During this time, I was eagerly awaiting the jeep that would ferry us back to Shillong.

The jeep finally arrived along with a courier who brought a letter vide which I was instructed to report to the field Camp Officer, who had his temporary Headquarters at Dimapur (Nagaland). I was assigned to take over as the Camp Officer of the camp since the present incumbent had to be moved out immediately due to some emergent circumstances. I was taken aback mainly because my wife was alone in Shillong with our little child and the fresh assignment only meant that I would not see them for a few more months.

I relieved all the staff except my camp Khalasi (the cook). My jeep with a trailer load attached, left for Dimapur, early in the morning. I planned my halt again at Jorahat, which was enroute. My cousin and his wife were pleasantly surprised. It appears that the Battalion Commander, Colonel Tripathi, who was in Jorahat for the meeting, had called on my cousin, whom he had met while both were posted in, Kanpur a few years back. They happened to develop a strong friendship, which till then I was unaware of.

My cousin told me that the Colonel had just left for Tobu, the Battalion Headquarters, from where I had arrived. They say the world is small and it really is. During his conversation, Colonel Tripathi had casually mentioned about a Kashmiri officer, Captain Koul, who was carrying out survey work in his Battalion's area of responsibility. He had also mentioned that the officer had broken their record of marching time while going from one disturbed village to the other, adding that he was working without security cover. My cousin felt proud and told him that the officer he was speaking of was none other than his own cousin. No sooner had the Colonel left than I entered. My cousin and his wife hugged and congratulated me for the good work I had done. My cousin remarked lightly, "Are you planning to become a General?"

# Chapter 18

# NAGALAND— THE ADMINISTRATIVE HEADQUARTERS

The next morning we left and reached the Dimapur Camp Headquarters. I met the Camp Officer who started the handover proceedings. He told me that the 'Administrative Headquarter Survey Project' had been going on for a few years and spread all over Nagaland. Most of the job had been completed but since the Nagas were very sensitive to the boundaries of their areas, the work of many disturbed Administrative Headquarters had been suspended, thus piling up over the years. This was currently assigned for completion. He said that the work might last for eight to nine months, which gave me a strong feeling that more of Nagaland was at hand.

He had already deployed a number of his field staff in some places establishing his 'Camp Headquarters' in Dimapur, in a small building that belonged to Director Land Records, Government of Nagaland. The place suited him because it was centrally located and facilitated efficient inspection of the field hands. I told him frankly that being a fresher, I would like to undertake some 'On the Job Training', under him, for a couple of days. He was gracious enough to agree and I chose a disturbed Administrative Headquarter called 'Zubza'.

I had heard something about this place, while I had been in Shillong. On a few occasions I had seen a 'Khasi' official, Sh. Amotam Singh, in our office in Shillong, behaving absurdly; at times even going to the extreme of creating a scene in the main hall. I was told that he used to be very efficient and had done wonderfully well during the 'Indo Burma Joint Survey'. He was later inducted to' Zubza' for some fieldwork where he lost his mental balance. They attributed this to some evil spirits or something inexplicable and paranormal, beyond anyone's comprehension. I worked under the Camp Officer for two days and picked up a few tricks of the trade, until I felt that I could confidently exercise my administrative and technical control over my field hands, deployed all around Nagaland. The next day the jeep dropped us at the Camp Headquarters in Dimapur where I took over as the Camp Officer. After a thorough evaluation of the work assigned to my camp, I came to the conclusion that the work would take at least another seven to eight months. This horrified me for I had already been away from my family for a long time and there seemed to be no end to the ordeal.

The next morning, I woke up and took a strong decision to close the Camp Headquarter, only leaving a few security guards behind. I also decided to visit the Camp Headquarter only during the last week of each month. In case of any emergency the field hands would know where to contact me since they always knew my approximate location. As per instructions, the field hands sent status reports of their fieldwork, bills and other official documents to the Camp Officer, reporting the progress of work during the last week. The Camp Officer, in turn, compiled the records of all the field hands under him and forwarded it to the Party Headquarters, in Shillong, through a courier to reach them on the last day of each month. I chose not to deploy any field hand in 'Zubza' and started the work myself wishing not to meet the fate of Amotam Singh.

I started with a bang and learnt through a courier, who had arrived from Shillong, that my Officer-in-Charge was likely to cross Kohima a day later and would see me enroute. My Officer-in-Charge arrived as scheduled. He was very happy to find that I worked independently like other surveyors in the field in spite of being a Camp Officer. He brought me a letter from my wife and some snacks. He reviewed my work and was very satisfied. While having lunch he remarked that my son, Navin, was growing fast and had started crawling. I joked and said, "Sir, one day you may come and tell me that Navin is getting married". His facial expression immediately changed. Although he was the ultimate in a unit but as regards the officers, their leave or withdrawal from the field needed the approval of the Director. He knew that my son's birthday was on the 1st of April, which was a fortnight away. He asked me to come to Shillong for a day, with official records, so I could spend time with my family, while attending to office work. I thanked him and he left for Kohima. I completed the work at 'Zubza' without meeting any evil spirits and left, as I had arrived, fighting fit.

I went to my Camp Headquarters in the last week of the month to prepare the monthly returns of the camp and various other documents. Unexpectedly, a courier arrived from the Party Headquarters at Shillong which contained official mail including a Demi Official (DO) letter from my OC, addressed to me. Vide this mail he regretted that the Director had not approved my visit to Shillong, as planned and thus it would not be possible for me to be with my family on the 1st of April. He philosophically observed that in life at times 'Duties' need to be given priority and this was one such instance. I took it in a positive spirit, completed the records and dispatched them to Shillong, through the courier.

In the days and weeks ahead, I joined my field hands deployed at very sensitive locations. They were very bright and experienced. We worked on equal footing and I learnt a lot from them. They were conscious of the fact that normally Camp Officers never worked independently, but were supposed to supervise and monitor the work done by people deployed under them. I was practically doing both.

In the evenings, after returning from the field, we would all assemble in front of my tent and make comparisons about who had done the maximum work. I sure took a few days to reach their efficiency but never felt shy to compete. I could never out beat one brilliant traverser, Sh. Chakarvorty.

I found that this attitude of not only inspecting your men but working with them created wonders and the results were incredible. We finished the work in about five to six months, including that at the sensitive Administrative Headquarters, which had been untouched for years. I sent a courier to Shillong and informed my Officer-in-Charge about the completion of the work. At the beginning he didn't believe it. Thereafter, I rang him up from Dimapur Telephone Exchange. He instructed me to hold on until the Director inspected the same. A few days later, he himself came for the field inspection of the camp. Fully satisfied he allowed me to de-induct the camp.

Thus, after carrying out nine to ten months of fieldwork, most of it hands on, I returned to Shillong. My Director was in the habit of keeping a close watch on the work carried out by young officers. On arriving at Shillong my Officer-in-Charge mentioned that he, the Director, was happy with my work. I had been in a godforsaken place and worked not to impress anyone but to satisfy my conscience. If in the bargain such good things happened, it was welcome. I was received very well by the so-called daredevils of No. 29 Party. I felt sorry for my wife and son who had been all alone during this time except that in between my younger brother, Ramesh, had visited them for a spell and stayed on for my son's first birthday.

My son obviously didn't recognize me and started weeping to find a stranger continuously in the house.

This continued for about a day or two until he was sure that the stranger was not in a mood to leave. He then started referring to me as 'Uncle' for a few days and then finally called me 'Papa'. At times, I narrate this incident to my friends and relatives and we end up laughing.

During my absence my wife had organized the house and bought certain items. The recess was tremendously enjoyable for another four to five months of productive work in office. Every Sunday, all the officers and their families visited one picnic spot or the other. Shillong had no dearth of picnic spots, which were situated very near to our location and we made the most of them. These picnic spots and the lush green parks were the lungs of Shillong, which kept it lively and in good humour.

We were blessed by a few visits of my cousin, along with his family, who was otherwise at Jorahat. During one of his visits, we visited 'Cherrapunji', the place that records the maximum rainfall in the world. We were surprised to see that the locals in 'Cherrapunji' had an acute scarcity of water because all the rainwater would ultimately pour down the hills.

The famous 'Lady Hydry Park' of Shillong was adjacent to our house and in the evenings as well as on holidays we would put our son in the pram and spend a lot of time there. My son practically learnt to walk in that park. He was very cute. I remember that at the park gate many young 'khasi' girls would literally snatch the pram from our hands, take him with them and later thank us for allowing them his sweet company. All good things come to an end and so did this sweet punctuation at Shillong.

# Chapter 19

# MORE OF NAGALAND

Planning of the next field assignments was at an advanced stage. I was told by my Officer-in-Charge that I would be deployed as one of the three Camp Officers with my Camp Headquarters at Kohima. The job involved generation of modern topographic maps of a vast area of Nagaland, including its capital city, Kohima. The area of responsibility was very large and so were the number of the Surveyors, rather field hands.

My men and I planned the fieldwork thoroughly and accordingly collected relevant records and reports from the Directorate library. I also gave responsibility to some field hands to collect the tentage and other field stores. I then sent an 'Advance Party' to Kohima so that they could reconnoiter and identify a suitable location for the Camp Headquarter. Soon, I left for Kohima in a jeep along with my camp Khalasi (cook) and the office helper. I called on the Assam Rifles Headquarters at Kohima and was happy to learn that Major R. P. Singh, of my Regiment, was posted there on deputation and held an important appointment. He told me that one Brigadier Gupta was their commander. Incidentally, Brig Gupta, recipient of the 'Vir Chakra' for his bravery during the Indo Pak war of 1971, had been our Battalion Commander of Alpha Training Battalion, in the Indian Military Academy, while I was a Gentleman Cadet (GC). As a result of this, I got a lot of help. I was allowed to establish my Headquarters at 'Jotsoma' Hill where a platoon of Assam Rifles was also deployed.

For the first time, I got my authorized snow-white tent with printed inner lining. The tent was huge and delightful. It had a small verandah/drawing room, a big bedroom with an attached washroom. The office tent was gigantic with considerable overhead space and could accommodate a number of people. The Camp Headquarter (CHQ) was laid aesthetically and blended very well with the topography of the lush green hill from where one had a bird's eye view of Kohima and its environs.

I gave instructions to the surveyors to move to their area of responsibility, along with their squads. The scene was thus set and the work commenced. As usual, I planned to stay with each field hand for a night or two and inspect their work thoroughly. I was blunt while making my remarks and was never shy to shower appreciation or point out any limitation that I would observe during the course of my inspections. The boys, as expected, worked very well. In the meantime, a message from my OC, through a courier, intimated me about the dates of the Director's inspection. I sent a courier to all my field hands to inform them about the inspection program and instructed them to be in a state of readiness. The necessary arrangement for the stay of the visiting officers was also made in the circuit house.

One fine evening, both the Director and the Officer-in-Charge arrived in their staff car. The inspection commenced the very next morning. The Director wanted to go to a far off place where one of the field hands camped in a thick and hilly terrain. We headed out in my jeep. The Director and Officer-in-Charge sat in the front seat and the two office boys and I sat in the rear seat. We carried a packed lunch, tea and some snacks. The terrain was mountainous with narrow hilly roads. On the way, while driving down from the top of a hill the driver cried out, all of a sudden, that the brakes had failed. Owing to the decent, the vehicle picked up speed, as if it was in top gear. It was about to run down a cutting and headed for a fall of a few kilometers when the Director instructed the driver to dash the vehicle against a huge rock embedded in the hill, which he did. There was a resounding bang. The vehicle was thrown to the other side of the road and rolled down the cutting. I was conscious and tried to maintain the gap between my head and roof of the jeep, which was crumpling due to the constant jolts against the ground, as it rolled down.

Now with the end seemingly near, with just a few seconds of life left, intending to make the most of it,

I thought of my son for, he would have a difficult life ahead. In the meantime, after one and a half roll as the tyres looked up, it appeared as if some external agency had suddenly stopped the vehicle from rolling down further. We emerged out of the jeep with great difficulty mindful not to disturb its critical balance. The people sitting in the front seats had a difficult time since they were stuck between the steering and the seat. We realised that we were saved because of a stone that protruded out of the ground and balanced the vectors coming from the different directions of the jeep while it rolled down. This was a miracle, by any standard.

It happened just adjacent to the village of 'Phiso', which was native to the Naga Leader, with whom the Government of India had negotiated for a long time to solve issues related to Nagas amicably. Some village women came to the site and one of them who knew a little Hindi said with a sense of astonishment, "Ek bhi nahin mara"—not a single person has died! Seeing the intensity of the accident, she naturally thought that everyone would have died. The vehicle had almost perished. My office orderly took out the belongings and found that all the office crockery had broken into pieces except my personal thermos flask which still retained some cups of hot tea.

It was nice that I had called on the Army Div. Headquarters to establish a liaison while setting up the camp. I had apprised them about the presence of my field hands who were deployed over the vast area. I swung into action and requested the DQ of the Army Div. Headquarters for help. He was kind enough to send a recovery vehicle and the jeep was brought down to Dimapur for major repairs.

It is very important to liaise with people and the administrative authorities beforehand whenever such projects are taken up. I have seen in my career that many officers shy away from establishing a relationship that at times is detrimental to the Government work, when a situation arises which warrants their help or guidance or both. My Director was very particular about such things and saw me in action. He mentioned this to my Officer-in-Charge during the inspection itself.

The inspection resumed the next day and everything went off very well. The Director inspected other field hands and made exemplary remarks, which boosted their morale and as well as mine. I was told that the inspection remarks made news again, for it had spread to other units as well and was displayed prominently on the notice boards of all the units in Shillong.

Mapping Kohima was one of the important assignments and needed a different approach to accommodate its dense details due to limitations of scale. I monitored the work of the surveyor very closely to make sure that the map stood the test of time.

I visited the War Cemetery in Kohima, located on Garrison Hill, which is maintained by the Commonwealth War Graves Commission and is counted among the best maintained War Cemeteries in the world. I saw an emotional Epitaph carved on the memorial of 2nd British Division in the memory of a thousand Allied Forces who had laid down their lives while engaging the Japanese troops in a fierce battle at the Indian front, bringing their advance to a grinding halt. This battle was fought on the tennis court of the Deputy Commissioner of Kohima and thus known as the 'Battle of the Tennis Court', which lasted from 4th April, 1944 to 22nd June, 1944.

The carved message, displayed graciously at the entrance of the Cemetery, reads:

"When You Go Home, Tell Them Of Us And Say,
For Their Tomorrow, We Gave Our Today".

The seasonal roses compliment the lush green carpet of grass in the cemetery just as the grave stones compliment the bronze plaques and make the valued sacrifice of each brave heart meaningful and thus immortal.

I met the caretaker of the cemetery who told me very interesting facts about it. I also learnt that there was a small library within the cemetery, next to his residence. I took permission to use the library and spent a few days reading some important literature and publications, relevant to the cemetery. I told the officer that I intend to write a small brief about the cemetery and file it in the relevant sheet file of the map sheet so that in the days to come people will come to know about this whenever they open the sheet file. I made a brief and filed it.

Work continued and once on returning from an inspection tour to my Camp Headquarter (CHQ) at 'Jotsoma Hill', I was shocked to find the camp razed to the ground. The tents were torn to pieces and my security guards were holding onto some important records. I was told that a huge storm had struck at night and turned the Camp Headquarter (CHQ) upside down. I decided not to ask for fresh tents from Shillong and instead liaised with the Assam Rifles Headquarters who in turn provided me some hutments, where I established the Camp Headquarter (CHQ). They also provided me a telephone extension, from their exchange, which facilitated my work.

All the field hands put in their level best and completed their targets in record time. This while taking special care of district boundaries, depicted notionally, but in many cases whose delineation did not exist on the ground. My instructions were to take signatures and thumb impressions of the village heads on these documents after understanding their version of the boundary in each village and its faithful depiction on the records. This could become a valuable supporting document at a later stage.

While the camp was at the penultimate stage of its closure, my wife and son, who stayed with my cousin in Jorahat, were scheduled to join me in Dimapur after a span of about six months. My cousin, who was in the Air Force, had arranged her move in an Army convoy. Unfortunately, my wife moved the same night when there was a huge massacre between tribal groups in the Nowgong area of Assam. This had arrested the attention of the entire nation for, the number of deaths that took place that night were comparable to what occurred at any one time during the Second World War. She had crossed the area along with my son that night while I waited for them at Dimapur praying for their safe arrival. She had been very tense but arrived safe and sound. We went to the Camp Headquarter (CHQ) where I monitored the winding up of the camp and after a few days, we left for Shillong.

My acquaintance with Nagaland was probably ending. I had no regrets as I had experienced and learned a lot. I had cut across its thick jungles, climbed some of its highest peaks, walked miles and miles over the boundary hill ranges, got closely acquainted with many of its tribes from the most forward 'AO' tribe to the most backward and wilder ones such as the 'Konyak' tribe with whom I had lived and slept many nights. Bereft of fear they, as I discovered, were very good hosts, unless of course they found out you were from the Army or the Assam Rifles.

These 'Konyaks' had a lot of pride to an extent that there were no thefts in their area. One could leave one's valuables on the side of a track or a footpath and surprisingly find it untouched on return. I thought that we, in the so-called civilized world, had a lot to learn from them. I don't know whether they retain this valued integrity over the years and secretly and sincerely wish they have.

I was told that in olden times these tribals would offer their women, as a gesture of their hospitality to the visitors, from the so-called civilized world, on occasions when they visited them in these godforsaken locations.

I also gathered that the Christian Missionaries were probably amongst the first to travel to these terrains, located in the interiors, penetrating into their ancient civilizations and bringing some refinement, probably to the extent that discouraged exploitation of their women by so-called civilized visitors. I was also surprised to see that these missionaries had translated 'The Holy Bible' into nearly seven Naga dialects, back in those days. This factual aspect must have bound them together and done some good to the tribals. This was borne out by the fact that in 'Yimpang' village I saw a few sparsely dressed men and women reading out the bible, in their own dialect, during the conduct of the prayers when I was invited to their wooden church, in spite of the restriction as explained before.

This enriching trip to Nagaland had made me wiser, in many aspects while gifting me three additional lives. The first life I owed to the trailer, which balanced the jeep when the rear tyre parted ways from us while we were speeding to Jorahat. The second one in 'Yankhoe' village while face to face with 'Khaloe', the 'Self Styled Brigadier' of the Naga rebels; this time I owed my life to Mr. Chetri, the Deputy Commissioner of Tuensang and Chander Singh, my Khalasi. The third life I owed to the strength of the stone that held our rolling jeep from falling down the cutting near Phiso's village, Jotsoma, after the brakes of our jeep failed. I had experienced and mostly enjoyed every bit of it and was prepared to experience more as per the diktats of time.

We arrived at Shillong, which once again received us warmly with its lush green vegetation, vibrant flowers, clean roads and bewitching weather. Office work started as usual, interspersed by the weekly picnics, evening get-togethers and regular visits to the Army Rhino Theatre, twice a week.

## Chapter 20

# THE OLD NEFA HILLS (ARUNACHAL PRADESH)

One fine morning, I was ordered to take over the command of the 'High Hill Unit', called No. 5 Party (North Eastern Circle). It was a prestigious unit with a wide area of responsibility, right from Assam to the high hills Of Arunachal Pradesh, which included the then old 'NEFA Hills'. It had always been a challenge to map this difficult area accurately, for it extended right up to the McMahon line on the Indo China boundary.

I felt a sense of pride in taking over the No. 5 party because of the challenges it posed. I was intimated by the Directorate Headquarters to induct the field to survey the high hills of Arunachal Pradesh, which included the hills as high as fifteen to sixteen thousand feet, with permanent snow features. Camps here should have ideally been inducted in the summer but it was delayed and it could not be helped, at that stage.

At the very outset, I called the staff, addressed them collectively, apprising them about the tough challenges ahead, the priorities and my expectations. Without wasting any time, I studied the area and instructed the Planning Section to plan the execution of fieldwork. Suitable Camp Officers and field hands were subsequently identified. Induction of field in such areas, especially in winter, warranted appreciable administrative arrangements, since the areas were covered with permanent snow features. This sometimes involved about three to four days of uphill march, from the last road head. This was also the time when the 'Long Range Patrolling' by the Army or the 'Paramilitary Forces', whosoever was responsible, didn't exist on ground, as reported by my field hands, because of extreme weather conditions.

Finally, the field was launched. To begin with, nearly hundred porters were recruited, in addition to our existing staff that generally carried instruments and other technical equipment. Adequate technical and administrative instructions were given to establish the lifeline, which involved the transportation of rations and goods of the field hands working as independent entities, under the Camp Officer (CO). They were spread out far and wide in the area. The Camp Officer had a challenging task and success of the survey missions, in such tough areas in particular, lay with him. The communication of the Camp Officer with the Party Headquarters was through monthly or special couriers. He in turn depended on his field hands who forwarded information through their monthly couriers to the Camp Headquarter (CHQ). We had no choice but to establish the Camp Headquarter (CHQ) at the road head, outside the area of responsibility where there were some minimum facilities like a Post Office or a Police Station. In ideal circumstances, the Camp Headquarter (CHQ) is located centrally at a suitable place within the area of responsibility for obvious reasons. At times, we could reach our first field hand only after two or three days of an uphill march over the treacherous mountains. These surveys were no less than expeditions and deserved to be dealt with adequate regard during their planning as well as execution.

I informed the Camp Officer (CO) about my inspection program about a fortnight in advance to make it clear that I was with them during these difficult tasks and emphasizing the fact that I meant business. In turn, he had sufficient time to intimate his field hands.

I left Shillong by jeep for the Camp Headquarter (CHQ), which was located at Dirang (Arunachal Pradesh). This small place between Bomdila and Tawang, about 47 kilometers from Bomdila, is situated on the road adjacent to the Dirang river, locally known as Dirang Chu. The road further goes up to the famous Sela Pass and then to Tawang. All these places had been in the news during the 1962 operations. I found Dirang, located at a height of about 4900 feet, a very scenic place.

The Camp Officer had set up the Camp Headquarter (CHQ) strategically across the road by the side of the river, yet away from it. In the evening, we had elaborate discussions regarding the inspection program. I desired to inspect the oldest and the youngest surveyor, deployed at the heights of about 9000 feet and 13000 feet respectively, on the same axis. The Camp Officer kept about twenty porters ready to carry stores and rations to the field hands as per their request. We prayed for good weather conditions to enable us to climb from 4900 to 13000 feet, crossing the 'Changla Pass' on our way. Incidentally, this was one of the three axes from where the Chinese had rolled down in the 1962 operations and killed a number of the lesser-equipped Indian troops, left with no option but to climb up to fight while the Chinese troops rolled down to hunt.

We halted for the night with the oldest surveyor at about 9000 feet. I was advised to take plenty of lukewarm water after which I felt refreshed. The mountains were laden with thick snow but I had a good sleep in the arctic tent. Early the next morning we got ready in our windcheaters, hunting boots and anklets to march to the youngest surveyor, at 13,000 feet. The weather was kind and we commenced our climb.

I had not yet acclimatized myself and it is never advisable to climb from 4900 to 13000 feet at a stretch. Overlooking this, I advanced mainly because I had to inspect another huge camp located in Dibrugarh (Assam) where 'Brahmaputra Bridge Survey', a very important project of national importance, indented by RITES, had been inducted and the work was in progress. A special mission of aerial photography had already been flown to photograph a considerable area for the purpose.

I was also to inspect an independent detachment, deployed in lower moderate hills where the field hand had been surveying in thick jungles of Assam, infested with wild elephants. The surveyor had intimated, through his courier, about the fear caused by the wild elephants and I therefore wanted to be with him, not that I was any match for the elephants, but simply to boost his morale.

Coming back to the inspection of the youngest surveyor, I was very keen to see him, that being his first field. The weather conditions started deteriorating around noon and after some time thick clouds covered the sky, which wore a furious look. I, along with Sham Bhadur, the office orderly who was from the family of 'Sherpas' and my Nepalese Camp Khalasi, who was equally strong, walked ahead followed by the CO, his staff and then a beeline of porters. It soon started snowing and the size of the snowflakes grew bigger and bigger. Day light began to fade but our climb went on undeterred. At one point, while crossing the 'Changla Pass', I looked behind, through the thick snowflakes, but to my surprise I couldn't see any one following us. Thinking that they may be climbing up slowly, we three kept continued to maintain our pace. The last hint of daylight started giving way to darkness and the snowfall became more intense. It would have been suicidal to stop since there was no place to rest in the absence of any form of vegetation.

As we continued to climb forward, through rough terrain of boulders and naked soil, clothed sparsely with the blanket of snow devoid of any vegetation as we had seen in the lower hills. I began to feel that we had reached a very high altitude as my lungs started grasping for every breath. Continuing the climb we reached a hilltop. The snowfall was at its peak and the last glimpse of day light made matters worse. The combination of the white sky, thick snowfall and snow-covered hills, beneath, led to a loss of perception of undulations.

I continued to walk ahead when Sham Bhadur, the man from the Nepalese family of Sherpas, caught me by my collar, pulled me behind and cried out loudly, "Sir, this is the end of the top, another few steps and you would have fallen miles down the cutting". He had practically pulled me back from the gorge of death.

Holding my hand he guided me down the hill with his 'Sherpa' intuition. We made the best of the last bit of day light and reached a frozen lake. By this time, the day had bid adieu and Sham Bhadur spotted, what he thought was the profile of some tent nearby. Walking ahead we came across a hill tent with another slightly bigger tent adjacent to it and breathed a sigh of relief. Sham Bhadur called out and to our pleasant surprise, my youngest surveyor came out of the tent and greeted us. He swung into action, lighting a small fire with his limited stock of firewood and we immediately started drying our wet hunting boots, socks and jackets.

My Camp Khalasi joined his Camp Khalasi and together they prepared a mild dinner while we discussed the technicalities and challenges of our work. We chalked out our morning plan to inspect him at a hilltop, if the weather permitted. My arctic tent was pitched and furnished with the luxurious air mattress and a comfortable sleeping bag. I did not sleep well as dark shades of worry about my people who were stuck enroute, in the freezing cold, kept biting me all through. I didn't pass this on to the young surveyor who, I am sure, must have been equally worried.

The next morning we were greeted by clear weather. We had a quick breakfast and took the luxury of donning dry clothes and good quality snow glasses, not only to neutralize the UV rays but also the intensity of the reflection of bright sunlight from the fresh snow. We went to the same mountaintop from where Sham Bhadur had pulled me by my collar the previous night. I looked around and thanked him in my heart of hearts, as it was now clear that a few more steps would have led me to the other world. I inspected the surveyor from this mountaintop because it had a good view.

I was impressed with the work of the surveyor, so without wasting any time, we marched back to our Camp Headquarter (CHQ), hoping to find our Camp Officer and his boys safe and sound. After marching down for a few hours, we spotted a line of people coming up from a distance. They were our people led by my CO. The sight of us brought a smile to each and every face. It seems they had almost written us off.

The Camp Officer said that all of them hid under some protruding boulders through the night since they could not climb ahead due to heavy snowfall. I took the

Camp Officer back with me, and the porters went with the rations and other stuff, to be delivered to the young surveyor, who rightfully deserved the replenishment. We reached the Camp Headquarter (CHQ) and I left for Shillong, via Dibrugarh, the next morning.

The return to Shillong was an adventure in itself. After reaching the plains of Assam, one had to cross Brahmaputra River by a huge ferry, in my case one which also accommodated my jeep. The ferry ride, which was enjoyable, took a few hours to reach Dibrugarh. Sitting in the jeep while we were being ferried, I prepared the inspection notes so that after supplementing it with the notes of Dibrugarh camp, I could readily give it to my office staff in Shillong for typing, cyclostyling and circulation not only amongst the Directorate Headquarters but also the field hands of all my camps and independent detachments, even if they were not connected with the work. I have always been particular about the inspection notes and ensured their transparency so that everybody in the unit and higher Headquarters is abreast of the nature of the work, its progress and the limitations, if any.

On reaching Dibrugarh I was informed, by the Camp Officer, that a telephonic message had been received from the Headquarters about Sh. R. P. Dhobi, a surveyor, of Dirang camp who had just expired. This was probably due to the 'High Hill Effect' after his return to Camp Headquarter (CHQ), at Dirang, on completion of his work. He must have arrived at Dirang just after my departure and expired the same night. He was a very sincere surveyor and the incident shocked me for I really liked him. I was conscious that the news might affect the morale of all the field hands deployed in the high hill areas. I was told that the Director had asked me to speak to him immediately after my arrival to Dibrugarh. I went to the telephone exchange and spoke to the Director who further informed me about the incident and also that the mortal remains were on their way to Shillong, escorted by responsible officials deputed by the Camp Officer of Dirang Camp. He asked me not to panic but ensure that the morale of the other field hands was taken care of, particularly at this stage.

I suggested that, if permitted, I would like to revisit some more field hands deployed on the high hills to strengthen their morale. He was more than happy to learn this and commented that he had heard that I did not respect the high hills and carry on without getting properly acclimatized. He went on to say that it was very important for me, in particular, to respect the high hills since everyone else in the camp was already acclimatized. I decided to revisit the high hills after completing inspections of the Dibrugarh Camp and the surveyor working in the elephant infested area.

Dibrugarh was another scene, much different from the high hills, as it was located in the plains. Moreover, the Camp Officer had nine jeeps, a huge truck and two mini ships, driven by what they called the pilots, to ferry field hands along with their vehicles off and on, across Brahmaputra, as required

From here, I went to see the surveyor deployed in the dense jungles of Assam, infested with wild elephants.

The young surveyor had already expressed his apprehension as mentioned before. I worked with him for a day or two. He was doing well but felt genuinely concerned about the elephants which were spotted, a few times, at places not very far from his location. I advised him to use firewood at night, for which he was authorized. He asked me, "Sir, what do I do if they come very near?" I patted him and smilingly said, "Show them your 'Survey of India Identity Card' and they will leave you unharmed." He laughed and we bid farewell.

I took the ferry back across the Brahmaputra River, reached the Dirang Camp and inspected a few field hands including the one at the famous 'Sela Pass', located at a height of 13,400 feet and is the world's highest motorable high altitude pass connecting the Tawang city and Guwahati. Known for the whistling winds and freezing cold, Sela pass had been in the news during the 1962 operations and it was here that many Indian troops fought bravely, though sparsely equipped, against the Chinese till their last breath.

While inspecting the surveyor's work, at the Sela pass, he suddenly exclaimed that he was unable to see. I was shocked and thought there may be another tragedy. However, I suddenly remembered that during the course on 'High Altitude Warfare' in the Indian Military Academy we had learnt that sometimes temporary blindness is caused due to the effects of high altitude. I made the surveyor relax for some time, amidst the gushing winds and after a short spell his vision was restored. I urged him not to panic and made him aware of the problem of 'Temporary Blindness'.

Revisiting and inspecting the field hands must have helped send a positive signal that I was with them in difficult areas and in difficult times. After inspecting the camp, I dashed to Shillong and was told by my wife that my son had been suffering with the intermittent pangs of high fever. However, on seeing me he became very excited and soon returned to being normal. That sure saved us from further visits to the doctor.

I visited the bereaved family of Sh. Dhobi, arranged for the temporary employment of his wife and calendared a cultural evening in his memory, in which many artists from Shillong performed. This included a female dancer who worked in Assamese films. The program was a hit. I mentioned in my 'Handing Over Notes' that this activity should be observed, each year, by the office in his honour as a mark of respect to his dedication and hard work to the extent that he breathed his last after completion of his work in all respects.

The next time I visited the then NEFA Hills, Arunachal Pradesh, was during an inspection tour when one of my Camp Headquarters (CHQ) was established in Tawang, the last Indian township of that area. This time too, may be unfortunately, our Camp Headquarter (CHQ) had to be established much before and outside the area of our responsibility. My first surveyor was a day's march away from the road ahead and others were still further. I recollect that there was an infantry Brigade Headquarter located there. Even though I was a young Captain, I commanded a very important high hill unit and believed in establishing proper liaisons, both with civilian and Army officials.

I stayed in our Camp Headquarter (CHQ) for the night and decided to call on the Brigade Commander, Brigadier Mahindru, in his office the next day. I was told to meet his staff officer, who was a Major, first. We shook hands and I was pleased to see the 'Para-commando' officer whose tag displayed the name Lahri.

He welcomed me saying that they had been endorsed letters from their channels about our work and the general area of our deployment. I expressed a desire to meet the Commander but got the feeling that he did not encourage the idea, probably thinking that a junior Captain could be disposed of at his level itself. I told him frankly that he could speak to his Brigade Commander in this regard and if he was busy then I would try another time. He picked up his intercom and informed the Commander that a youngster, Captain Koul, who had come from Shillong, wanted to meet him. The Commander replied, "Call the youngster for lunch today with all the officers". The staff officer conveyed this and I thought that my job was done.

While chatting over a cup of coffee, the two of us had a strong feeling that we had met before and all of a sudden, it dawned on me that we had met in the deep deserts of Rajasthan around Pokharan, about seven years back, during an Army exercise while I camped with my troops in tents. I remembered an officer, dressed in a 'Para-commando' battle rig, landing from a Jonga in front of my tent. Covered with dust he was probably carrying half the dunes of Rajasthan on his shoulders. He introduced himself as Captain Lahri.

I offered him my tent. He had a wash in my tent and I didn't allow him to depart until he agreed to have lunch with me.

He was impressed when I pointed out the addition of his moustache. He assured me that he would extend all the required help in our work right up to the McMahon line and smilingly said, "Not beyond". Later, I enjoyed a good lunch with the Brigade Commander and his officers. The Commander assured me of all help and enquired about my future program. I replied that after inspection of my camp I was scheduled to have a meeting with Ms. Neeru Nanda, the then Deputy Secretary Home, Government of India and Mr. Battacharjee, Secretary Home, Government of Arunachal Pradesh, in Itanagar. On a lighter note, he said he had to take the youngster in me seriously and smiled. Lahri and I shared our experience with him to which he commented that the world was a small place for sure and it is always exciting to meet known people, especially at such godforsaken places.

The next morning, I marched off to inspect my surveyor who was camping near 'Bumla Pass', on the Indo China boundary line. Bumla had been in the news during the 1962 operation since this is where the Chinese had mercilessly attacked Brigade strength of Indian troops who fought tooth and nail until their last breath, despite being sparsely clothed and poorly equipped.

I reached in the evening and camped in the Army location, which was a stone's throw from Bumla Pass. In the morning while climbing up Bumla Pass, I met an officer who was coming down after inspecting his gun positions. He introduced himself as Major Shah who, as I learnt later, was the famous actor Naseeruddin Shah's brother. He is probably the same officer who later on rose to the level of Deputy Chief, Indian Army. I inspected the surveyor on the borderline at Bumla. While preparing to come down, I couldn't resist myself from going ahead for about 100 meters, just to satisfy myself of having walked on the Chinese soil, but returned soon so as to avoid being caught.

The following day I left for 'Khinzamane', a place on the borderline, also in the news during the 1962 operations. It may have been a matter of coincidence that all three axes from where the Chinese troops had rolled down in the then NEEFA Hills in 1962 operations, were now being mapped under my command. We did so successfully in spite of winter being at its peak. I owe this success to all the field hands who had nerves of steel to execute my instructions in extreme weather conditions. In spite of all odds, they completed the government work setting the highest standards of surveying, which brought laurels to my unit, the No. 5 Party of North Eastern Directorate, and kept its flag flying high.

This claim is further strengthened by the fact that during that very year three field hands were awarded the 'Honorarium', for their dedicated work, by the Surveyor General of India, in the whole directorate comprising of about eight units. All three were from my unit, which included the youngest surveyor whom I had inspected at a height of about 13000 feet. This gave a lot of fillip to the whole unit and became a matter of pride for me as well.

By now my acquaintance with Arunachal Pradesh and Assam was also probably concluding. I was being considered to undergo an advanced one-year course of 'Advanced Photogrammetry', at the Survey Training Institute, currently called the Indian Institute of Surveying and Mapping, Hyderabad. It was the same institute where I had studied 'Survey Engineering' for two years and had a short tenure as an instructor and course officer for a year.

Finally, with bag and baggage we left for Hyderabad and joined the long course on 'Advanced Photogrammetry'. Soon after, in about two and a half months, we were blessed with our daughter, Smriti, on the 6th of March in the Military Hospital, Secunderabad. Going forward, I was lucky to be posted to Hyderabad itself, after the completion of the course. Meanwhile, I was also sponsored by the Department to undergo a two-semester course, 'Post Graduate Diploma in Computer Methods & Programming', in Hyderabad. Some of the other course mates were officers from Electronic Corporation of India (ECIL) and the majority were freshers, either engineers from B.tech or M.tech streams. The course was conducted in the evenings and was on the pattern of the 'Credit System'. It involved frequent internal and sometimes external examinations and warranted a lot of studies.

To my good luck, I had a very rich library of 'The Survey Training Institute' within the office premises which I made full use of. Initially, I found it difficult to balance office work during the day, classes in the evening and studies at night. I wanted to withdraw from the course but was very apprehensive that it would cause my wife to doubt my capability, a prospect I couldn't accept. Finally, I made up my mind to continue and do well in the course. I started leaving the house for office in the mornings when my children would be asleep, devote the forenoon to office work and study in the library thereafter, leave to attend the classes in the evening and finally return home late when my children would be fast asleep. During this time they hardly saw me, except on Sundays and thus I became, what I called, a 'Sunday Father'. I went on to complete the course successfully and pass it with a distinction.

# PART IX

# Mapping Goes Digital

# Chapter 21

# THE AMERICAN EXPERIENCE

The Survey of India, under the Ministry of Science and Technology, is one of the oldest Government organisations in our country and has always kept itself abreast with the latest technologies. During the pre-independence era, it had well known Royal Sapper officers who were regarded all over the world for their contribution to the science of surveying and mapping.

As mentioned before, Colonel George Everest, in whose name the highest peak of the world is named, was the Surveyor General of India more than 225 years ago. He gave the world a new mathematical surface, 'Everest Spheroid', as a reference spheroid to which India and adjacent countries were mapped. The organisation had stalwarts like Brigadier Bomford whose books on Geodetic Science are, even today, referred to in many universities in the world. The contribution to survey sciences from Lambton, the famous Royal Sapper Officer and many others who, while on the staff of Survey of India, has been remarkable.

The survey technology has always received a fillip, from time to time, mainly due to its defence applications. The faculty of 'Photogrammetry', making of maps using aerial photographs as data source, got a boost during the Second World War due to obvious reasons. This led to the development of 'Analytical Photogrammetry', which involved simultaneous solutions to innumerable mathematical equations. However, this demand for a strong 'Computation Support' couldn't be met by computing systems that were available at the time. The Photogrammetric Science per force transited to the so called 'Analogue Photogrammetric Systems' and further development all over the world resulted in more sophistication of 'Analogue Photogrammetric Machines', manufactured by 'Wild Switzerland', 'Kern' and some other manufacturers with optics generally from 'Zeiss'. The Survey of India imported sophisticated systems and used the latest technology for generation of maps like any other advanced country in the world.

The powerful computer systems with advanced architecture, supported by sophisticated operating systems, in the early eighties made not only simultaneous solution of hundreds of equations possible but also enabled their computation in real time. This lead to the new era of 'Photogrammetric Workstations', enabling synchronization and perfect registration possible, in real time, between the 3-D model of the earth's terrain, generated within the workstation, and the corresponding digital map superimposed over the terrain. Thus, it became possible not only to generate digital maps but also to store them on the computer systems, which further facilitated the user-friendly process of map updating.

However, there was a substantial and deliberate lag in the manufacture of such equipment because by that time high end manufacturers from all over the world such as 'Wild Switzerland' had invested a lot in the analogue technology and had thus set up the manufacturing lines at their plants specifically intended for 'Analogue Photogrammetric Machines'. They delayed adopting the digital technology but couldn't withhold it for long after giant computer corporations took the lead in countries such as America, Norway, Germany and Switzerland.

In India, the Ministry of Science and Technology decided to go digital and procure expensive digital mapping systems, which offered an end-to-end solution in the digital environment. After a lot of deliberation the decision was taken in 1987 and two huge configurations were identified, one financed by the United Nations and the other by the Government of India. The first configuration was from 'SYSCAN', a Norwegian Company and the other was from the famous Intergraph Computer Corporation located in Huntsville, USA. India raised two 'Digital Mapping Centers', one located in Dehradun, which was of a much bigger configuration and the other in Hyderabad. The Norwegian system was installed at the Modern Cartographic Centre in Dehradun.

I happened to be one of the officers who were selected for posting to these centers in 1988. We were deputed to undergo basic training with agents of Intergraph Corporation in Mumbai. After completion of the basic training, five of us were deputed to the United States to undergo advanced training at Intergraph Computer Corporation in Huntsville, Alabama. This place was and is best known for the NASA Space Centre where Armstrong, the first human to step on the moon, had been trained before his historic journey to the moon.

We took a British Airways flight to London. On landing at Heathrow Airport, I felt as if we had landed at Ludhiana because many of the counters were manned by Sikhs. We intended to shop at the duty free counters but finding everything available to be pretty expensive, ended up just window shopping. We then proceeded to Huntsville via Chicago and landed at midnight. An officer, deputed by Intergraph Computer Corporation to receive us, took us directly to Hotel 'Ramada Inn', where we stayed for the night. The next morning we were given the option of either staying at the hotel or opting for a fully furnished apartment, authorized to officers of Intergraph Corporation. This was in accordance with the Memorandum of Understanding (MOU) signed between the Government of India and the vendor. This was very thoughtful on the part of senior officers who drafted or rather finalized the MoU.

We immediately opted for the double room apartments in order to give each other company. The apartments were luxurious and fully furnished. The NASA Space Centre was a few houses away from my apartment and had a common wall with our colony.

The first day we took a cab to reach Intergraph Corporation, which was about ten to fifteen kilometers away and our training commenced with immediate effect. To make things even better, we were provided the use of an attractive Toyota van without a driver, for the duration of our training., This came as a great relief because travel by cabs proved to be rather expensive.

In those days, Huntsville was a nice city, a quiet place devoid of any railway line and passenger buses. We learnt that it was called the science city. The headquarters of Intergraph Computer Corporation, one of NASA's known centers and various other scientific organisations were located there. The Intergraph Computer Corporation was an ocean to the human eye. Their workshop was massive. We were taken for a visit to the workshop in a small train, which was an astonishing and great experience.

The instructors were a dedicated team and experts in their own fields and some of them had been professors in reputed American universities. This included Dr. Don Woodley from the U.S., Dr. Algarf from Egypt and Dr. Mustaffa from Iran. We would take notes of everything possible, both in the class or the lab keeping in mind the fact that, on our return, we were expected to install and operationalise these systems.

The instructors and lab assistants were cooperative and often went out of their way to address our queries. On Friday, most of them would turn out in shorts, eagerly waiting to drive off with their mobile homes or trailer boats towed to their vehicles, for the weekend.

We completed our assignments on time so as to avoid having to make the long drive on Saturday, and would instead visit prominent places, located further away. During one such drive to Birmingham, a historic city in Alabama, which was a few hours' drive from Huntsville, we encountered an experience which could only be termed 'bitter'. It appeared, while on our way, we had erred while driving and to top it we failed to respond to signals given by the traffic police, asking us to stop. Innocently, we continued to drive and before we could even realise, a fleet of vehicles surrounded us. We were driven to the side of the road, escorted by two or three police vehicles in front, two at rear and two on our left side. All the vehicles were flashing sirens and dissipating bright lights.

The police instructed us to sit motionless in the vehicle and physically pulled out the officer who was driving, searching him thoroughly while pointing pistols at each of us. We happened to be accompanied by the wives of two colleagues who were scared, to say the least. The situation was akin to a Hollywood movie. Finally, after checking the driver's license and papers related to the vehicle, we were allowed to proceed. We then asked them the reason for the entire episode and they replied that since we hadn't responded to their signals, from Birmingham itself, they had suspected us for Mexicans on an illegal mission.

While in Intergraph Corporation, we found a smile on every face, which spoke volumes about the general level of satisfaction of people and their prosperity. Whenever we requested any one for the location of a post box, to post our letters, they would offer to post the letters themselves. As a result, we never saw the location of a post box in the premises. Such was the extent of their courtesies to foreign guests.

While walking the corridors of the huge training centre, whenever they observed us approaching the glass doors they would hold the doors open until we had crossed and give a parting smile as well. Every stranger wished us when we crossed their path as if they knew us intimately. It was a good training ground to learn the day-to-day positivities and courtesies. These finer things matter a lot in life and make it worthwhile to live.

There were many Indians in the NASA Space Centre. One evening they arranged a get together in one of the scientist's houses, where we enjoyed Indian dishes and learnt about their experiences. I also learnt that most of them wanted to come back to India but couldn't because their children had assimilated into the American culture and would probably, genuinely, find it difficult to adjust in an Indian environment.

One day we visited the NASA space centre which, as mentioned, was extremely close to our location. The entry tickets, we felt, were not very cheap but the visit that lasted for almost a day was worth it. On entering, there was a huge compound with a prominent long pole, which had a fulcrum in the centre. The pole was fixed to a tall and wide base in such a way that the long pole revolved round its fulcrum, with the support of a motor, and made a very huge circle with the radius of the height of about a two-storey building. It had a simple hand rest fixed to one extreme end, without any seat belts or any other support whatsoever. Only those visitors who volunteered were allowed to try it. The volunteer would sit on the extreme end of the pole with the help of the hand rest and legs placed on either side of the pole. The revolution of the pole started from a point, which was a little higher than the ground, and it took the volunteer to an extreme height, without any support other than the hand rest.

I volunteered and by the time I reached the topmost point, I sweated from every pore and cursed myself for having volunteered for the ride. After a few revolutions, the motor stopped and in my heart of hearts, I thanked the stars for the safe landing. I got down from the pole sporting a tired smile just to show my bravery to my friends and other visitors.

My colleague, Dr. Darmar, also volunteered after seeing the appreciation I got from people around us but by the time he started going up the colour of his face started fading slowly but steadily. To his bad luck, when he reached the top most position, the motor developed a defect and he had no choice but stay at that position for quite some time. I am sure he must have cursed himself for having tried it but, like me, he also pretended that everything was fine. Unfortunately, his facial expressions didn't support his false gestures for too long.

The museum was impressive and amongst other things, we saw the space suit that Armstrong wore while landing on the moon. We also saw the fragment of the space lab, which had fallen on Australian soil when the Americans had destroyed their disused sky lab in space. This fragment had generated a buzz in the whole world and resulted in some unpleasant arguments between Australia and United States, back then.

Another memorable experience was watching a movie in the NASA theatre that was simulated such that the viewer felt as if the voyage from earth to moon and back was real. The intensity of this feeling, of traveling in space, was so great that I was convinced that the strict instruction given at the beginning of the movie, to fix and tighten the seat belts, was not only justified but also required. I remember feeling the jitters, sensation of fear and a sunken stomach that one experienced during the travel and more so towards the end when one landed on the earth.

The state of the-art expertise in robotics was also on display when a robot received us at the entrance of the museum and extended all courtesies just as a refined human would normally do.

On completion of the course, we visited Los Angeles via San Francisco. We were eager to see 'Disney Land' and 'Universal Studios' in Hollywood. Our official itinerary gave us a few days off which we spent in Los Angles because our flight from Hong Kong to Delhi was scheduled only once a week.

We checked into a Hotel near 'Disney Land' and later took a guided tour of this wonder. It was a different world and a memorable visit. We saw advanced robotics in action while listening to the famous speech of Abraham Lincoln. The robot was such a lifelike replica of Lincoln that it felt as if the former President of the United States was delivering his famous address in flesh and blood. We also saw huge photographs of Walt Disney along with famous personalities such as John.F.Kennedy and our very own Pandit Nehru and Raj Kapoor.

Towards the culmination of this visit, in the later part of the evening, we witnessed a breath-taking scene of a caravan embellished with illumination and beautiful dancing girls, a vision that cannot be expressed in words.

The visit to Universal Studios was a revelation as well. Preserved sets of box office hits such as 'The Ten Commandments', 'Jaws', 'Earthquake', 'King Kong' and many others were astonishing as were the sets of the ever famous 'Star Trek' serial. It was nice to find an Indian restaurant in Hollywood that came as a welcome rescue. We also saw the 'Walk of Fame' with names of famous Hollywood actors engraved on it and walked along its side to see who all had earned the honours. We later took a guided tour to see places of interest in Los Angles including the streets, best known for infamous gang wars.

We finally took the Hong Kong flight via Tokyo after a night spent visiting various places of interest, including the 'Metro Rail', which I was seeing for the first time.

Our visit, which was a once in lifetime experience, came to an end as we boarded our flight to Delhi.

## Chapter 22

# DEHRADUN BECKONS

After landing in New Delhi, I rushed to Hyderabad to meet my family. Here I learnt that I had been transferred to the Digital Mapping Centre, Dehradun. We thus packed our baggage and moved. By this time, the Digital Mapping Centre was already set up. The systems, which had been shipped from USA, were already installed, as per the design planned, by American engineers of Intergraph Corporation and their Indian agents. We five officers, freshly trained, joined them and commenced the Site Acceptance Test (SAT).

As per the contract, we were imparted an additional three months training on the system by the engineers of Intergraph Corporation, which also included Dr. Don Woodley and Dr. Algarph, our instructors in USA. In the meantime, about a dozen junior officers were deputed to International Training Centre, located in Holland, to undergo a three months course. The five of us were made responsible to operationalise the systems. These systems had also been installed, around the same time, in Australia and Japan. I was designated Division Head, Photogrammetry and DTM (Digital Terrain Modeling) and oversaw 'Engineering Software Packages'. We worked day and night to operationalise all systems and passed on the knowhow to the junior officers who returned from Holland after completion of their training.

Soon we started getting a lot of important visitors and final year students from some of the IITs. We had a number of foreign visitors as well. Along with my team, I was driven to do a lot of research on the systems. Results began to show up in the production pipeline and this earned the praise of the senior echelons, on many occasions. The success, of my division, was mainly because of the dedication of my team members who worked hard day and night.

During this period the 'Everest Bicentenary Celebrations' were held in London and India. India was given the responsibility of bringing out the first digital map and a great quantum of the work fell on my shoulders. One of the major tasks was to generate a Digital Terrain Model of Mount Everest itself.

We were beginners and I was given a few days to complete my part of the job. We were yet to operationalise the corresponding software modules. I generated the binary files but had a tough time to generate its graphics. I used to be in the computer centre, sometimes alone until midnight for a few days. I remember that one late night I was alone in the computer centre with a security guard, who had been waiting for me to close so that he could seal the centre. I referred to the notes I had prepared during the course of my training in USA and found a small clue. I applied some permutations and combinations, based on the clue and succeeded. It was the early hours of the morning and I remember almost jumping with joy. In the excitement, I forgot to note down the line of flow and after the successful processing, for reasons unknown, I ended up deleting the products generated. I guess the pressure of having to produce the desired result, within the specified timeframe, coupled with the loneliness of the computer centre at night as the culprit. To say I was very upset, would be an understatement. However, I decided to call it a day.

I reached home but could not sleep well. Starting fresh and early the next morning, I worked for a few hours remembering all that I had done the last night and by God's grace succeeded, yet again. This time round, I took the precaution of taking notes of all steps and processes followed. The Director was very happy and immediately rang up the Surveyor General of India. Owing to this experience, I ensured that in future no officer or operator ever worked alone in the computer centre, at night, since a very strange psychology often creeps in and makes one commit blunders, unintentionally.

My innings at the Digital Mapping Centre (DMC) was peppered with many satisfying moments. This included successfully setting up the first SPOT stereo Model in the Analytical Photogrammetric Workstation in India and the technical paper, related to it, was selected for oral presentation in an International Workshop conducted by the 'International Institute of Photogrammetry and Remote Sensing' in Vienna (Austria).

Meanwhile, I learnt that I had been selected to participate and lead the 'Survey of India' team in the Indian Scientific Expedition to Antarctica for the year 1991-92. I have penned down the overview of the experiences of this great and unique journey in a subsequent chapter, 'The Journey to the Least Known Land', only to give it the respect it deserves.

# Chapter 23

# DEPUTATION TO BHUTAN

The posting at the Digital Mapping Centre did me a lot of good. I was later deputed to Government of Bhutan, as a 'Senior Level Expert', to work on the 'Indo Bhutan Survey Cooperation Project (IBSCP)' at Thimphu, the capital city of Bhutan. This included acceptance of Photogrammetric Systems from Switzerland and some software modules from the University of Austria, on behalf of the Governments of both India and Bhutan. It was a great experience which provided more than one chance to visit Bhutan and each such trip has been memorable.

I preferred to fly by 'Druk Air', the Royal Airlines of the Govt. of Bhutan, mainly because it would directly fly to Bhutan with an intermittent halt at Kathmandu, the capital of Nepal. More importantly, it would fly very close to the Everest Peak, which I was very keen to see in order to check the extent to which it agreed with the simulated digital terrain model that I had generated for the map brought out by India, on the occasion of 'Everest Bicentenary Celebrations'. To my bad luck, on the first two occasions, the peak was surrounded by very thick clouds, standing like an iron curtain between the Everest and me.

During my third trip, two foreign women tourists were seated next to me. One was a florist from the U.S. and the other was a professor probably from Oxford. They were visiting Bhutan together, for a couple of days, after which they planned to fly back to their respective countries. To my relief, as we approached Everest, there was not even a wisp of cloud, as was the case before. The grace of the world's highest peak mesmerized us beyond words. I remember, I was sitting on the window side and the women wanted me to exchange seats so that they could get a clear view. With a heavy heart and what would be termed as 'ungentlemanly', I refused. I later apologised to them and explained my reasons. Having viewed Everest from a close range, I was convinced that we had depicted the digitally generated simulation, of the peak, on the map, reasonably well.

Thimphu, the capital city of Bhutan, is about half an hour drive from the airport, which is located at Paro. It is a lovely, small city covered by lush green mountains. People are mostly Buddhists but there are as many Nepali migrants settled there. I found a 'Son of the Soil' sentiment prevalent leading to a sense of insecurity within the Nepalese community. Apart from this I found the Bhutanese very warm and possessive about India, whom they considered a great friend.

I was on foreign deputation to the Survey of Bhutan. My itinerary had been synchronized with the itinerary of an expert Swiss engineer whose company supplied the systems. It was a nice experience to work with the engineer who had come to install and operationalise the systems and thereafter the additional responsibility to design and supervise the training of the Bhutanese officials, in using the systems for generating products.

The assignment imposed a great responsibility on me to not only accept the systems transparently but also ensure there were safe guards if it developed problems later. The expert from Switzerland had configured the software modules in the hard disk of the systems in Switzerland itself and expected me to accept the system after he had run them successfully. He wanted to handover the huge stock of compact disks and floppies to the Bhutanese officials since he had already completed loading and configuring the same back home.

I disagreed and expected him to load each of the software modules in my presence to make sure that the content of diskettes and configuration of the software were correct. It appeared that he had come to Bhutan just to get enough time to go around the hills and advocated a short cut that could be followed for acceptance of the system. I was forthright and meant business. He said it would take too much of time if he followed my way of acceptance of the system but he realised that I was firm about it. The matter soon took a serious turn and he threatened to fly back to Switzerland that very day, if I insisted on redoing the entire process. He stated that he had to attend to other assignments in various countries. I humbly left the decision to him and started doing my job.

Taking his brief case he went out of my chamber fuming. I was sure he had left for his hotel to pack up and was a little worried because such an eventuality could have resulted in some sparks flying and probably things boomeranging back to me. The matter was sensitive, more so because I was on a foreign mission. I was however, confident in my approach since I knew I was right in my request. It was only being fair to the Survey of Bhutan.

After a couple of hours, as I worked in my chamber gloomily, to my surprise I found the expert from Switzerland enter along with the Project Coordinator. As expected, he glowered but sat quietly. It seemed he had complained about me to the Project Coordinator and repeated his threat. Thankfully the coordinator understood my logic completely and apprised him that things would go against him and his company, if he followed through with the threat. With the odds stacked against him, he agreed to carry out the process as requested. I must mention that I found him to be a very capable and knowledgeable person. During the process he cooperated completely and we developed a good understanding. It was on my insistence that he went around Bhutan, during the last two to three days of his stay.

I wrote a detailed report on the installation and acceptance of the system ensuring that it covered not only the salient details about the equipment but also helped solve operational problems which could arise, while running the system, in future. The Deputy Director of 'Survey of Bhutan', Mr. Ugyen Tenzing, was kind enough to offer me a stenographer for secretarial services, who helped key in the elaborate report, observing minimum breaks, for days together, thus allowing me to submit it on time.

My wife and 12-year-old daughter joined me in Thimphu, during the last two days of stay, by which time I had completed my work in all respects The Secretary Survey, Govt. of Bhutan made certain that we traveled around Bhutan and visited all the important places. Finally we went to Phuentsholing, on our exit route and stayed in the famous Druk Hotel for the night and thereafter drove to 'Bhagdogra', which is the border town in India, to take the afternoon flight to Delhi via Calcutta.

During our return we had a strange experience, which left a permanent impression on our mind. The flight was late because of the delayed landing of an incoming flight from Delhi, which finally landed towards dusk and all the passengers including a number of foreigners, hurried to board the aircraft. Those days, passengers had to identify their baggage before boarding the aircraft. After identifying the baggage we were about to take our first step on the stairway of the aircraft, when all the lights within the aircraft went off. We were sent back and informed that there would be a little delay.

To our horror, the delay had no end and we were finally told that to rectify the issue, a major part needed to be transported from Delhi, which was possible only the next day and hence we were put up at a very standard hotel. All of us thanked our stars that a serious tragedy was averted since the same problem could have occurred midair. My family enjoyed the hospitality of Indian Airlines, not only during the night, but the next day as well. We came back to Dehradun and that brought me to the culmination of a very interesting short and experiencing tenure in Bhutan.

After a few months, I was ordered by the Surveyor General of India to open a new office, the first 'Geomatics Centre' in New Delhi. We moved with bag and baggage to Delhi and I, along with my team of officers, took about one and a half years to set up the 'Geomatics Centre' and to bring it to the initial level of production mode.

Meanwhile, there was a strong rumour that I was being considered for a posting back to the Army. I learnt through reliable sources that a letter to that effect had been floated from the Department of Science and Technology (DST) to the Ministry of Defence (MOD). Perhaps my long tenure in the Survey of India (DST) was at the penultimate stage of culmination. This long tenure in civil and a scientific environment at that had done me a lot of good and I flag it as an important milestone in my whole career. It provided a fertile platform to blend the professional experience of a sapper and a surveyor. This 'blend' went a long way in helping me administer and launch survey operations in some of the toughest and most hostile areas of north east; explore and map the challenging terrain of Antarctica, which at times warranted risk to life as elaborated ahead and execute the 250 kilometer long Oil Pipe Line Survey, from 'Manmad' to Bharat Petroleum Corporation (BPCL) Refinery in Mumbai, which went across the toughest Western Ghats and densely populated areas of Mumbai.

I do not shy away from noting that my reputation of being a hard task master had travelled both in civil organisation and Army circles. I had the fortune to work closely with subordinates right down to the operator level, both in field and office. This brought me face to face with them several times over the same tables and terminals. This aspect made me wise on both technical and administrative fronts, which led, if I may so remark, to my success. I should also be frank enough to reveal that I have always been bestowed the confidence and love of my seniors, in spite of my forthright attitude.

# PART X

# Voyage to the
# Least Known Land

## Chapter 24

# INDIAN EXPEDITION TO ANTARCTICA

The desire to visit and explore least known lands had probably been in my subconscious mind always. The feeling was, however, dormant maybe because I had never got a chance to vent it out until I was commissioned in the Indian Army and subsequently transferred to the North East Region, the experiences of which I have detailed in the previous chapters.

It was in 1981 that media reports started to appear about India's plan to send its first expedition to Antarctica. The inherent wish to see the unknown land simmered deep in my mind but I didn't discuss it with anyone. To my good luck, I came across a notification, issued by the Department of Ocean Development (DOD), Govt. of India, calling for volunteers to participate in the Antarctica Expedition. Without any hesitation I volunteered immediately and put forward a written request, which had to go through official channels, with the recommendations of my Officer-in-Charge, to start with. This was the period when I was being inducted to 'Mon' and 'Tuensang' area of Nagaland to carry out the independent surveying and mapping work. It appears that my Officer-in-Charge was against me participating in the expedition, because of the risk involved. He silently informed my wife about the issue and apprised her about the risks involved, probably feeling that it was not a responsible decision on my part.

When I went home for lunch that day, I found my wife in a pensive mood. She told me frankly that she was not in favour of my participation in the expedition. I assured her that I shall not opt for it without her consent though she should know that there was no lesser risk involved in the field work that I was assigned to carry out in the militant hit 'Mon' and 'Tuensang' area of Nagaland. Thereafter, my Officer-in-Charge summoned me to his office and told me that he would forward my application to the Director's office only after I had given it due consideration, which I never exercised, thus missing my first chance to see Antarctica.

In the months ahead, my wife realised that my life was equally at risk, if not more, while I worked in the militant hit area along the 'Indo Burma Boundary Hill Ranges', as it was perceived in regard to Antarctica. My Director, the then Colonel S.M. Chadha, learnt about this much later and felt very sorry for, he always liked young officers to undertake adventure.

A decade later, the Department of Ocean Development (DOD) approached the 'Survey of India' to participate in an expedition to the unknown land and inducted the first team of Surveyors, in 1990, to provide control work in the near vicinity of the Indian station 'Maitri'. As destiny would have it, I once again came across the notification, in 1991, issued by the Surveyor General of India calling volunteers to participate in the 'Indian Scientific Expedition to Antarctica' while I was posted to 'Digital Mapping Centre' at Dehradun. Many other officers had also volunteered. When the results were announced I was surprised to find that not only I had been selected but was also designated the team leader, of the survey team.

Many organisations were eager to take part in the expedition but owing to the fact that the strength of the scientific team was limited to only twenty five members, the Department of Ocean Development initiated and followed a strict selection process. The sub team leaders were required to present the objectives of their respective organisations to a board of officers, under the Chairmanship of Mr. V. K. Raina, the then Deputy Director General—Geological Survey of India (GSI), a famous scientist and mountaineer, who had led the second Indian expedition to Antarctica. He was the one who had recommended 'Maitri' as the alternative location for the Indian Antarctic Station when the first Indian Station, 'Dakhsin Gangotri' started sinking in the ice shelf.

On behalf of Survey of India, I made the presentation and pronounced very crisply our aim to provide GPS control points in farther areas of 'Gruber', Wohlthat Massif and Petermann mountain ranges, as far as 150 to 200 kilometers from the Indian station at 'Maitri'. Our team was finally selected and we were subjected to a very strict Medical check-up which was carried out over three full days at Ram Manohar Lohia Hospital, Delhi. The standards of the medical test were very high and understandably so. In fact, one of the team members was rejected on medical grounds. Surprisingly, the official who came in as a replacement was also rejected. Thus my team was reduced to only three members instead of four, as planned.

We were to be part of the 'Summer Expedition'. Each expedition had two teams; one the 'Summer Team' which returned after about six months and the second was the 'Winter Team' which was left behind to live through the winter in Antarctica, which lasted for about a year and a half. The 'Winter Team' was left on their own, well-equipped but with no ship to their rescue and were brought back along with the summer team of the subsequent expedition.

Director, Geodetic and Research Branch of Survey of India was responsible for coordinating the activities of our team, within 'Survey of India'. I was directed to provide the GPS control during the expedition. However, on my own initiative, I told my team to collect additional Electronic Measurement Machines (EDMs) and related instruments, which may enable us to generate a map of Indian Station 'Maitri'. This was beyond the requirements and tasks assigned.

The national team included 25 scientists supported by 75 Army, Air Force and Naval personnel, including naval cooks, pilots, air craft maintenance team, sappers and two medical officers, one each from the Army and Air Force. We were deputed to the Indo Tibetan Border Police (ITBP) Training Centre, Joshimath, near the famous Badrinath temple, to undergo 'Snow and Ice Training', for 2 weeks. Everyone in the team was treated at par, without any distinction whatsoever, which was the norm during such expeditions.

A member from the 'Film Division of India', Sh. Udai Shankar, a reputed photographer, was a part of the team, assigned to film the expedition. A journalist, Sh. Pant, who was a mountaineer as well and a medical specialist from the All India Institute of Medical Sciences, who was there to carry out studies on polar medicine, were also part of the team. The training, which took us to many avalanches, not only sharpened our skills of 'Snow and Ice Training' but also provided a platform for all the team members to interact with and understand each other prior to the expedition. This was a great advantage. After the 2 weeks, we went back to our respective places and remained in a state of readiness to move at short notice.

The day of departure soon arrived and our team was given a farewell, organised in the office of the Surveyor General of Indian Dehradun. A number of Directors of the department, from across the country attended the ceremony. The Surveyor General handed me a memento to be presented to the Station Commander of the Indian Antarctica Station who was wintering at the station along with his team.

I assured the Surveyor General and all the senior officers in attendance that we would put our best efforts, not only to complete the assigned task but also to keep the flag of Survey of India flying high through the course of the expedition. All members of the national expedition team reached Goa, a couple of days in advance, to board the Swedish Ship 'Thuleland', which was one of the best ships in the world those days for sailing to 'Antarctica'. We heard that the particular Swedish shipping company had two such ships, meant for sailing to the Polar Regions. However, they had lost one after it collided with an iceberg, in the Arctic region. The ship had seven to eight storeys, which included luxurious, well-furnished air-conditioned cabins fully equipped with inbuilt wardrobes, small refrigerators and various other utilities. It also had a mini cinema hall, a huge gym, a sauna bath, huge well-furnished dining halls and many more utilities complimented by a huge and long deck. It had the capacity to accommodate five to six choppers inside and two on the deck, at any time.

While in Goa I suddenly remembered that I had forgotten to pack an important personal item. My wife had packed my *Pheran*, the Kashmiri robe, and a pack of leaves of 'Kashmiri Kahwa Tea', also called *Moghul Chai* in Kashmiri. Unfortunately, I forgot to carry it along when I left home. I had planned to take a photograph, on the ice shelf of Antarctica, wearing the *Pharen*, with a cup of 'Kashmiri Kahwa' in my hand. This was a wish that was never to be realised. Even today, whenever I think about it, I feel bad.

During the four to five days when the ship was being loaded, the team was taken to different beaches in Goa each morning for 'Yoga', under the instructions of a professional 'Yoga Master'. Apart from a huge consignment of supplies and equipment two big Air Force choppers (MI-8s) and three naval choppers (Cheetas) were loaded onto the ship.

On the 'D Day', all team members assembled at the Goa port, with a lot of fanfare involving TV reporters, journalists, senior officers of each participant organisation, families and VIPs, including the Columbian Ambassador and the Secretary Department of Ocean Development, Govt. of India.

The moment of truth arrived and the name of each member was announced, who then shook hands with the VIPs before climbing the stairs of the ship. While I shook hands with the Secretary of the Department of Ocean Development, he requested me to create a map of the area, for which the government had been spending several crores of rupees, each year, without much success. I couldn't get myself to tell him that I had been assigned to provide the GPS control points during the expedition and not the map. His direction, as a humble request, kept simmering in my mind, as it was very genuine.

Finally, after the last member climbed the ship, the Naval Band swung into action and filled the environment with lively tunes. This, merged with the loud voices of the people and resonated to wish the members a safe voyage to the least known land. Finally, the pilots of two boats, belonging to the Port Trust of

India, blew their hooters to indicate that the ship was ready to start. At that stage, the mighty 'Thuleland' blew its horn with full might and began her voyage, with two pilot boats guiding her out, on either side for some distance and finally leaving her to sail to the far off ice continent.

After sailing for about two days many members fell victim to 'seasickness'. Their condition was pitiable and started becoming pathetic as we continued. They would feel nauseous all the time, coupled with headaches and restlessness. As a result they never stepped out of the cabins and kept low all the time. This continued until we reached Mauritius. We were told that the precedence had been that on reaching Mauritius the ship was not officially anchored at the shore. Instead, in the past, the Captains had anchored ships in the middle of the sea and boatmen would arrive from the shore to take the members to the port. The members would then tour Mauritius and return to the ship at night and the ship would resume sailing in the morning.

To our surprise the ship touched and anchored at the shore and thus entitled us to land in Mauritius officially. We later learnt that since the Govt of India was bestowing a chopper upon the Govt. of Mauritius, which had been loaded on the ship, the ship was allowed to touch shore. After docking, the Govt. of Mauritius sent a number of beautiful cars and we were taken around to experience the breathtaking views of this beautiful place.

The ship had to wait for some consignments from Norway including inner thermals for the team members, which hadn't reached India in time. They were couriered by the Norwegian firm so it could be delivered to the leader of the expedition in Mauritius. This was a blessing in disguise, for us, as we remained in Mauritius for a few more days. The following day the Prime Minister of Mauritius hosted a lunch in honour of the team members of the Indian Scientific Expedition to Antarctica, which was a pleasant experience.

Once the Norwegian consignment was received the ship resumed its sail from the port of Mauritius. Those who suffered from seasickness had a wonderful time in Mauritius but started suffering again and this time around they knew it would last longer as Antarctica was still far away.

The ship continued to sail day and night, over the blue waters of the sea and under the umbrella of the blue sky. I remember the scenic beauty of the sea, which I would generally enjoy during sunset sitting silently on the deck of the ship. One got a feeling that the ship was lost in the infinite waters of the sea for there was no sign of life except water everywhere. The ship was equipped with a rich library, which I utilised to the fullest. Valuable books on the subject put me wise on some of the interesting facets of the least known part of the world, to the extent that I made some broad notes related to its evolution, exploration, wild life, weather, Aurora and other interesting aspects, which make it different from the other continents. I retain these notes even today in the original rough format and append them as and when I come across other interesting aspects, on the subject, from the newspapers or while surfing the internet.

It is interesting to know that Antarctica was formed as a result of the breakup of a much larger Super Continent known as Gondwanna, millions of years ago, which included Australia, New Zealand, South Africa, South America and India. The fact has been supported by a theory that the Gondwanna continent broke away and resulted in the movement of landmasses to their present positions. The science related to 'Plate Tectonics' explains the movement of the Earth's crest and its plates which is a slow but continuous process. In their explanations about the massive breakup of the super continent, the scientists have analysed and concluded how the plates subsequently fitted together like a jigsaw puzzle. The ultimate coming together of the landmasses and existence of similar rocks and fossils found across these break away continents strengthens this theory further.

As regards the exploration, no one had ever seen the ice continent until 1819. The ancient Greeks, however, followed the myth of 'Terra Australis Incognita', in accordance to which they believed that the earth was round. They strongly believed in the existence of a large southern landmass which balanced the weight of the known part of the world in the northern hemisphere. The Europeans, however, opposed this myth until a new wave of exploration swept through Europe in the fifteenth century. Bartholomew Diaz and Vasco de Gama explored and opined that Africa extended only to the Cape of Good Hope. Expeditions by Ferdinand Francis Drake in 1577-1580 and some others led to the discovery of Australia. As a result of this, the myth of 'Terra Australis' continued and geographers assumed that the story didn't end there. This encouraged further exploration.

James Clark Ross, J. R. Foster, G. Foster and James Weddell have been some of the famous explorers who made a mark in their valuable explorations of the unknown land. The famous explorer James Cook crossed the Antarctic Circle in his voyage of 1772-1776 and explored further sub Antarctic Islands. He was the first human to encircle Antarctica.

On 27th January, 1820, a Russian Admiral, Thaddeus von Bellingshausen, became the first to sight Antarctica. He had been sent by Tsar Alexander to explore the southern harbours, for the imperial fleet. His was the second expedition to have encircled the Antarctic continent.

The British Royal Navy Officer, Edward Brainsfield went on to become the first person to sight the Antarctic Peninsula. As per records of his midshipman, Bone, they unexpectedly saw the landmass at 64 degrees latitude. This further encouraged explorers to venture towards the long-sought after southern continent.

The first official landing, on the continent, was made by Henry.K. Johan Bull, a Norwegian who had migrated to Melbourne, when he led a commercial expedition down south to Ross Sea. The ship left Melbourne on 26th September, 1894 and the main landing was made on 24th January, 1895. They say that commercially the expedition was a failure but became highly valuable on account of the geographical findings which boosted the urge to explore the unknown continent. Another landmark expedition, led by Shakleton in 1907-1909 with Edworth David, Alastair Mackay and Douglas

Mawson as other members, was launched with the aim of reaching Southern Magnetic pole. In all, they travelled 2360 kilometers without dogs and ponies.

This race to conquer the South Pole continued and initiated many more expeditions. Robert Scott's Discovery expedition (1901-1904) was one such which unfortunately failed. Sir Ernest Shackleton then led the British Antarctic expedition which sailed over the Weddell Sea for the South Georgia Island, with the aim of establishing a shore station to support the exploration of the interiors of Antarctica.

There is an interesting story behind the two overlapping expeditions—Roald Amudsen's Fram expedition (1909-1912) and Robert Scott's Terra Nova expedition. Each of them wanted to be the first to reach the South Pole. Amudsen kept his aim, of conquering the South Pole, a guarded secret. Amundsen's superior planning, comparatively favourable weather and above all the secrecy of his mission, keeping Robert Scott in the dark, enabled him to reach the South Pole first.

Robert Scott's Terra Nova expedition set out for South Pole on 1ˢᵗ November, 1911 along with his four companions Evans, Oates, Bowers and Wilson. They faced tremendous hardships and deadly weather but succeeded in reaching the South Pole on 16ᵗʰ January, 1912. They were, however, shocked to find the tent and flag left by Amudsen, who had conquered it thirty three days earlier. Sadly, harsh weather perished Scott and his companions on their return journey. In his attempt to save Bowers and Wilson, Oates walked into a blizzard and succumbed. Evans died of a fall while Scott was the last to die because of acute exposure and starvation.[3]

The British, shocked on hearing news of the death of Ronald Scott and his team mates, declared them national heroes. It seems their tragic deaths overshadowed the victory of Amudsen.

A search party, launched by the British, under Surgeon Attickson succeeded in finding the dead bodies of Scott and his two other companions, Bowers and Wilson. The three bodies were lying in a tent—Wilson with his hands across his chest, Bowers wrapped in his sleeping bag while Scott lay half out of his bag with one arm stretched towards Wilson. One of the search party members, Tryggve Gran in envy said, "They died having done something great—how hard must not death be having done nothing".

Attickson took charge of the diaries and letters which told their story of hardship and extreme bravery. One gets a glimpse of this as best described by Robert Scott in the following few lines penned down by him on 29th March, 1912:

"We took risks, we knew we took them . . . Had we lived, I should have had a tale to tell of the hardihood, endurance and courage of my companions . . . These rough notes and our dead bodies must tell the tale . . ."

---

[3]   Time Magazine—January 1990 issue

Attickson then read out the account of Oate's death. This was followed by the burial services and all of them sang Scott's favourite hymn 'Onward Christian Soldiers'. The tent was collapsed and a small snow cairn, built with a pair of crossed skis, was planted on top.

"Here they would lie until one day, drifting with the barrier, they would find their final resting place in the sea".[4]

Led by Attickson, the search party retraced their steps along the path which was believed to be followed by Scott, while on his search for Oates. Approximating the spot where they felt Oates had fallen, they erected a cross with the following inscription:

"Hereabouts died a very gallant gentleman, Captain L.E.G. Oates of the Inniskilling Dragoons. In March 1912, returning from the Pole, he walked willingly to his death in a blizzard to try to save his comrades, beset by hardship".[5]

Man's inquisitiveness ensured that the exploration of the continent continued. The 'Mechanised Age' dawned around 1923 and modern means of mechanical transport swapped age old methods of skiing, man hauling and dog sledging. Some of the famous explorers of this era include Sir George Hubert Wilkin from Australia, Sir Richard Evelyn Bryd who was an American naval officer, Lincoln Ellsworth, the son of an American

---

[4]    Oraclequest Education Foundation
[5]    Oraclequest Education Foundation

millionaire and Sir Vivian Ernest Fuchs who led the first land crossing of Antarctica in 1957, covering about 3473 kilometers from Weddell sea, across the south pole, to the Ross.

Another noted explorer of the 'Mechanised Age', who explored Antarctica, was Sir Edmund Hillary, the world famous New Zealander who had already created history by being the first human to set foot on the highest peak on earth, Mount Everest, on 29th May, 1953. This he did along with the Nepalese Sherpa Tenzing Norway. In Antarctica, he used converted farm tractors to cross the ice continent and was the third to reach the South Pole by overland journey. During the 1967 expedition to Antarctica he also made the first ascent of Mount Herschel.

All the men who led or took part in expeditions to the deadly ice continent had interesting stories to narrate which speak volumes about their strength, both physical and mental. Their narrations speak of their common traits—courage, dare devil endurance, utmost dedication towards the mission and above all the iron will to achieve the goal, at any cost.

The broad notes, I had prepared while on the ship, appended until date, have much more to offer, in addition to the above-mentioned facts of interest. These I shall share with you as we go ahead.

Our life on the ship varied each day but there was a sedentary element that I broke up undertaking some form of physical exercise. I made it a point to run a few kilometres every day on the deck of the ship. Additionally, I joined the 'Yoga Group' and attended classes daily which were run by the medical specialist from the All India Institute of Medical Science.

The scenes of sunset and sunrise started to get more mesmerizing as we approached nearer to the tip of South Africa. 'Thuleland' kept on sailing day after day in its attempt to take us closer to the ice continent inch by inch.

After about three weeks of sailing, we crossed a small South African Iceland, almost at an arm's length. The Captain of our ship said that it housed some scientific laboratory in a few sparsely populated buildings that existed. We saw some men in a distance and were tempted to go near and talk to them. The ship, on our request, made two to three rounds of the island, but didn't touch the shore for a major part of the world, India included, had cut off interaction with South Africa, in those days, due to its policy of apartheid. As we progressed, the days became longer to the extent that we had the company of the sun until dinner time which, in the beginning, was a strange feeling.

As we continued, the weather started to get rough. Wind speeds increased forcing the captain to have all the exit doors locked and issue strict orders against any team member venturing on deck. The ship now began rolling and pitching in an awkward manner making everyone alert. The rough seas warranted that all crockery in the kitchen and the huge dining halls to be adequately secured. We were advised to use ropes to secure the chairs and tables in our cabins.

Soon we began to feel as if we were caught in a deadly storm. It was a frightening sight when we looked through the glass panes of our cabins. Waves came like mountains of water and lashed at the ship, time and again, throwing about all the loose items lying in the cabins and other places. We were told that we had entered the corridors of what is called 'The Roaring Forties'. The situation only worsened as we sailed ahead and entered the region called the 'Furious Fifties'. The amplitude of the rolls and pitches of the ship increased manifold.

Readers may know that the 'oceans around Antarctica provide an almost uninterrupted corridor for circumpolar westerly winds, which blow around the main latitudes. These latitudes earned the sobriquets of 'Roaring Forties' and 'Furious 'Fifties' in the nineteenth century when the sailing ships used these winds to enhance their fast passage around the earth. The westerlies extend through the entire depth of 'Troposphere' (the lowest level of atmosphere) and give birth to these great atmospheric depressions which move around Antarctica and generally spiraled in towards its coast.

A few days later, we emerged out of these roaring and furious latitudes and the sea became comparatively calmer. To our dismay, the weather worsened which seriously affected visibility. By now we were drawn into the region of floating icebergs where visibility was important. All at once, we felt the ship come to a standstill. In spite of the fact that it was day, intense bad weather had made it pitch dark. Visibility dropped to almost zero and gave us a feeling as if the night had spread its paws again. The Captain of our ship was supposed to be one of the best in the world as regards competency to sail in Polar Regions. He was known to be gifted with great intuition when it came to weather forecast or sailing on rough seas. He, in his wisdom, had decided to halt the ship. I remember going to the bridge where he showed me, massive icebergs in the immediate vicinity of the ship, on his radar. Sailing further, in almost zero visibility, could have been catastrophic. After sometime, using his skills, he began to steer the ship forward slowly but steadily. Suddenly, the weather conditions improved and it turned bright. The Antarctic environs, under the light of day, started opening up with spectacular scenes that one could only dream of. The rays of the sun made the floating icebergs look like mobile pearls, some small and some big, spread all over the chest of the blue waters of the ocean, under the veil of the light blue sky.

For us this was a pleasant punctuation, after the harsh treatment of the 'Roaring Forties' and the 'Furious Fifties'. All the expedition members were excited to have first-hand experience of these scenes, which one generally read about in books or watched on television.

During this time I learnt that Mr. Peter, a painter on the ship was actually a very famous photographer who took up employment on such ships, the world over, so that he could embark on expeditions to the Antarctica which he photographed extensively. We further learnt that he contributed his pictures to the National Geographic Journal for many years. Without wasting any time he started clicking some beautiful shots.

At this stage, it may be worthwhile for readers to know some more salient facts about Antarctica, based on the extract of my broad notes[6]. Antarctica is the highest of all continents with an average elevation of 2300 meters. It covers an area of about 14,000,000 square kilometers and contains about 90 per cent of the world's ice. The Antarctic continent is classified as a desert since the annual precipitation in Antarctica is lesser than many deserts. Its climate limits plant life to very hardy lichens, mosses and algae in some coastal areas and scattered mountains.

Nearly three dozen species of birds ranging from the magnificent Albatross to gulls, cormorants, terns and other visit the sub Antarctic islands. The animal life mainly consists of penguins, squas, seals, snow petrels and whales. Penguins are the most personable and are more active than the seals, squas or petrels. They are by far the most interesting of all the Antarctic animals. These animals are rarely found on land and depend on the sea for their food, mainly 'krill'.

'Krill' is a Norwegian term and means 'small fry'. It is the main source of food for Antarctic animals and birds. Nature has gifted it with five pairs of legs which probably enables it to stay afloat despite being heavier than water. Mature female krills lay about 2000-3000 eggs at a time which sink deep into the sea and are pushed southwardly towards the coasts, by the under currents. Here they hatch into larvae and subsequently

---

[6]   I incorporated a similar note in the topographic map 'Maitri and Environs' brought out by Survey of India in 1992.

mature and rise to the surface, after two to three years. In summer they live on a variety of microorganisms whereas in winter they survive on algae, which is available on the underside of the pack ice.

Another interesting Antarctic creature is the 'Ice Fish'. It is the most unusual among vertebrates in Antarctic waters and lacks appreciably in haemoglobin, the red pigment in the blood which carries oxygen. They have only ten per cent of the oxygen carrying capacity, as compared to other fish, but nature has bestowed upon it some spatial features which help it adapt to its environment. The body of Ice fish contains anti-freeze molecules because of which the body fluids remain still and don't freeze at sub-zero temperatures. They say it is still not fully understood how their system works.[7]

There are about 18 species of penguins which include the Emperor, Adelie, Gentoo Chinstrap, King, Rackhoppe and Macaroni penguins. Emperor penguins are generally about a metre tall and weigh about 30 kilograms. They lay eggs, about 13 centimeters long which weigh approximately 0.4 kilograms. They hold the eggs on their feet and cover them under their special abdominal skin. It is the male who first takes charge of the egg within a few hours and the female proceeds to the sea to feed herself for a period of one month, while the starving male incubates the egg at temperatures as low as –45 degrees Centigrade, against heavy blizzards and in the process sheds about 40 per cent of its weight.

---

[7]    Oraclequest Education Foundation

The males get relief only after the females return. It is astounding to see them recognise their partners with precise accuracy. At this stage the chick, which has by now hatched, is transferred to the mother's feet while the male leaves for the sea to have his first meal after four months. The swapping of responsibilities continues till mid-December when the chicks reach about 60 per cent of their adult body weight. At this stage they venture out to their next environment, the sea. Similar is the case with other types of penguins except for some small variations.

Seals are by far amongst the best adapted animals to the cold waters of Antarctica. They are various species such as the Leopard seal, Ross seal, Crabeater seal, Elephant seal, and Antarctic Fur seal. The longest amongst them are the Elephant and Leopard seals, which measure about 3 meters and weigh about 400 kilograms. Antarctic Fur seals are the shortest, the males measure about 2 meters and weigh about 100 kilograms while the females measure about 1.5 meters and weigh less than 50 kilograms. Unlike other species of seals, the Antarctic Fur seals can walk and even run on the steep ground

There are two main categories of whales—'Baleen' and 'Toothed'. Baleen whales are differentiated into Blue whale, Fin whale, Sei whale, Southern Right whale, Humpback whale and Minke whale. Toothed whales include Orca whale, Southern Bottlenose whale, Sperm whale and Southern Four tooth whale and Dolphins. Toothed whales are smaller, both in size and weight but not necessarily in strength.

Blue whales are considered to be the largest mammals in the world. They are generally 40 meters long and weigh about 84 tonnes but the recorded weight of some Blue whales has been 180 tonnes. Fin whales are about 20 meters long and weigh about 40 to 50 tonnes and do not venture as far as the Blue whales, instead limiting themselves to the extent, which can allow them to feed mainly on krill. The Sei whales are about 18.5 meters in length, weigh about 29 tonnes and have a life span of about 70 years while the Southern Right whales, although only about half a metre longer than the Sei whales, weigh about 96 tonnes. Humpbacked whales usually weigh about 31 kilograms. They are known to produce the longest and the most varied songs in the animal world. The Minke whales have an average length of 6 to 8 meters and weigh about 6 tonnes.

In the 'Toothed' category, the Orca whale, also called Killer whale, is about 9 meters long and weighs about 6 to 7 tonnes. They feed on Ice Fish but prefer warm blooded prey. They are very strong and are known to attack and feed on Fin whales and other bigger whales.

Antarctica has a unique climate as a result of high latitude, perpetual snow cover, and great heights of ice plateau, and the vast extent of its surrounding ocean. It is very different from the north polar zone which, although at a similar latitude, is essentially an ocean surrounded by land. The Antarctic weather is dominated by extreme cold and varies in average and extreme temperatures. The world's lowest known temperature, −89.2 degrees Centigrade (126.6 degrees Fahrenheit), was recorded at Vostak (USSR) station in 1983. Winds, some of which have been clocked at 320 kilometers per hour, come up and turn a pleasant day into a day where survival may become difficult. Whiteouts occur very often when the surface definition is lost due to the absence of shadows which makes travelling hazardous, due to the loss in the perception of undulations.

One of the most spectacular natural phenomena that exists in Antarctica is Aurora Australis, which consists of spectacular patterns of light that are visible in the night skies. It is caused by a magnetic field, which gives rise to many complex reactions in the magnetosphere. Some particles of the solar wind travel down to the thermosphere into auroral ovals and initiate vast systems of electric currents that excite the polar aurorae.

During the last fifty years, Antarctica has attracted the attention of every major scientific community of the world. It was only after 1956 that inland stations were built. At present Argentina, China, Russia, USA, South Africa, U.K., Germany and India have established their permanent stations. In 1987 scientists of the British Antarctic Survey reported the detection of a 'hole' in the Ozone layer in the earth's stratosphere. This major breakthrough in scientific research stunned environmentalists and the phenomenon is constantly studied in most of the scientific stations, in Antarctica, including the Indian station. Scientists are also exploring the existence of various minerals and efforts are being made to relate the scientific studies carried out in Antarctica to the recent environmental changes so that effective management and conservation studies can be carried out.

Like the other members, I became impatient to reach the stunning continent due to these interesting features. Day by day, hour by hour we inched forward to the Antarctic shore. Excitement was at a crescendo as we approached the shore and the Captain finally anchored the ship very near to the ice shelf. This sent ripples of happiness across every face. Those who were seasick started to regain their balance. One could see happiness on their face. The sky was so clear that one got the impression that Antarctica was devoid of clouds.

I was standing with the Expedition Leader, Dr. Mukerjee and Dr. Dhargalkar and we were in a celebrative mood due to the safe arrival after a month's sailing. Dr. Dhargalkar was a reputed scientist and the first Indian to have 'Wintered in Antarctica' with the Australians. We were good friends and I found him to be a nice human being. Dr. Mukherjee decided to call on the Indian Station at Maitri straightaway. It meant flying choppers for less than an hour one way. This didn't matter for there was only day and no night. I personally felt that he could have positioned the calling for the next day. Dr. Dhargalkar also felt the same, but we did not obstruct his decision.

Dr. Mukerjee identified a call group and two choppers, one MI-8 of the Air Force and another 'Cheetha', from the Navy, were brought up to deck and kept in a state of readiness. Dr. Mukerjee asked Dr. Dhargalkar and me to be careful and take care until they returned. The leader, along with Mr. Udaishankar, the photographer from the Film Division, hopped into the naval chopper and both the choppers flew away. The weather appeared to be ideal for flying since there wasn't even a trace of cloud across the blue sky and wind had literally gone to sleep.

Dr. Dhargalkar and I together appreciated the surrounding scenery. It was a breathtaking sight to see penguins come towards the ship in hundreds with their 'quack quack' sounds, without much hesitation. The seals, in dozens, lay on the shore motionless and unfurled despite our presence. Some members started taking photographs and some got busy recording video. After about three to four hours, Dr. Dhargalkar and I started to get concerned as we expected the call group to return by then. To our dismay, this didn't happen. In the meantime, the weather got bad. Wind speeds started to increase and the visibility fell drastically.

The radio officer confirmed that both the choppers had left the Indian station Maitri more than an hour and a half back. Anguish started to build but we didn't reveal it to other members. By now, the visibility had reduced further and we could hardly see anything beyond the ship.

All of a sudden, we heard the sound of a chopper and soon the Air Force chopper landed on the ship. I signaled the pilot, Flt Lt Cheema and went to him, while the rotor of the chopper was still running. He enquired the whereabouts of the naval chopper and was taken aback when I informed him that it had not yet returned. He mentioned that it had left much before his. This was now a matter of serious concern and soon all the team members were aware. Flt Lt Cheema consulted his senior, Wing Commander Gill, and loading a substantial number of fuel drums on to their chopper, left on the rescue mission. With the weather only getting worse we waited endlessly for both choppers, but in vain.

Apparently, while returning from the Maitri the weather turned nasty causing the pilot of the naval chopper to lose track, due to poor visibility and gushing winds. After flying for a long time he realised that he had exhausted his fuel dangerously and thus decided to land on an iceberg, next to the shore while keeping the rotor of the chopper running with the two pilots, leader and the photographer inside. Just when fuel was about to get exhausted, which would have resulted in them freezing to death, Flt Lt Cheema, despite poor visibility noticed something resembling a blue dot on the iceberg, through a gap in the clouds. On closer examination, Flt Lt Cheema and his senior pilot were relieved to find the naval chopper, almost totally exhausted of fuel. Hovering at an optimum height they pumped substantial fuel into the naval chopper from the fuel drums they had carried

The two choppers then flew back together, salvaging the situation. Incidentally, the pilot of the naval chopper, Raj, was a decorated pilot and flew with confidence but on that particular day, the Antarctic fury went against him.

Antarctica thus, in its own way, showed us its colours on the very first day. This was an important lesson indicative of the fact that Antarctica was never to be taken for granted. Bright weather changed to furious in no time; silent winds changed their tempers going from zero to hundreds of kilometers in no time; where everything looked beautiful only till an incident occurred and when it did it was usually catastrophic.

The next day various teams were flown to Indian station Maitri, one after the other, in accordance with the priority of work. I, along with my team, flew with our machines and other instruments. My team had the maximum outdoor fieldwork scheduled. Help was limited and team members had to do everything including but not limited to unloading of multiple helicopter sorties, lifting and hauling cement bags and other construction materials, on their shoulders.

Maitri, located in Schirmacher Oasis, is one of the smallest Antarctic Oasis and a typical polar desert. It is about 25 kilometers long and 3 kilometers wide with an area of about 34 square kilometers. It is about 100 meters above the sea level and is situated in the Schirmacher Hills on the Princess Astrid Coast in Queen Maud Land, East Antarctica.[8] On reaching Maitri, I entered the allotted hut with a very heavy haversack on my back, worn over my overalls. While removing the haversack, a member of the previous team, who had a long beard, wished me from a distance. I reciprocated and got busy arranging my possessions. He remained standing and asked me, "*Kausher chha yiwan?*", meaning do you know Kashmiri (in the local dialect). I was shocked and equally thrilled that someone was talking to me in Kashmiri and that too in Antarctica. He introduced himself as Dr. Hanjura, the then Station Commander of Indian Station and leader of the previous expedition. I had heard his name and that he was a reputed scientist from the National

---

[8]    Indian Antarctic Program—Wikipedia the Free Encyclopedia

Physical Laboratory, but was completely unaware of the Kashmiri connection. I later heard that he had been a brilliant student and was further surprised when, in passing conversation, I realised that we had a very close common friend, Dr. Inder Bhat, my course mate and room partner in the Engineering College, about whom I have mentioned before.

Members of the Indian expedition received the best possible rigs and food at par with the richest countries of the world. The station also had well equipped labs, to carry out necessary scientific research.

The leader inducted all the teams and discussed my plan of work. We depended heavily on the leader, for the logistics, but were independent while carrying out our technical work. During the discussions, I indented for helicopter sorties to enable my team provide GPS control points in some far off mountains such as Guber, Wholthot Massif and Petermann mountains. He informed me that ours was the only team, which had such intense requirement of helicopter sorties, due to the nature of our work and assured me of all possible help. He, however, added that these mountain ranges were about 150 to 200 kilometers away from the Indian Station.

It appeared that each sortie would involve about one to one and a half hours of flying, on either side. Guber, Wohlthat Massif and Petermann mountain ranges were known to be hostile with regard to wind speeds, which increased from zero to two hundred kilometer within no time. Each sortie, was thus required to be launched with utmost care and precautions. I was asked to give in writing an undertaking that we would work, in these mountain ranges, at our own risk. I had no issues with this demand and did so immediately. Keeping in mind the element of danger associated with all the three ranges, the leader instructed to fly two choppers instead of one. The additional chopper was just to boost the morale of the leading pilot and to help in crisis management, which may erupt anytime.

Dr. Mukerjee was an experienced leader and had already taken part in more than one Antarctic expedition. As mentioned already he had also wintered in Antarctica and was thus more than aware of the hostile mountain ranges because a few scientists had actually lost their lives, in one of the ranges, during an earlier expedition.

We were also aware of the fact that the number of clear days would be very less and my team needed to start their fieldwork immediately. The deal was sealed and I called my team to brief them. I grounded one of the two members in Maitri so that he could carry out GPS observations at the station, since observations had to be carried out in differential mode which meant that observations had to be carried out at two stations, simultaneously. The other team member accompanied me to the mountain ranges with the second GPS.

The following day was clear and we were permitted to fly. Both the choppers were ready and my teammate and I flew with Raj, the ace flier. The other chopper flew empty behind us. Mid-way through our flight the pilots realised that a strange phenomenon occurred, which caused a breakdown in communication with Maitri, after we crossed a particular location. They attributed it to a magnetic storm. The pilots, thereafter, remained incommunicable with the Indian station. We took more than an hour to reach Gruber mountain ranges and were dropped at a place that was suitable for landing. From there, my team member and I had to walk over the thick ice cap to reach the hilltop where we wanted to take an observation.

Being a hostile area the pilots had instructions to drop us in the area of work, fly back to Maitri and then returns to the mountain ranges to bring us back. This was to ensure they remained out of the danger zone, at any given time, except when they transported us. Logic was that should the weather turn hostile, during our observations, at least the choppers, which were the lifeline of the expedition, would be safe.

The pilots told us to be available, at the exact place where they left us, in two and a half hours. This was the minimum time we needed for our satellite tracking by GPS. The choppers flew back to Maitri and I recall that we were the only two creatures left on the vast ice sheets, which ran for miles and miles, plain at some places and mountainous at others. The weather was thankfully good with bright sun and no wind.

Suddenly, both of us heard strange sounds, which resembled the shatter of glass breaking all around and beneath us. I became very alert. I carried a GPS on my back along with a sleeping bag and emergency rations in the haversack. I asked my teammate to maintain some distance and walk behind me because the sound of breaking glasses made me believe that there might be crevasses underneath and if one of us fell into the crevasse at least the other would be safe.

I had never walked slower in my life than I did that day to cover a distance of about hundred meters. We soon started our observations but to our bad luck they failed because there was no satellite tracking. I tried all means at my disposal but in vain. In the middle of all this, we were delayed in reaching the designated spot where the choppers had already landed. This is generally not done and the senior pilot did not hide his displeasure. Such delays, in such conditions often lead to tragedies. I apologised, knowing he was right. I myself was in a very bad mood due to the failed observations but didn't share it with anyone. When we returned, the leader greeted and congratulated us on the eve of the first successful observation. I thanked him but didn't share my agony.

In the evening, I told him that we needed to go to Guber again. He almost sprang up on hearing the request and refused to allot a sortie. We argued and I told him that I needed to strengthen the observation further and if the particular sortie was not cleared, I would not observe at other mountain ranges. Finally, he relented and we flew the next day. He also sent Sh. Udaishankar, the photographer, to film us in Guber Mountains, taking observations. Luckily, the observation was successful that day. As a result, I was excited and not only hugged but also kissed my teammate when the instrument started tracking the satellites. Udai silently captured this joyous demonstration without letting us know and it was included in the film. After finishing our work, we reported at the designated place, on time and the choppers came and picked us up.

I had detailed discussions with my team members regarding us taking up additional work to survey around the Indian Station during clear evenings and nights, since there was no sunset during the period of our stay in Antarctica. Fortunately, we had brought all the necessary instruments with us. My team was supportive and soon we started to carry out the additional work, in our spare time as well as on days when we did not receive clearance to fly to the mountains, due to bad weather.

The next few days were busy and pretty non-productive until one day we were cleared to fly to Wohlthat Massif. As usual, we flew with Raj and the other chopper flew behind. The pilots faced the same phenomena resulting in a break in communication with Maitri Station, when we crossed the particular area, mentioned before. On reaching the mountain ranges, the pilot hovered for some time and selected a suitable spot to drop us. While dropping us the pilots had a quick discussion and informed me that the wind speed had started rising and as such they didn't want to risk leaving us behind. Hence, they decided to keep the rotors of both the choppers running and stay. They asked us to finish our observations within an hour. We accordingly completed our observations and flew back safe.

While hovering over Maitri Station, before landing, we saw that all the members had crowded around the helipad. On landing, we learnt that the leader had become very tense because the choppers didn't return immediately, as was the norm, after dropping us. The decision taken by the pilots couldn't be radioed back to the station since our communication had broken down. We later learnt that the leader had been waiting by the helipad for quite some time and had not even had his lunch, fearing for the worst. He was therefore very thrilled on seeing us, as were all the other members. We were received like war heroes.

Work went on and we completed the observations at Petermann Mountains where Raj made one of the most difficult landings in a gulley, since there was no other suitable place to land in the area. I later heard that he had been recommended for an award for that particular landing. I am, however, not sure about the authenticity of this information.

By the end of our trip we had completed all assignments, including the additional work of surveying Maitri Station and its surrounding area. During our four-month stay in Maitri, we witnessed blizzards, whiteouts and all other forms of Antarctic weather. We enjoyed the hospitality of the 'Antarctic Day' as we never came across night, in Antarctica.

We undertook 'Galley Duties' that were allotted to each member as per the roster. Members had to carry out duties that included serving food to the expedition team, cleaning plates, cooking utensils, station premises and packing burnt human excreta, which was automatically burnt, to ashes, in specially designed electric toilets, fabricated by the Defence Research and Development Organisation (DRDO). The ashes and other filth was kept in a packed state, ferried in the ship on its return journey, and dropped into the sea at specific latitude per diktat of international conventions.

We found that the Indian station followed the international conventions very strictly. As a result, the Indian Station and its environs were clean compared with that of the USSR. I have also read international literature on the subject where many countries have been blamed of accumulating reservoirs of filth in some pockets of Antarctica.

The USSR station and East German Stations were nearby, at a distance of few kilometers and sometimes we paid them customary visits. I remember they visited us on 26th of January and enjoyed the hospitality we extended. They loved the Indian rum and ice cream. The Indian and Russian leaders were good friends and we found the Russians very hard working and helpful. They helped Indians with their heavy machines whenever there was a requirement.

Those days, during Gorbachev's Presidency, the USSR was going through both political as well as economic turmoil. To say that the economy was in shambles, would be an understatement. The Russians offered their personal items including cameras, watches and typewriters for sale at petty prices, just so they could take back dollars. In fact the situation was so grim that they were not even sure when their government would send them ships to take them back from Antarctica.

On 'New Years Eve', our leader identified a 'Call Group' of five members to go to the USSR Station to represent Indians and to celebrate the New Year with them. They hosted us really well. It was a sight to see them celebrating the New Year and raising toasts according to timings of their various regions and this continued for a long time. It was a memorable night. A year later the USSR disintegrated and as a result I guess the length of the ceremony the next year would not have been as long.

Back at the station scientists carried out various studies on geomagnetism, meteorology, geology, oceanography, communications and polar medicines. A member, Mr. Pant, worked on journalism and the other, Mr. Udaishankar, made a film on the activities of the expedition. I extended substantial help to Udai whenever required. He ensured that my team had good coverage mainly because our work was outdoor oriented and had an element of adventure.

The time to depart from Indian station Maitri finally came and the teams were flown to the ship. I remained on at Maitri till the last day since I was giving final touches to my work and had to complete some more observations. My leader, Dr. Mukerjee, requested me to leave behind a trace of the large-scale map, as it would be very useful for the expedition. He forwarded this request in the form of a letter. Additionally, he gave another letter addressed to the Surveyor General of India with a request to give utmost priority to the generation of a large-scale map, of the Indian station, with intimation to the Secretary Dept. of Ocean Development. I accordingly left a copy of the Survey with the leader before my departure.

After completing the last GPS observation, I boarded the chopper and the pilot asked me if I wanted to fly to any nearby place, as it was to be my last sortie. Incidentally, my team had utilised about 80% of the helicopter sorties of the naval choppers. I told him to fly to the Rookery of 'Emperor Penguins' that I had heard was not very far. He flew me there and I finished one full film roll while photographing some of my favourite shots of the penguins and then with a heavy heart returned to the ship.

By now fatigue had set in and without realizing why, I opened the camera and in the bargain exposed the entire roll. I am dismayed, even now, when I think about the event, for the roll that was exposed had some of the best shots I had taken, including those of penguins and squas, at very close range. Looking back it was as though I had lost control on myself for a moment.

On reaching the ship, we were greeted by a rare sighting of blue whales and rare species of seals and penguins. The next day, while photographing on the deck, I sighted what was to be a once-in-a-lifetime view. Blue whales formed a backdrop while a squa and a snow petrel flew over, next to the ship. Just as I was about to take the photograph, Peter, the photographer on the team, came running causing the snow petrel to fly away, before I could shoot the picture. He probably didn't want me to take that photograph because such a combination of Antarctic animal life is very rare. I had an intense argument with him and warned him to be careful in future. None of the members, who were present at the scene, appreciated what he had just done.

The ship then started its return journey. We faced alternate patches of calm and rough seas, mainly when we reached the corridors of 'Roaring forties' and 'Furious fifties'. One night, while getting down from the leader's cabin, I spotted the Chief Engineer of the ship climbing up the stairs in a hurry. He was heading to the bridge of the ship. On enquiring, he told me that there was a fire alarm. I froze and stood still on the step. It was almost midnight and most of the members would have been asleep. If the alarm was true it would mean the end of everything, especially at such a Godforsaken place. I remained composed for half an hour till the Chief Engineer came down smiling and informed me that everything was fine, adding that it was a false alarm. I heaved a sigh of relief and went down to my cabin.

After a few days we reached Mauritius. This time round the ship didn't anchor at the shore and instead we went to the shore by boat. We went around and did some last minute shopping. Setting sail we soon reached Goa where my wife, Kunti, and our two children, Navin and Smriti, had come to receive me. Officially, a very senior officer of the rank of Additional Surveyor General was deputed to receive the 'Survey of India' team. The expedition members were received in style with the naval band in attendance. My children were excited to see the magnificent ship which I gave them a tour of. They were most excited to see the choppers on the deck. They wished to relax in my cabin, which they did for a few hours until we finished our custom clearance and other formalities.

We remained in Goa for a few days and then went back to Dehradun. I was received in the office with great excitement. The Surveyor General was very happy on learning about the tasks we carried out. I handed over the letters from the Commander of Antarctica Station regarding the urgency of the map, which we had surveyed as an additional job. He placed utmost priority on the generation of the map and instructed the Director Geodetic and Research Branch that I should not report to the Digital Mapping centre, my parent unit, until I designed and monitored the publication of the map, based on the surveys carried out.

I was also asked to give a detailed presentation to the officers and staff of Survey of India, with the Surveyor General in attendance. I made a hybrid presentation with slides, videos and the text files, which was well received. The Surveyor General instructed his concerned officers to recommend us for 'Certificate of Honour'.

Subsequently, I got busy in designing the first Indian map of the Indian Antarctic Station. I called the map 'Maitri and Environs' which was liked by the Surveyor General. I invested extra efforts to make it special and different from the usual maps. As mentioned before,

I had prepared some detailed notes about the 'Ice Continent', after studying relevant books in the ship's library, which I included as broad textual notes along with valuable photographs in the map. I also included the weather summary of Maitri over the period, which I had noted down in my diary, as the thematic information.

The Director Geodetic and Research Branch and the Surveyor General appreciated the mockup of the map. The notes and records sure came handy although I had not prepared any of these with the intention of incorporating it in the map. The map was finally published and distributed to all the 'Map Sales Offices' of Survey of India, across the country. It sold like hot cakes both at these offices and at exhibitions. The news about the map along with my photograph was covered and broadcast on the Doordarshan news channel, during the main English Bulletin at 9:00 P.M. My parents, who were in Udhampur, were thrilled to see me on national TV. I was showered with praise and appreciation by both colleagues and family. This gave me a great sense of having accomplished a good job in Antarctica.

After about two months, participants of the Antarctica Expedition (1991-92) were called to Delhi to meet the Prime Minister, Late Sh. Narasimha Rao. On the scheduled date, he fell sick and we were kept waiting in Delhi for a few days, in accordance with his directions, since he was very keen and particular to meet each member personally. Unfortunately, he did not recover soon enough and instead deputed late Sh. Kumaramangalam, the then Minister of State, Dept. of Science and Technology, to do the honours.

A function was also organized by the Department of Ocean Development, at the India International Centre, New Delhi, with the media in full attendance and the Honorable Minister was the Chief Guest. The film produced by the Film Division of India and photographed by Udai Shankar was shown and the chief guest personally presented mementoes and a few other gift items to each expedition member. The film won a lot of appreciation from the Honorable Minister and Dr. Rama Rao, who had, in the meantime, taken on additional charge as the Secretary Dept. of Ocean Development. The film finally went on to win the coveted National Award that year. Udai received the award from the President of India, Late Sh. Shankar Dayal Sharma.

The film was also shown in cinema halls all over the country as a prelude to the main movie, playing at the time, giving us all a lot of publicity. In the meantime, Dr. Rama Rao, Secretary, Department of Ocean Development and Secretary, Science & Technology, Govt. of India, had to give a presentation to the Prime Minister of India, Sh. Narasimha Rao on the work carried out by the Indian expedition teams in Antarctica, in response to a question posed in the Parliament. The Secretary instructed the Surveyor General to send me to him, with all the slides that I had photographed in Antarctica. Several of these slides were selected to show the Prime Minister during his presentation. He was thoughtful enough to mark my slides with some dots so that he could return it to me. After his presentation, he again called, thanked me and returned my slides, which I have retained with the markings, made by him, till this day.

The author with Dr. V. K. Dhargalkar, on the deck of Thuleland,
awaiting the arrival of the 'Call Group'

A penguin rookery near Schirmacher Oasis

(Photo presented to the author by the Russian Team Leader
during the New Year Celebrations in the Russian Antarctic
Station)

# PART XI

## Back to the Army

# Chapter 25

# TROOPS IN HIGH-TECH ENVIRONMENT

I was posted back to the Army, after a long and successful tenure with the Survey of India, in the year 2000. I reported to the Additional Director General Military Surveys, under the Director General Military Operations, who posted me to a specialized unit with an intention that I would take over as the Deputy Commandant. The Commandant of this unit had been trying to get me posted here since a couple of years. I reported to him towards the concluding part of his service. The officer who went on to replace him was also on the verge of superannuation and thus I practically commanded the unit for a long time.

The unit, a huge computer centre, was equipped with powerful computer configurations. The Commandant of this unit was always kept on his toes because of being in close proximity to senior officers in Delhi. The unit further had dozens of officers on its strength, including a number of women officers and a few hundred troops.

Commanding this 'High Tech Unit' was always a challenge primarily because of the type of work involved. I didn't have to do much to introduce myself since most of the officers had at some time or the other heard about me. I was very particular about the physical fitness of the officers and troops. I made certain that officers attended Physical Training (PT), along with the troops, as a matter of routine and qualified the physical tests regularly in accordance with existing guidelines. This was to ensure that their physical standards didn't suffer due to their high tech work. I would be sure to attend the PT parade with the boys or would generally be around during such activities, to boost their morale.

I would often make surprise visits to the computer centre just to see for myself whether shift timings were being respected. While doing so I observed some laxity especially in the second shift, which was being terminated much before the scheduled hour. I conveyed my zero tolerance policy towards such laxities clearly and mentioned that if there were some problems that came in the way, the same should be shared with me so that we address such issues optimally. In the days and months ahead I found that things, on this front, had improved considerably. One evening, after the second shift, I slipped into the *Jawan's Langer*, the soldier's mess and was shocked to find them eating cold food. I then got to know that the majority of the sappers, who worked the regular shift, got to eat hot meals but it was people in the second shift who were not as fortunate.

I discussed the matter with my Adjutant, Capt. Mangal and the Centre Subedar Major (CSM) and then realised that in fact the early closure of the second shift was mainly because these men wanted to avoid eating cold food. I felt very guilty and ordered a 'Board of Officers' on priority. We were fortunate to have a very smart and hardworking Adjutant. He arranged to procure some big and heavy-duty food warmers, which were sufficient enough to store warm food for those on the second shift, or for that matter whenever the requirement arose. The men were, as expected, very happy and their punctuality improved appreciably.

One of my other observations was that the men drank tap water, though there were several expensive water purifiers which were dusted regularly but not functional due to one defect or the other further complicated by delayed repairs. We immediately ordered all the purifiers to be placed under an 'Annual Maintenance Contract (AMC)' and thus, going forward, the men didn't ever have to drink tap water again.

My surprise visits to the *Langar* during the day also threw up a few shocks. I was surprised to find innumerable flies swarming around the area. My Adjutant took the initiative and arranged to procure a few electric flycatchers immediately, which tackled the menace effectively. One day I told my Adjutant and

Subedar Major to accompany me on my visit to the Langar at 5:30 A.M.. We were shocked to find filthy utensils lying around the cookhouse, which had not been washed after serving dinner the previous night. These utensils had become a breeding ground for flies. The Subedar Major was caught off guard and had no explanation. I cautioned him and 'Mess-in-Charge' to ensure they followed the normal practice of cleaning all utensils, after the men had finished their dinner since they had adequate staff. Knowing that old habits die hard, I again visited the place the very next morning, at the same time, something which the men and the Subedar Major would have never expected. To my dismay, I found the situation unchanged clearly indicating the fact that my instructions had not been taken seriously. I gave the Subedar Major and 'Mess-in-Charge' a tongue lashing until they almost shivered in their pants. I repeated my visit yet again the next morning and was happy to notice that things had improved. Such surprise visits conveyed to the officers and men that I was serious about such things and the fact that they should not take me lightly as I did not follow a periodic routine of my visits, to ensure the element of surprise.

As a leader I was particular that the officers put in their best effort to reach their targets and made them accountable whether it was PT attendance, drill parades or monitoring production in the digital mapping environment. Over a period, a sentiment spread that I meant business but at the same time took good care of the troop's welfare. My wife in her own way contributed to look after the welfare of sapper's families. Wives of other officers also extended all help in this regard. In due course higher formations started to recognise this unit. Support, whenever needed, poured in from all quarters.

We, as a team of officers, took a lot of interest in developing religious places such as the 'Mandir' and 'Gurudwara', which were authorized in accordance with the strength of the troops. I also suggested that my Adjutant and Subedar Major advise the 'Mess-in-Charge' to be sure that special dishes were made on the eve of 'Eid' and 'Christmas' although we had very few Muslim and Christian soldiers in our centre. This was to strengthen the feeling of togetherness. All and all I had a very good innings at the centre and thanks to the support and cooperation of each and every member of the unit, to whom I owe a lot, we were able to achieve all targets set.

One day I had visited the Base Hospital, Delhi along with my wife. After finishing our work, we decided to go around and see if we could find some of our men and their families since I saw our 'Three Tonner' parked nearby which usually transported sick families to the hospital. I then noticed one of our men along with his wife and children. On enquiring we were told by the sapper's wife that one of their twins, aged four years had an acute handicap and was like a vegetable neither being able to walk or crawl. She mentioned that they had been given a quarter on the fourth storey of the building, which was the top most floor. Life, for her, was difficult as the child cried, most of the time to be brought down to the compound. A major part of her day passed doing so.

We were horrified to learn about the plight of these parents and were further touched when we saw tears rolling down her face. My wife asked her how we could help the situation to which she replied that her husband had requested for a change of house to the ground floor, a number of times, but it had not been approved. I made note of it and on reaching the office asked for my Quartermaster. I advised him to look into the matter on priority basis, which he did. Eventually, it might have brought some solace to the suffering family for the long pending approval was finally made. Such instances further contributed to my job satisfaction.

I was always keen that the men have clean 'Rest Rooms' and made it a point to check for myself their condition. Initially, I had to ensure that all necessary items, required to give a new look to the washrooms and toilets, were provided. I firmly believed that the Commandant's surprise visit, to such places, once a while made a difference. In the monthly *Sainik Samelans* also known as *Darbars*, where the officers and men were collectively addressed, I ensured to advocate the point that one of the salient factors in judging the personality of a man is by the standard of cleanliness of his washrooms, whether at office or at his residence.

At times, I had the dirty wash rooms cleaned in my presence and in the presence of concerned officers, not with the intention to embarrass them but rather to drive home the importance of cleanliness. This worked.

Looking back I owe the trait of cleanliness to the *Safai ka Hafta* that we observed in our school, as elaborated in the beginning.

We had two female officers in the centre, Capt. Richa and Capt. Sini. Both of them were very professional and worked at par with their male counterparts whether it was PT, Drill Parade, performing the duty of a 'Weekly Duty Officer' or attending to routine work in the Centre. I understand that Capt. Sini was a topper in her course. Seated in my chamber I could gauge whenever Capt. Sini was the 'Weekly Duty Officer' because during her tenure there would be a clamour in consequence to the special activities initiated by her.

I remember an instance when there was an emergency declared in the office around forenoon. The Additional Director General called to inform that the Ministry of Defence requested for a particular plot of a particular graphic file, on a transparent film, related to a patch of the Indo China Boundary. This was meant for Mr. George Fernandez, the then Minister of Defence before his scheduled departure to China along with a team of officers, the next day. Such transparent films, that could retain the printed matter permanently, were not readily available in India, those days and generally had to be airlifted from Singapore. This gave me the jitters as I had done substantial research on it during my stay in Digital Mapping Centre, Dehradun while on deputation with the Survey of India where I had faced this problem.

I was apprehensive to explain this to the Ministry of Defence, though I shared it with my Additional Director

General. I, however, instructed my 'Duty Officer' to call the right offices, in both the Civil and Army, requesting them to spare one tracing paper roll each, even though I knew that the print would be smudgy. A few tracing rolls were thus collected, literally on a war footing. Capt. Richa tried the roll on the printer, in my presence. To our good luck the bluish tracing paper roll, collected from the 'Boundary cell', worked and gave a neat transparent print out during the initial sample trials.

I asked Capt. Richa to complete the job before going home since it was now pretty straightforward and would thus not take more than half an hour. All the other officers were allowed to go home. I kept waiting and after sometime went to the particular section where I asked the Shift-in-Charge about the delay. To my surprise, he told me that Capt. Richa had taken the print out a long while back and had left for home. I was shocked that in spite of having completed the work she had not bothered to submit the completion report. I instructed the Adjutant to get the print out properly packed and arranged to deliver it through the 'Duty Officer'. I also asked him to inform Capt. Richa to meet me the next morning.

In the morning, Capt. Richa arrived and as instructed met me in my chamber. I, as expected, gave her a piece of my mind and asked her why she had not submitted the completion report, especially keeping in mind the fact that this was no ordinary assignment. She replied that she had completed the work and handed over the output to the Shift-in-Charge and left with her father-in-law, who generally drove her home. I guess the confusion was due to a communication gap and I told her to be extra careful in future, especially with regard to important assignments.

That evening while I worked late at the office my Adjutant came and told me that one Major General (Retd) Gyan Sagar had been waiting outside, in our office lawn, for a long time. I asked him if he was the same General officer from the Corps of Engineers and from the 104 Engineer Regiment. He affirmed the same and I asked him why he had not made the General Officer comfortable inside the office. He then went on to tell me that the General officer came every day to fetch Capt. Richa who happened to be his daughter-in-law. He, however, never stepped inside the office.

I immediately sprang up from my chair and went out to pay my regards to him. The General Officer looked quite feeble due to his age. Incidentally, he was one of the few Engineer officers who had commanded the Infantry Formations and enjoyed a very high reputation in the Army. I had met him in the College of Military Engineering, back in 1977 when he was a Brigadier and commanded an Infantry Brigade. I was allotted the 104 Engineer Regiment on the very day he had come to attend a conference in Pune. I remember some officer pointed to him, from a distance, while mentioning that he had been the former Commanding Officer of the 104 Engineer Regiment. I walked up and introduced myself and he congratulated me on learning that I had been allotted 104 Engineer Regiment. The whole incident played out before me ever so clearly. I compelled him to come to my chamber and told my Adjutant to take good care of him. In the meantime, I went to Capt. Richa's section and asked her why she was delayed. She replied that since I had been unhappy with her, the day before, so she had chosen to stay on late to complete some routine office work that was pending. I felt guilty and told her that she needed to understand the gravity of the day before which was a very different situation. I asked her to pack up immediately and join her father-in-law, the general officer.

When I returned to my chamber and told General Gyan Sagar that I was from the 104 Engineer Regiment, he got up and practically lifted me with his feeble arms, which showed the regimental spirit that ran in his blood. I also recalled how I had met him when he was the General Officer Commanding (GOC), Shillong but he could not place me. Capt. Richa later informed me that he had developed Alzheimers and was surprised that he remembered the roads so well and hardly ever got confused while driving.

I later saw him escorting Capt. Richa to the PT Parades each morning. He used to take her back after the Parade, drop her to the office at 9 A.M. and again escort her back home in the evening. He had passed on many of his traits to the young officer, which am sure must have benefitted her in her later years. I had heard several stories about him in the Regiment. He had been a very strict Commanding Officer and known as one of the most punctual officers the Regiment ever had.

After a few years stay at the unit, I was given the command of the Defence Institute of Geospatial Information and Training (DIGIT), which had just been set up and was in its infancy.

# Chapter 26

# AT THE HELM OF THE INSTITUTE

I took over the Defence Institute of Geospatial Information & Training (DIGIT) from Major General P.K. Gossain. The institute was established to impart training to officers and men in Digital Mapping and Geographic Information System. There were initial hiccups, on expected lines, which are characteristic to any newly set up organisation. Being new, the institute had not yet gained any of the required visibility in the defence environment. I had a choice to either lie low or labour hard to bring it into the limelight, which obviously would fetch the institute a lot of work and responsibility.

I analysed and concluded that the institute had substantial potential to do wonders. This was reason enough to decide against the first option of lying low and instead I decided to start with a bang. I made my Deputy Commandant draft a few courses for the officers and men, some of long durations of more than a year and some as short as a week. I didn't shy away from calling on senior officers of the level of Engineer-in-Chief in the Indian Army, Director General Information Systems, Deputy Chief of Army Staff, Additional Director General Military operations and Additional Director General Military Training. I remember that I was initially ignored and at times even avoided by some of the officers, mainly because, at the time it seemed as though I was asking for too much, for the infant unit.

We, however, followed a two-pronged approach to develop the institute; one was long term and the other short term. For the short term, we immediately started courses of short durations, for both officers and men, after receiving approval from the Headquarters. The reputation of these specialized courses spread not only to the Army but also the Air force and Navy. In spite of the tight schedule, we accommodated and ran courses for 'All Arms' and a few specialized courses for the Air force.

In the meantime, the Para Military Forces approached us, as they were keen to get trained in Geoinformatics. I personally ensured that we walked an extra mile and my officers, with the cooperation of other junior instructors, put in their maximum in imparting the training to these organisations. In turn, they were extremely thankful and happy for having received our help. The institute in its infancy thus started bubbling with energy mainly due to the floating population of officers and other ranks, not only from the Army but also from the other services, including the Para Military Forces. This elevated the morale of my staff, both officers and men.

As regards the long-term strategy, we were allowed to initiate certain actions which gave us the must needed encouragement and confidence to impress upon very senior officers about the requirement and importance of these courses. I ensured that all the senior officers visited the unit and were briefed properly, through presentations and training materials that we had developed and also witnessed live training sessions. The very fact that we had gone ahead without waiting for further resources helped us in getting maximum support and cooperation from concerned senior officers.

In the meantime, I received invitations to deliver lectures to senior officers of the Military College of Telecommunication Engineering (MCTE) Mhow; National Institute of Forensic Sciences (NIFS), New Delhi; as well as National Institute of Technology (NIT), Hamirpur (H.P.). I also chaired many 'Board of Officers' related to Geoinformatics with members from the Army, Navy, and Air Force, as well as some scientists from the DRDO. This definitely added another dimension of strength to the institute. Director General Information Systems visited DIGIT several times and expressed his satisfaction and appreciation. We received his encouragement from time to time. He subsequently became the Vice Chief of Army Staff and was always a source of encouragement for us.

Chapter 27

# CHINA AND RUSSIA—
# GLIMPSES

I was deputed to proceed to China to participate in the Workshop conducted by the 'Permanent Committee on GIS Infrastructure for Asia and Pacific (PCGIAP) Working Group' in Chengdu, the capital of the Sichuan province of China. This was scheduled to be followed by the technical tour of Tibet.

PCGIAP is a committee, under the umbrella of United Nations, whose vision is to develop Asia Pacific Spatial Database Infrastructure in the form of a network of databases located throughout the region and thus providing the fundamental data needed to achieve economic, social, human resource development and environmental objectives in the region.

I flew to Hong Kong, after a span of about sixteen years, took another flight to Chengdu and checked into the hotel arranged by the Indian embassy. Chengdu, nicknamed as the science city of China, is a well-known city with a long-standing history and civilization. It covers an area of about 3861 square. kilometers. and is full of vigour and vitality. It has moderate climate during both summers and winters, with average temperature of 21.4 degrees Celsius. The city is located adjacent to the Yangtze river, which is its major source of water. In those days, Chengdu was being developed with a view to attract international investment. The roads that connected the city with other places, of the Sichuan province, were in excellent condition and very well maintained. One could find a lot of infrastructural development taking place day and night, which was indicative of the prosperity of the region.

We saw some part of the major railway line under development from Golmud to Lhasa whose estimated length was 1000 kilometer of which about 500 kilometer was already completed. We also understood that the contract for the construction of this ambitious railway line had been given to various foreign companies. It involved construction of about 2000 tunnels along the route. The construction of this line, which forms the main artery that connects Tibet to main land China, was completed only a few years back. One had to praise the dedication and competence with which the Chinese were developing their infrastructure, even back then. By saying so I am not demeaning the competence of Indians but the fact is that we have a lot to learn from them.

The workshop scheduled, for about a week, was very educative professionally and was attended by delegates from Australia, Japan, Malaysia, Thailand, Republic of Korea, Indonesia, Vietnam, Iran and India. Surprisingly, I didn't find any representation from Pakistan. The organizers arranged a visit to the Remote Sensing and Cartographic facilities located in Chengdu. Men and women, clothed in white aprons, worked like robots in these centers.

The Chinese officers treated us with care and warm hospitality. Communication proved to be a big problem and we couldn't function without the support of an interpreter.

I was surprised to find women working in all fields that one could imagine, including 'Rickshaw Pullers'. One day I spoke with a Chinese woman officer of the 'Survey Bureau of China' while she was detailed to receive the Surveyor General of India at the Chengdu airport. It so happened that the organizers of the workshop asked me if I would like to join her. I accepted the offer mainly because of two reasons. Firstly, while in India, the Surveyor General had telephoned me on learning that I had also been detailed to participate in the workshop. Secondly, it was a pleasure receiving a very senior officer from the Govt. of India on Chinese soil, extending all courtesies deserved keeping in mind that he was the head of a reputed organization back home.

Fortunately, the lady officer was fluent in English. We waited for a few hours, late night, at the Sichuan airport because of the delayed flight. During this time we had elaborate discussions on various aspects related to the rich cultures of our respective countries. I learnt that she had a five year old daughter and thus advised her to go home since I was sure her young daughter would be waiting for her. I assured her that I would take care of the arriving officer. She then told me that her child, like most children in China, was used to it since it was common for most women to work. I also learnt that the women who did not work were, in a way, looked down upon, by society and one could hardly find women who didn't go out to work.

She went on to mention that Indian film music used to be their best source of entertainment in her school days. She in fact mentioned about a few old evergreen Hindi songs, though she didn't know a bit of Hindi. It was probably for the first time that I spoke to a Chinese national for that long. Finally, the Surveyor General of India landed. We accompanied him to his hotel and thereafter left for our respective places.

Life would have been very difficult in China but for the interpreter who was a young woman with a good command over the English language. I once asked her as to why she had chosen the English language. She said that she had never thought of learning English, let alone becoming an interpreter. It so happened that while she had been away from her office, on maternity leave, her mother-in-law advised her against wasting time at home and instead encouraged her to learn English at a coaching class next to her house. She attended these classes, developed a lot of interest in the language and finally joined the Ministry of External Affairs, as an interpreter.

While in Chengdu, I had two strange experiences due to the communication gap. Realising the grave communication problem that existed, the very first day we wrote the names of the two hotels on two sides of a paper, in Chinese script—one where we resided and the second where the workshop was being held. We would show this to the cab drivers, depending on where we wanted to go. This worked well, however, one evening we left the workshop venue and took a cab back to our hotel, which was about 10 kilometers away. Initially, we indicated the direction to the driver by pointing our finger. After driving for quite a distance we realised that we had not shown him the name of the hotel, inscribed on the paper and did so immediately. After some time he stopped at the gate of the hotel asked us to get down. We were shocked to see that it was the same hotel from where we had set out. It was then that we realised that we had probably showed him the name of the wrong hotel, on the paper. We couldn't stop ourselves from laughing aloud. We then made sure we showed him the name of the hotel, written on the other side of the paper and finally reached comfortably.

The second experience occurred when one evening, after returning from the workshop, I entered my room and didn't find fruits kept in the room, which the hotel did as a matter of routine. I was annoyed and expressed my displeasure, over the phone, to the receptionist, who fortunately understood English. I asked him to send 'the boy; to my room, along with the fruits, meaning 'the waiter'. After some time, I got a call from the receptionist who appeared to be thoroughly confused. He hesitantly asked me in hushed voice, "Sir, you asked for boy or girl?" It was then that it dawned upon me that he probably had a limited understanding of the English language. Shocked and embarrassed I at once dropped the phone, rushed down and explained to him that I had asked for a waiter which he had misconstrued.

The workshop proceedings were rich and provided valuable learnings in many aspects. After the day's proceedings the hosts generally arranged dinner, in different hotels of international repute. This continued all through the duration of the workshop. While this gave us a lot of respite, after the day's business, we also had a tough time as regards the food since we found 'authentic' Chinese food to be very different from the Chinese food that we were accustomed to in India. Apart from being devoid of any condiments, we were also not comfortable using chopsticks and it was not easy to make the waiters understand when we asked for knives and forks. We therefore, would most often be content with a soup along with a little rice, served in the small soup cups and the dessert.

We attended a few good cultural programs, which exhibited the rich Chinese culture. Our visit to the museum in Chengdu was a worthwhile experience. One could learn a lot from the spick and span layout of the articles and the way visitors were guided using running commentary, through headphone sets provided. Chengdu is also famous for 'Pandas' but we were not able to visit the particular location due to paucity of time.

We were also told that there is a noticeable difference between the culture of Chengdu and North China. At Chengdu, people liked to interact amongst themselves and were fond of having tea together in teahouses. It may be interesting to know that the 'Gaiwan Tea' was first invented in Chengdu. 'Tea doctors', who are the attendants in tea houses, serve tea and can pour the tea, holding bronze pots with long necks, from about a meter's height without spilling a single drop. They were highly skilled and thus served multiple customers, quickly and accurately.

After the culmination of the workshop, some of the delegates were taken on a technical tour of Tibet, for about a week and I was lucky to be a part of it. It was generally rare that an Indian official would officially be taken to tour Tibet and that too the interiors, for such a long duration. We were not many in number since a majority of the delegates had already left in the absence of a proper sanction by their respective Governments.

## Technical Tour of Tibet

From Chengdu we were flown to Lhasa, the capital city of the Tibet Autonomous Region (TAR). Tibet is known for its spectacular landscape and is also known as the roof of the world because there are about fifty peaks measuring more than 7,000 meters above mean sea level. It has a population just exceeding 2.3 million.

'Lhasa', in Tibetan language, means 'Holy Land'. The city towers at a height of 3650 meters above the mean sea level with an average temperature of 21.8 degrees Celsius and is one of the highest cities in the world. It is located on the northern bank of the Lhasa river. It has a rich heritage and is famous worldwide for its historic Tibetan Monasteries. It is also known as the solar city because of the longer durations of sunshine.

Some of the delegates started to feel the effects of high altitudes immediately on arrival in Lhasa, probably due to the lack of oxygen. To begin with, they complained of sudden giddiness. One of the delegates, Prof. Ian Williamson of the University of Melbourne, known worldwide in the GIS community, almost fell down the very first day and therefore couldn't accompany us during the first day of our outing. I was cautious to increase my intake of fluids and suggested to the others to do the same. I also advised other delegates to walk or climb with small steps until our bodies acclimatized. Both suggestions helped.

Our hotel was located near the grand 'Potala Palace', which is the jewel of the city and was set up in seventh century during the reign of King Sogtsen Gampo, over an area of 48 hectares. This palace comprises of 13 storeys, is about 115.7 meters high and consists of White and Red sections with 1000 rooms. It had been the Headquarters of the Dalai Lamas and is a treasure house of traditional Tibetan culture. There are many other famous places of tourist attraction, which include the renowned Jokhang and Sera Monasteries. One such monastery was inhabited with only female monks with shaven heads. I remember a pair of twin sisters amongst them who took out a photograph of 'Madhuri Dixit', the Indian Film actress, from under her pillow and indicated to us that she was her fan.

The development of Tibet was high on the priority of China. It is understood that all the provinces of China contribute financially for this. The results, seen on the ground, were eye opening. The city was divided into two parts, New and Old Lhasa. Old Lhasa had all the temples and monasteries whereas New Lhasa was developed as a modern town, with all the requisite facilities. The habitants of Old Lhasa city were mainly Tibetans whereas many Chinese had settled down within the New city limits.

We also observed that China was making attempts to change the demographic pattern of Tibet. It encouraged Non-Tibetans to migrate and permanently settle down in Tibet, against the wishes of the Tibetans. We also learnt that jobs were being offered to Tibetans in main land China.

We visited the markets and found many foreigners going around. We saw tourists mainly from other Chinese provinces, Japan, USA and Germany and surprisingly we did not spot any Indian. While resting in a park, located in the heart of Lhasa, we noticed some Tibetans sitting in small groups. We were surprised to find that the Chinese police, probably as a matter of routine, didn't allow them to sit together for long and asked them to disperse.

We also visited the newly developed modern shopping complexes with European looks. We were taken for a visit to the regional Directorate Headquarters of the Survey Bureau of China, located in Lhasa, where the Director gave a presentation about the activities of the Directorate.

While here we attempted to look for Indian food, though we had no expectations. We were thrilled when we succeeded in locating one such joint in one of the streets. We ate to our fill, even though the preparations were not that good, but it was a welcome change. We also visited the palace of Dalai Lama, where he lived before his exile. It was flooded with visitors since it is a landmark not only in Lhasa but also in the whole of Tibet. The palace was well maintained. We were given a tour and saw his sitting place and the library amongst many other interesting things.

After two days, we were driven up higher to a township known as Gyangze, located in the higher hills of Tibet, about 422 kilometers from Lhasa. It was a small but beautiful township inhabited mostly by Tibetans. The next day we drove much higher to a height of about 5130 meters where many of the delegates didn't feel like moving out of the bus due to high altitude. I went around small distances with the Chinese officers but walked with small steps and with utmost caution. Here, I drank yak milk for the first time in my life and found that it tasted good.

It was very interesting to see the Chinese part of Tibet, for me in particular, because I was aware that somewhere on the other side, though very far, were the high hills of Arunachal Pradesh, rather the 'Old NEFA

Hills'. This area was surveyed and mapped partly under my command when I held the Charge of No. 5 Party, the High Hill Unit of Survey of India, during my posting in North Eastern Region. I found the same terrain, similar people and followers of the same religion here as well. One could appreciate that the Chinese had a great advantage of height, which gave them the strategic advantage during the 1962 operations.

Finally, the 'Technical Tour' culminated and we came back to Lhasa, from Ghangtze. From here we flew back to Chengdu. This was around four years before the Beijing Olympics and serious preparations had started in full earnest. The Chinese officers, with us, were very proud of it. After being together for about a fortnight we thanked them for their hospitality and left Chengdu.

On our return we flew to Hong Kong, where we stayed for the night. The next day we took a guided tour of the city. Our guide was a former pilot of 'Cathay Pacific Airlines'. I could not believe that this was the same Hong Kong which I had seen about sixteen years back, then under the occupation of Great Britain. One never got the feel that it was now a part of China. The currency was still the Hong Kong Dollar, as had been the case during British rule. There was unbelievable infrastructural development all over including the airport, roads, huge and long bridges, buildings etc. Frankly, I could only recognize one prominent square with a big market around it while the rest had undergone a sea of change. The sight of the Hong Kong port left one breathless.

That evening, we boarded a Cathay Pacific Flight, from Australia. The Australian passengers were hooked to their radio sets and informed us that India was on the verge of winning a cricket match, which was being played at the time, a fact we were ignorant about. We soon landed at Delhi which brought us to the end of a visit that had made us richer, professionally. This trip, apart from making me wiser on many aspects, fulfilled my childhood desire of visiting China. The other half of my childhood desire, to visit Pakistan, appeared almost impossible, at that stage.

## The Russian Experience

After a few months, I got a call from the Additional Director General, who informed me that I had been deputed to lead a 'Committee of Officers' to Russia, in connection with a technical task. I was happy to get this opportunity because it would be very satisfying, professionally. Two other officers were shortlisted to accompany me. One of them, a very dear friend, arrived from Bangalore two days prior to our scheduled departure. I remember it was a Friday and we had to fly on Saturday evening to Frankfurt from where we were to board another flight to Moscow as there were no seats available on the direct flight from Delhi to Moscow. It was pouring heavily and I got a call from the officer who out of respect suggested that I need not bother coming to the Headquarters to collect my passport, tickets and foreign exchange since he had already picked it up on my behalf. He promised to hand them over, in the evening, at my residence. I thanked him and invited him over for dinner.

That evening after reaching our house, despite a heavy downpour, he got down to handing over the items collected. I remarked that the passport was not seen. He tried locating it but was unable to find the document, even after checking the vehicle in which he had traveled. There was a sense of emergency as both of us revisited all the places he had gone to during the day. By this time it was very late and we finally gave up the futile search and returned home to have dinner. My friend was pale and couldn't get himself to have dinner. My wife assured him that everything would be all right. While we forced him to have dinner, I couldn't help get worried within, not because I would miss this foreign visit but because my absence could probably have led to some official implications, as I was to lead the delegation. Finally, after dinner, the officer left, very morose. I asked him not to worry adding that I had visited enough foreign countries; as regards the official front, I was confident of taking care of it. On Saturday evening, I made certain I was at the airport to see off the two officers and told them to enjoy the trip but I could see from their faces that they were affected by my absence.

I am deliberately narrating this incident, in detail, to convey that there are still some good people around, probably a minimum of one on each street, a few in each town, may be a few dozens in our country, who are dedicated, feel your pain and go all out to help strangers, probably, more than I have ever done. These are the people, who have been taking our country forward in spite of all negativities.

The next morning, I informed the police about the loss of my passport and took other necessary actions. Even though it was a holiday, being Saturday, I contacted the officer in charge of the passport office in Delhi to enquire if he could help me to get the passport issued that very day, on an emergent basis. I explained to him the gravity of the situation. He was very kind and assured me that he would find out if the concerned officer was in Delhi and if so would get the office opened and the job done. Unfortunately, to my bad luck, the officer concerned was out of station. However, he reassured me that the passport would be issued on Monday, as soon as the office opened. He asked me to send a card or a chit with a reminder on Monday, so that he would initiate the action on priority.

In the meantime, the Indian Military Attaché's office in Moscow called up asking me to fax a copy of my new passport the moment I received it. My friends in Russia had probably, by now, intimated them about the mishap. I also contacted the duty officer concerned with the air ticket to request him to see if he could accommodate me in the Aeroflot flight that flew direct from Delhi to Moscow, on Monday evening. He expressed his regret since there were no seats available. However, understanding the emergent situation, he went out of his way and after interacting with his superiors, accommodated me under an 'Emergency Quota', kept up their sleeve, for exactly such situations. He also asked me to contact him immediately on receipt of the passport.

Come Monday, I was issued my passport, by the kind officer, by lunchtime. I faxed the copy to the Military Attaché while the airline officer arranged my direct ticket to Moscow.

I came home in the evening, picked up my bags, hurriedly wished my wife goodbye, left for the airport and flew to Moscow by the overnight Aeroflot flight. At Moscow Airport, I was received by a representative of the Indian Military Attaché, accompanied by Russian officials who transported me from the airport to the railway station in a very stately car. I had never seen such dense traffic in my life as I witnessed that morning, while traveling from the airport to Moscow city. The traffic inched forward slowly, much slower than even a snail's pace. I was apprehensive that I might miss the train to St. Petersburg, which thankfully I didn't. The Russian representatives persuaded me to have breakfast, seated me comfortably in the train and saw me off with full courtesy.

The journey to St. Petersburg from Moscow, by train, took around 7 hours. At the end of it all, I reached St. Petersburg on time while my counterparts had taken double the time to reach Moscow via Frankfurt.

There was a middle-aged Russian couple in the compartment who in spite of the communication gap, made all efforts to make me feel at home. The woman was very sociable and in due conversation I learnt that her husband used to be a pilot. They communicated with me using improvised sign language to the best of their ability and so did I. The woman mentioned the name of Raj Kapoor and indicated that he was very popular amongst her generation. She sang a few lines each of '*Eecheck dana beechak dhana . . .*' and '*Dum dum diga diga . . .*' It seemed her generation enjoyed old Hindi film songs a lot, though they hardly understood its meaning.

The train, on its journey, passed through lush green and scenic terrain. I was fortunate to have taken the day train else I would have missed the charm of some of the most scenic frames I have seen in my life, which kept unfolding in continuity as the train gushed ahead, towards St. Petersburg. We had a sumptuous lunch served by the Russian Railway Service. On reaching St. Petersburg I realised that women passengers, in Russia, expected men to leave the compartments first so that they could dress up at their convenience. The woman hinted this and I accordingly vacated the compartment first. The couple bid me farewell and said something in Russian, which unfortunately I couldn't understand. All and all the journey was a memorable one.

As I alighted from the train, I found my friends, who had arrived earlier that morning and a few Russian officials, at the railway station, to receive me. The officer friend, who had lost my passport, was excited, relieved and on top of the world.

I was immediately driven to the hotel, where I checked in and we immediately left for work. I chaired the first meeting where I found a substantial presence of Russian officials, many of whom were not seen from the next day. Even though language was a barrier we were facilitated by an interpreter who was a young Russian woman. During the course of the meeting, she interpreted all the proceedings very efficiently and displayed her command over the English language. She even managed to interpret technical terms precisely so that they didn't lose their essence, even after translation. She later told me that she had done her masters in English from Los Angeles.

During the very first meeting, I discovered that we had a few serious differences with the Russian team. I also found that the Russian delegates retained sentiments of being a super power and intended to force certain things on us, which were not in our favour. As a result of this, some of the arguments remained inconclusive. Through the interpreter I conveyed to our Russian friends that our intention was not to argue but rather to work along with them, to the best of our ability—nothing less and nothing more.

Gauging by her facial expression, I understood that the interpreter was awkward to convey this to the Russians. She in fact asked me if she should use the exact words. I asked her to convey the message, not only in the same words but also with the same emotions. She blushed and interpreted the sentiment faithfully after which there was a few moments of pin drop silence.

I further discussed the issues, in question, with their software expert, who was an important member of the Russian delegation and convinced him that we were in no way asking for the moon but were rather precise and logical in our request. After a few hours of discussions, the Russian team and we finally got on the same page and during our further sittings they extended their complete cooperation.

The first day we returned to the hotel rather late and went for a late but long walk. The bewitching beauty of St. Petersburg at night stunned me. We decided that we would go for early morning walks every day, starting the very next morning. The morning scenic beauty, of the city, was equally captivating. The city was situated on both the banks of River Neva and the mesmerizing oceanic beauty, created by Neva, was aptly complimented by the old European architecture, full of Roman essence, which was further balanced by the aesthetically planned infrastructure across the city. We visited many places of tourist interest on our off days and discovered many more breathtaking scenes of natural beauty. I am originally from Kashmir and have been lucky to visit some of the famous places around the world, but as regards both scenic and human beauty, I place St. Petersburg only next to Kashmir, if not at par.

St Petersburg, Russia's second largest city after Moscow, was founded by Tsar Peter the Great in 1703 It is also the northernmost city in the world to have a population of over one million. It had been the capital of Russia from 1713 to 1728 and further for about 86 years from 1732 to 1918. It is known as the cultural capital of Russia. Hermitage, one of the largest museums of the world is situated in this city.

Peter the Great founded the city as he wanted Russia to have a better seaport than the then existing Arkhangelsk, situated on the White Sea, to the north and which remained closed during winter months. It was during the great northern war that Peter the Great captured Nyenskans and laid down the first brick and stone building in the city, then called Peter and Paul Fortress, way back in 1703. He used conscripted peasants from all over Russia and Swedish prisoners of war to build the city and later moved the Russian capital here from Moscow. It remained the seat of the Romanov Dynasty and the Imperial Court of Russian Tsars as well as the Russian Government for another 186 years until the communist revolution of 1917. It suffered deeply from the catastrophic yearlong fires, in 1736.

The Russian revolutions of 1905 and 1917 began in this historic city. During World War I, the city was renamed Petrograd which meant 'Peters City'. It was in March 1917, during the February Revolution, that Nicholas II ended the Russian Monarchy and over three hundred years of Romanov Dynastic Rule. In 1924, Petrograd was renamed Leningrad, five days after Lenin's death.

During World War II Leningrad was besieged by the German forces following an invasion in June 1944. The Siege lasted from September 1941 to January 1944 for 872 days. The 'Siege' is known as one of the longest, most destructive and most lethal sieges that any major city has undergone in Modern history. It isolated the city cutting off most essential supplies. They say more than one million civilians died, mainly of starvation; while many others had either escaped or were evacuated causing the city to thin beyond limits.

The view of the city from my room was spectacular and it captured a major part of it in a panoramic vista that any professional photographer could only have dreamt of. One can never imagine that this city had undergone such manifold suffering; the pangs of battles and World Wars that caused her destruction all around; the wild paws of historic siege that resulted in the deaths of thousands of her determined citizens who preferred hunger to surrender; the blows that this land of Lenin, the Leningrad, received leading Russia to 'Communist Rule'. As I watched from the window of my hotel room, I couldn't help ponder how at the end of every war, dead bodies are removed and so it is with the rubble of destruction. After a bitter interlude, humanity starts all over again when the dead are mourned, victories celebrated and historians ready with their quills to record the wounds of destruction, making them eternal, sometimes factually and at times with distortions. I had read in some books about the bridges in St. Petersburg, over the Neva River, which could be separated in the middle, each half supported by the fulcrum at the two extreme ends. I checked with the interpreter who affirmed the fact and said that the activity was generally scheduled at mid night. I asked her if she had ever seen it to which she replied that she always wanted to but the inconvenient timings prevented her. Along with my two colleagues, I decided to observe this interesting activity, at the scheduled time.

We reached one of the huge and long bridges, which had wide roads, supplemented with rails for trams and which were illuminated on either side by magnificent tall iron lampposts. We hurriedly crossed it and came across a

Russian girl who borrowed a matchbox from my friend to light her cigarette. She advised us to rush back since after the separation of the bridge we would be stuck on that side of the shore until early morning. We thanked her and no sooner had we crossed back that the bridge began to separate. We witnessed the engineering marvel amazed at how the transition was incredibly smooth in spite of the power lines, lampposts, road and rails. We were told that the bridge would become one again at 5:00 A.M.. On further enquiry, we learnt that the activity had been taking place for decades to make way for huge ships to cross at night. It was nothing less than magic, something unbelievable and difficult to explain to someone who has not witnessed it.

I thought that it was similar to a scene from a Hollywood movie, probably 'The Earthquake', which is still preserved at Universal Studios. It is exhibited to visitors where a running train breaks due to impact of the earthquake, as do the concrete columns on the platform. However, on the press of a button everything regains its original shape as if nothing had even happened.

After a couple of days, we finished our assignment and packed off to board the overnight train to Moscow. Some of the Russian team members, including the interpreter, accompanied us. I noticed that she had a very serious countenance, which was unusual for her. I enquired about this from one of our Russian counterparts, who knew a little English and was shocked when he told me that her father had passed away that very day. I expressed my condolences to her. She then told me that her father had gone to withdraw money from a bank, in Moscow, that day and someone shot him dead as he came out of the bank and fled with his money. I again conveyed our heartfelt condolences and thanked her for the help she extended to us during our stay. We boarded the train and reached Moscow the next morning. We were scheduled to take a flight to Delhi that evening and thus had a full day at our disposal. We, along with the Russians, went around Moscow to see the 'Kremlin Square', the Moscow University and various other places of interest, before finally boarding our flight to Delhi. We reached Delhi the next morning and switched over to our usual routine, both at office and home.

After a few days the Additional Director General informed that, the Surveyor General of India had already taken up the case of my deputation to 'Survey of India' with the Ministry of Defence and sought its approval on a priority basis. Consequently, I stood transferred to the 'Boundary Cell', which was freshly organized and elevated to the level of a Directorate where I was to take over as the first Director of 'International Boundary Directorate'.

# PART XII

# Call from the
# Surveyor General

# Chapter 28

# INTERNATIONAL BOUNDARIES

One morning I received a call from the Surveyor General of India, asking me to take over as Director, 'International Boundary Directorate' (IBD), adding that the then existing 'Boundary Cell' had been reorganized and elevated to the level of a Directorate. He wanted me to join forthwith as international boundary matters with the neighbouring countries were likely to receive a boost in the very near future. I was happy on two accounts—firstly, an appointment in the 'Boundary Cell', now the 'International Boundary Directorate' was always considered prestigious and secondly, it did not involve a change of station. I received a fax from Army Headquarters, in respect of my transfer, shortly after the call from the Surveyor General.

The next morning I took over as the first Director of the 'International Boundary Directorate' (IBD). Officers posted to this office had to study a lot and keep abreast of complex issues related to international boundaries, some of which had crept up even centuries ago. As a result, senior officers relied heavily on personnel who had been in the office over a considerable period of time and who had dealt with these issues practically on a daily basis. It was not uncommon for some of these officers to hold onto crucial information, at times, probably to make themselves indispensable.

The then Surveyor General, Major General M Gopal Rao, was against this practice and so was I. He had studied the boundary matters thoroughly after taking over as the Surveyor General and thus guided and apprised me on some of the crucial issues during various discussions. I, on my part, also studied the issues in depth and got a lot of support from my staff in understanding some of the complex issues.

Fortunately or unfortunately, maybe as a matter of coincidence, activities related to the boundary issues with the neighbouring countries, dormant for quite some time, started to get activated, one after the other, soon after my arrival. This was probably in line with the expectations of the Surveyor General as hinted during our first call. I thus had to understand and analyse, in depth, issues related to international boundaries with countries concerned, along with their data.

Soon, representative delegations from these countries started visiting India, one after the other sometimes, within a span of about a month or two. I dealt with the delegations from Myanmar, Nepal, Bangladesh and Bhutan, generally held under the leadership of the Surveyor Generals of the two countries, as arranged by the Ministry of External Affairs (MEA), with due representation from the Ministry of Home Affairs (MHA) or any other organisation, depending on purview of the particular case.

I was particularly surprised to learn that we had a number of unresolved issues, with regard to the international boundary, with Bangladesh. I personally felt that we had missed the opportunity to conduct result-oriented discussions and take the matter to its finish, right at the time when Bangladesh was declared a Republic. It would have been a lot easier for the two sides to accommodate each other under the then fresh environment of friendship. I guess we had then taken the issue for granted not foreseeing its resurrection later or may be the Government of India had some political compulsions to leave some sensitive pockets, along the boundary, unratified.

It is worthwhile to understand that a boundary issue, however petty, has the tendency to be influenced by politics, snowballing into a serious issue, fuelled by hype that surrounds it. This subsequently attracts the emotions of the public, which further complicates the issue and comes in the way of a logical solution.

Around this time (2008), Bhutan was about to be declared a Republic. Better sense prevailed and the Govt of India was keen to resolve pending boundary issues, with the Royal Govt. of Bhutan before it became a republic. Bhutanese officials also understood futuristic advantages and cooperated. The hard work on both sides paid off. All issues, pertaining to the international boundary, between the two countries were resolved. The boundary was demarked crisply and vividly much before Bhutan transited into a Republic. The strip maps and the authentic documents, as regards the depiction of the international boundary between any two countries, were signed not only by the respective Surveyor Generals but were also duly attested by the plenipotentiaries of the two countries. I was very content with the achievement which was a result of the hard work of the concerned field directorates and the staff of the 'International Boundary Directorate' (IBD), under the efficient guidance of the then Surveyor General of India and Ministry of External Affairs (MEA). The event was adequately covered and appreciated by the media.

Nepal was another neighbour with whom we had a number of longstanding boundary issues. Many of these had, by now, run into complexities. I, however, give full credit to Maj Gen Gopal Rao, the then Surveyor General of India, who impressed upon and convinced the Nepalese logically. All but two glaring issues were resolved. These two issues had to be carried forward in his time. It was, under no doubt, a job well done.

# Chapter 29

# Sir Creek Talks— First Hand Experience

After a few months, the Surveyor General called me from his Headquarters in Dehradun and said that he had been asked by the Ministry of External Affairs (MEA) to come to Delhi immediately to attend an important meeting in the afternoon. He intended to come via my office, which was next to MEA and instructed me to join him. By that time I was reasonably settled as Director, 'International Boundary Directorate' (IBD).

We went to MEA for the meeting, as scheduled. The context of the meeting was that both India and Pakistan had mutually agreed, at the highest level, to depute their individual delegations to hold composite dialogue on the issue of Sir Creek. It appeared that both countries wanted to initiate 'Confidence Building Measures' (CMBs) and addressing the 'Sir Creek Issue' could probably be the most appropriate step in this direction. At that point, I left the meeting to muster up all the relevant records, in my office, while the Surveyor General attended another meeting in this regard along with the Chief Naval Hydographer, Rear Admiral B.R. Rao.

The next day, I was again summoned to the MEA and the Surveyor General asked me to get ready to leave for Pakistan as a member of the Indian delegation as his representative. The delegation would be led by Rear Admiral B.R. Rao, the Chief Naval Hydrographer with members from the Indian Navy, MEA and Survey of India. I was also told that I should feel free to propose, to the leader, our position on the land portion inclusive of the Creek. This was a great responsibility especially since it involved representing the country on a hot issue like 'Sir Creek'.

I updated myself thoroughly on the issue, which was expectedly very complex and involved digging more than century old records, which had their genesis in the era of the British colonial rule. I became conscious since my proposal to the leader, on the issue of land portion of the creek, would cast its effect subsequently on the limit of maritime boundary.

# The Dispute on Sir Creek

At this stage, it may be worthwhile to introduce the reader briefly to the dispute between the two neighbours on the issue. The 'Sir Creek' issue is a dispute between India and Pakistan over an estuary, about 96 Kilometers (60 miles) long, which flows into the Arabian Sea. It cuts across the marshy lands of the 'Rann of Kutch' region in the Indian State of Gujarat and the Sindh province of Pakistan. The Creek is named after the British representative and is locally called 'Bann Ganga'.

The factual position is that actual demarcation exists 'from the mouth of Sir Creek to the top of Sir Creek and from the top of the Sir Creek eastwards to a point on the line designated at the Western Terminus'. The boundary is further unambiguously fixed. One has to clearly understand that in this issue the demarcation of the border, on land, is of substantial consequence because it ultimately becomes the basis for determining the maritime boundaries, drawn as an extension onto the sea from the reference points on land.

India claims that the boundary should lie in the middle of the estuary, on the lines of the accepted practice as well as the pillars built mid-channel during the British colonial rule. Pakistan, on its part, states that the boundary should lie on the southeastern bank of the creek and bases this claim on the line shown on a map drawn by the British Governor of Bombay in the early 20th century. India claims this to be a ribbon line, as is the practice of cartographers to indicate the boundaries, which should not be misinterpreted as a line.

## Composite Dialogue on Sir Creek (22$^{nd}$ to 24$^{th}$ December 2006)

We boarded the Pakistani International Airlines flight from Delhi to Lahore on 21$^{st}$ December, 2004. At the entry point of the aircraft all the passengers had to undergo an additional security check, conducted by the Airline staff themselves, something which was out of the normal for any international flight. After a halt at Lahore, for about two hours, we boarded our flight to Islamabad.

The talks were scheduled over two days beginning on the 22$^{nd}$ Dec, 2004 in the Pakistan Defence Headquarters, Rawalpindi. I recollect that the visit to Pakistan had induced a strange excitement in all members of the delegation, clearly evident from their body language. It suddenly struck me that my second childhood desire, to visit Pakistan, had become a reality.

On the flight I spotted two known Indian faces that of Indian cricketers Mr. Yuvraj Singh and Mr. Nehra. I had a Pakistani woman passenger on my right who asked me if I was a part of the Indian Delegation on the 'Sir Creek Composite Dialogue'. I affirmed and asked her how she had guessed it. She then showed me a Pakistani English daily, which carried news about our trip and related details.

On arrival at Lahore airport, we were received very warmly, with full protocol, by the Brigade Commander of Lahore Area in the VIP Lounge. We then set off for Islamabad, the capital city of Pakistan. We reached Islamabad pretty late and were received with a lot of *Josh* by the Pakistani hosts. We were driven to the Hotel Pearl Continental, located at Sadar, Rawalpindi. I remember it was around dinnertime and one of our delegation members, Mr. Shyam who was Deputy Secretary, Pakistan Division in MEA, suggested having Chinese food. Just as we were about to enter the Chinese restaurant, in the hotel, I told Admiral Rao that we could have Chinese food back home in India, as well. Now that we were in Pakistan why not try Pakistani food. Everyone liked the idea, including Mr. Shyam and soon we were made comfortable by the hotel staff, in the restaurant serving the local cuisine. The food was lavish with a great variety of traditional Pakistani non-vegetarian fare. The vegetarian dishes were equally good. The atmosphere was complimented by live music comprising of old Hindi film songs.

The restaurant was packed with customers who looked at us with a lot of curiosity, I guess because we were from the Indian delegation. I forwarded *Farmaish*, a request to the singers to sing a few chosen *Ghazals* by Ghulam Ali and Mahindi Hasan, which I cherished since my childhood. By the end of the evening all members of the delegation enjoyed both the food and music to the fullest. Admiral Rao thanked me as he also had a ear for music, especially *Ghazals*. The evening rejuvenated each one of us to face the important business, slated for the next day.

The next morning we first called on the Indian High Commissioner's office. Here we met the Deputy High Commissioner, who was also a part of the Indian delegation along with Mrs. Devyani Khobragade, the First Secretary and Capt. Sanjay Bhalla, Naval Adviser in the Indian High Commission. The leader then identified a small 'Call Group' who called on the Rear Admiral Tanveer Faiz, Additional Secretary, Ministry of Defence of Pakistan. I was a part of this group and found him to be a very soft-spoken and a seasoned naval officer. He appreciated certain Indian TV serials such as, but not limited to, '*Kyun Ki Saas Bhi Kabhi Bahu Thi*' and '*Kani Ghar Ghar Ki*'. He told us that 'Tulsi', the main character in '*Kyun Ki Saas Bhi Kabhi . . .* ', had taken Pakistan by storm to the extent that his own wife refused point blank to serve the dinner when the serial was on. I invited him to visit India and on hearing this, he looked towards the sky and said, with a strange brightness in his eyes, "Hope so!". We also called on the Secretary Defence, Govt. of Pakistan, Lt Gen (Retd) Tariq Waseem Ghazi, who wished us fruitful talks.

We were then led to the main conference hall, which was in the adjacent block. The sea of journalists, both from newspaper and electronic media, was indicative of the sensation that the 'Composite Dialogue on Sir Creek' had created in the minds of the general public in both countries. The event was in fact a major headline, in the morning news, followed by various discussions by experts on the subject. While we were in the process of occupying our seats, in the conference hall, the journalists were allowed to capture their shots and were requested to leave to enable us commence business.

The leader of the Pakistani delegation Major General Jamirul Rehman, the Surveyor General of Pakistan, extended a warm welcome, with full diplomatic courtesies, to the Indian delegation and wished success for the talks. He introduced all the members of his delegation, including one Capt. (Retd) C.D. Bhatti who was the only retired officer in both the delegations.

The aim of the talks was mainly three fold: to arrive at a mutual consensus to carry out 'The Joint Survey of Sir Creek'; to identify the extent of the area, rather the limits up to which the joint survey would be carried out and to finalise the methodology of the survey which would jointly be carried out by Indian and Pakistani Surveyors.

As regards the first point, it was in fact the reason of the meeting as mutually desired by both the Indian and Pakistan Governments. The matter was nonetheless discussed and both the sides agreed to put their best foot forward.

The second point, regarding the extent to which the 'Joint Survey' would be carried out, was discussed at length, by both sides and partly agreed upon, after due deliberations. When the matter was further discussed, in the second session after lunch, both the sides failed to reach an agreement as regards the area of the joint survey, mainly because both the sides couldn't agree on some 'Peripheral Points'. I remained very attentive at this point because I was aware that my leader would expect my opinion, as it pertained to the land portion. The discussions went on for a considerable time with both sides trying to impress upon each other with their respective viewpoints.

When I look back, I can remember only two occasions in my life, this far, when I was a 100 percent attentive— first, when I handled the live mines (anti-personnel, anti-tank and fragmentation), as detailed before; second, during these talks, which expected me to propose to our leader the limiting points of the joint survey that pertained to the land portion of Sir Creek. A wrong suggestion, at this level, would have been catastrophic.

Towards the evening, the leader of the Pakistani delegation sounded his so-called final position. At this stage, Admiral Rao looked towards me and I gestured a 'No' since it was clearly against our interest. Both the delegations harped on the same point through the entire day, which was an experience for me. It sure inculcated patience and ensured that at no stage one spoke lightly, in spite of the disagreements and extraordinarily long arguments. Finally, both leaders decided to call it a day and meet the next morning to resume the discussions.

The Pakistan side had scheduled a sightseeing tour for us that evening. However, two of my colleagues from the Survey of India, one of whom was the Director of the field Directorate of Gujarat, under whose jurisdiction the area under question fell and the other officer, Brig Girish Kumar, though posted to our Directorate (IBD), was on short deputation to MEA and me collectively decided to give the sightseeing tour a miss and instead work out the methodology of 'Joint Surveys', with the Surveyor General of Pakistan and his land surveyors, provided they agreed. Admiral Rao agreed when I told him that we would join them for dinner, which was being hosted by the Additional Secretary Defence, Govt. of Pakistan, in honour of the Indian Delegation.

As discussed, I made the request to the Surveyor General of Pakistan who was very supportive, and readily agreed. Maybe he also realised the advantage of having a mutually agreed draft ready and handy. Both understood that it would be an asset, in the eventuality of both sides agreeing on the extent of area, the next day. The chances of such an agreement, however, seemed bleak, keeping in mind the events of the day.

Major General Jamirul Rehman, the leader of Pakistani delegation and the Surveyor General of Pakistan was objective and even though he had suffered a paralytic attack, in the recent past, we found him to be very active on the work front. He also commanded a lot of respect from his colleagues. We discussed the methodology threadbare including the data source, instrumentation, camping facilities and details about the security and joint movements.

Another major aspect that we had to decide on was the location where the two teams would camp, after completion of the fieldwork. This had to be authenticated by the Field Directors of the concerned Directorates of both countries.

I suggested that this activity could best be placed at the Indo Pak border at Wagah, near Amritsar. The Surveyor

General of Pakistan readily accepted it. We further decided that both teams would bring their computer systems to the border, at Wagah and Attari respectively, work jointly during day and retire to their respective locations on their Indian and Pakistani sides, at night. Having completed the proceedings planned we went to our hotel, changed our rigs and joined the other members of our delegation to enjoy the hospitality of the Additional Secretary Defence, Govt. of Pakistan.

During the course of dinner we had informal discussions with our counterparts from Pakistan. After an evening of delicious food and amazing live music, both sides exchanged gifts and then retired for the night.

The next morning, talks resumed on the same note and both sides, like before, repeated their stand and the disagreement remained alive even after a couple of hours' deliberations, on the very point which had been the bone of contention for the day and a half day. During the course of the discussions I noticed that a major part of the advice, on the Pakistan side, originated from Mr. Bhatti, the superannuated officer.

The talks were scheduled until 1:00P.M., that day, since we were to catch a flight for Lahore attending a luncheon, hosted by the Pakistan delegation in the Pearl Continental hotel. Finally, the talks concluded with the two delegations gracefully agreeing to disagree.

At the main gate, dozens of cameramen and press reporters waiting eagerly to know the outcome. Admiral Rao said to me, with a smile, "I am not a diplomat.

What should I tell the media since the talks haven't been very successful"? I replied, on a lighter note that he should wear the hat of a diplomat, for some time and we both laughed. In the meantime, we worked on the 'Press Release', which was jointly approved by leaders of the two sides and handed over to the waiting media. Admiral Rao and the Surveyor General of Pakistan had to answer some incisive questions from news reporters and handled it very well. We then rushed back to the hotel, took off our uniforms, slipped into muftis, packed our baggage and left to have lunch with our Pakistani counterparts. We planned to leave for the airport directly in order to be on time for the flight.

We had been told that the Government of Pakistan had scheduled a visit to the 'Anarkali', in Lahore and a message to this effect had already been conveyed to the concerned echelons there. I had heard a lot about the 'Anarkali' of Lahore. It is to Lahore what 'Karol Bagh' is to Delhi. All the members of the Indian Delegation were extremely excited about the visit.

Admiral Rao was discussing something with me while drinking soup when Brigadier Maqsood Ahamad from GHQ, of the Pakistan delegation joined us and said with a smile, "*Hum aapko ek tohfa dena chahtay hain*"— meaning "we want to gift you all something". At that point, the leader of the Pakistan delegation announced that in the best example of flexibility, they had agreed to conduct the joint survey, to the extent of the points, as proposed by the Indian Delegation. There was a strange sensation and members of both side celebrated. The 'Record of Discussion' maintained was elevated to the level of 'The Minutes of Meeting' and was again read, very carefully, by all the members of both delegations. Both leaders agreed to sign the 'Minutes of Meeting' hurriedly but carefully. The methodology of joint survey, in respect of the topography, which was finalized by the Surveyor General of Pakistan and me the previous night, came very handy and was annexed readily with the minutes of the meeting.

Two copies of the minutes were made available to the Indian side, one remained with the leader and the other was handed over to me for archiving in the files of the International Boundary Directorate, where original copies of 'Minutes of Meetings', related to international boundary matters, are lodged.

By this time we were already late for the flight and were only getting further delayed. We were, however, assured that the aircraft would be detained until such time we boarded. There was great excitement and we left for the airport where I spotted the Foreign Minister of Pakistan walking to board the same aircraft. I mentioned to my Pakistani counterpart that their Foreign Minister had been kept waiting in the aircraft, for almost an hour. He said it didn't matter since we were on an important job. At Lahore we were received by the local Brigade Commander as was the custom. We were all excited about the scheduled visit to the 'Anarkali'. We didn't waste any time to convey the same to the officer. The Brigade Commander was quiet and after a pause, informed us that the permission for the visit had been withdrawn, due to security reasons.

We were all disheartened as we were looking forward to the visit. The Brigade Commander was very apologetic but helpless. He, on his part, entertained us in the VIP Lounge from where we were driven to the Pearl Continental Hotel located at Mall Road, Lahore. It was a far bigger hotel than one at Rawalpindi. After freshening up we visited shops within the hotel premises. As expected, in hotels, the items were exorbitantly priced. I walked into a shop that sold shawls and at once the shopkeeper recognised me as being part of the Indian Delegation. He mentioned that he had been seeing us on TV all these days. I asked him for two shawls, one for my mother and the other for my mother-in-law. He was very gracious and offered a good discount, on the price, appreciating the fact that I was from India. My mother, even today, wears the shawl occasionally and refers to it as the 'Lahori Shawl'.

I was left with some Pakistani currency and asked the shopkeeper to give me coins in exchange. He didn't accept the currency and instead gave me a handful of coins absolutely free. I was impressed by his gesture and seriously thought that he, perhaps, mirrored the feelings of the people of Pakistan.

In the meantime, the local Brigade Commander sent an army officer to our rooms to collect the list of garments that we desired to buy from 'Anarkali'. Guess he had understood our anxiousness. In a few hours the clothes were delivered to us and thereafter, we flew back to Delhi.

On reaching home my wife informed me that the Sir Creek talks were very much in the news in India as well. She had in fact received a number of calls from our relatives who had seen me on TV but somehow had herself missed watching that particular segment.

As planned, fieldwork related to the joint survey of 'Sir Creek' commenced on 15th January, 2006 with the Governments of both countries extending their support in its execution. The most encouraging thing was the substantial goodwill between the survey teams on either side, which helped accomplishing the mission smoothly.

The Director of Gujarat Directorate kept us informed, on daily basis, about the progress of 'Joint Survey'. It was very heartening to know that everything was happening, amicably and as planned. After completion of the fieldwork, land surveyors from both India and Pakistan shifted to their respective border posts, located at 'Wagah' and 'Attari' respectively, along with their computer systems. Directors of either side finally authenticated the 'Jointly Surveyed Maps' thereby putting their seal on a job well done and most importantly in a cordial environment.

## The composite Dialogue
## (17th to 18th May, 2007)

It was again after about six months that the Surveyor General of India gave me a call, on this aspect, asking me to get ready to attend a meeting along with him in MEA. All the concerned officers of MEA, the Surveyor General of India and the Chief Naval Hydrographer, were present at the meeting. The Governments of both the countries had yet again decided to hold the 'Sir Creek Composite Dialogue' in Pakistan in June' 2007. The Surveyor General of India (Maj Gen M Gopal Rao) was to lead the Indian delegation, this time round.

Like before, the talks were scheduled over two days, on 17th and 18th May, 2007. I recall that it was very hot on 16th May, 2007 in Delhi. While leaving home I talked to the Surveyor General on the phone, he advised me to carry a blazer along and I stuffed a tie in one of its pockets and a few more of them in the suitcase.

At the airport, I saw Admiral Rao, the Chief Naval Hydrographer, also carrying a blazer in his hand. I asked him if he had a tie as well. He replied that he had not got one along so I told him he could borrow one from me, since I had brought a few. We boarded PIC flight (PK-271) from Delhi to Lahore. Yet again we underwent the security ritual at the entry to the aircraft. The Pakistani official, conducting the security check recognized me and said, "Sir, I think that I have seen you on TV". I told him that he may be right since he would have seen me during the news coverage of the last delegation. I smiled and told him that chances were he might see me on TV again the next day.

# Chapter 30

# FACE TO FACE WITH THE GENERAL

We reached Lahore at about 6:30P.M.. In spite of the hot and sultry weather I slipped on my blazer and tie while getting down from the aircraft. The local Brigade Commander received and made us relax in the VIP longue. From here we flew to Islamabad where we reached at about 9:00P.M.. The Pakistani hosts received the delegation with full pomp and show, here as well. We were driven to Pearl Continental Hotel and initially made comfortable in a room, next to the reception, under the supervision of Lt Col Taimur, the Pakistan Army officer who had been designated as 'Liaison Officer'. He was a tall Pathan with a long beard. He was very courteous and concerned about our comfort.

While we waited, Admiral Rao, sitting farther away from me, suddenly signalled to me pointing to his neck. Not sure of what he meant I asked him what he wanted. In a hushed tone he said, *"Kant Langote"*. I then understood that he was asking for a necktie. I then asked him, in a low tone, as to why he needed it. He replied that the Honorable President was coming. I asked him not to pull my leg. Just then Lt Col Taimur came in and informed us that President Musharraf would be arriving, with his wife and would join us for dinner. I apologised to Admiral Rao for, I had thought that he had been joking. Unfortunately I had put my ties in the suit case which had been taken to my room, by the hotel staff. I offered to go to my room and get a tie but he advised me not to since the President was expected to arrive any moment.

Soon, President Musharraf, along with his wife, arrived. It appears his decision to come was both sudden and unannounced. He looked very smart in his casual attire and stepped in like a breath of fresh air. We were introduced to the first lady of Pakistan Ms. Sehba Musharraf who was also informally yet gracefully dressed. Both added a pleasant aura to the restaurant and its environs. A foreigner forced his entry through us and introduced himself to the President who remained quite courteous and composed until the foreigner left.

The Surveyor General of India introduced the members of the Indian delegation individually. When he introduced me as Director, International Boundary Directorate, President Musharraf looked towards me and said with a smile on his face, "Solve the issue this time. I have told my officers to be very flexible and you should also show some flexibility". I told him that we would do our best. I could guess from his body language that he was serious about resolving the issue. Food was served and we enjoyed the evening with live music. This was one of the most memorable and historic dinners for most of us.

After dinner, we all assembled outside the restaurant for photographs with the President and his wife. He was kind enough to oblige. The camera of one of his staff developed a snag to which the President remarked, "Don't worry, I shall not leave until your camera works," and everybody laughed.

It was very evident that the President was seriously interested in a resolution of the Sir Creek issue from this gesture else no President, of any country, would have ever dropped by so casually, along with the first lady to meet a foreign delegation, the way he did. This probably further added the dimension of importance to the resolution of the issue, made evident by him without any ambiguity.

The next morning we headed to the Ministry of Defence to attend the Composite Dialogues for which the profile of leaders, from either side, had been raised to Additional Secretary level, as I mentioned before.

The Pakistan delegation comprised:

Rear Admiral Tanveer Faiz, Additional Secretary Ministry of Defence—Leader

1. Maj Gen Asif Ali, The Surveyor General of Pakistan
2. Mr. Zahir. A. Junjua, Director, Ministry of Foreign Affairs
3. Cdre Nasim Anwar, Joint Staff Headquarters
4. Brig Maqsood Ahmad, GHQ
5. Cdre Muhmmad Zafaryab, Hydrographer, Pakistan Navy
6. Capt (Retd) C.D. Bhatti, Ministry of Defence
7. Capt Javed Iqbal, Naval Adviser High Commissioner of Pakistan, New Delhi

The Indian delegation comprised:

1. Maj Gen M. Gopal Rao, The Surveyor General of India—Leader
2. Rear Admiral B.R. Rao, Chief Naval Hydrographer
3. Sh. Binoy Kumar, Joint Secretary, Ministry of Defence
4. Brig P.N. Koul, Director International Boundary Directorate
5. Cmde S.K. Jha, Directorate of National Hydrography
6. Brig Girish Kumar, Director Boundary Cell, Ministry of External Affairs
7. Sh. K. Jeeva Sagar, Director Ministry of External Affairs

Following were the three additional members from High Commission of India:

1. Sh. Manpreet Vohra, Deputy High Commissioner
2. Sanjay Bhalla, Naval Adviser
3. Dr. Devyani Khobragade, First Secretary

Rear Admiral Tanveer Faiz welcomed us and expressed hope that deliberations between the two delegations would be fruitful. He also applauded the efforts put in by surveyors of both countries to carry out 'Joint Survey of Sir Creek' successfully and in a cordial environment. He then introduced the members of his delegation.

Major General M. Gopal Rao, the Surveyor General of India thanked the leader of the Pakistan delegation for the highest standards of hospitality extended to the Indian delegation and hoped that the talks would be yet another mile stone in the resolution of the Sir Creek issue. The discussions took place at length and soon we broke off for a working lunch. The 'Call Group', identified by the leader, was scheduled to call on Mr. Kamran Rasool, Secretary Defence, Govt. of Pakistan, immediately after lunch.

I attempted to investigate the background of Mr. Kamran for he was the senior most bureaucrat of the Pakistan Government, whom we were meeting. I learnt that he had been a science graduate, had done his masters in English literature, followed by PG Diploma in Development Administration. He had then undergone training in the Civil Service Academy, Lahore for two years followed by further training in

Manchester University. He had held many important offices including the office of Cabinet Secretary Govt. of Punjab, before taking over as the Defence Secretary.

Deliberations resumed after the 'Calling On Session'. Both sides affirmed that the 'Jointly Surveyed Maps' were acceptable and mutually agreed to exchange the maps, after due authentication by representatives of both countries. This was a big step forward towards resolving the issue.

I had the privilege of signing the 'Joint Survey Maps', on behalf of India, while my counterpart from Pakistan did it on behalf of his country.

A brief ceremony to exchange maps was then held, where I handed over the maps to my Pakistani counterpart and so did he, in the presence of our leaders and other members of the delegations. Applause and cheers resounded in the conference hall. I was very happy to have been associated with the Sir Creek issue, especially during my tenure as the Director International Boundary Directorate. The jointly surveyed maps that we handed over to each other not only became an important mile stone towards the resolution of 'Sir Creek Issue' but also an important addition to the treasure of records, held by both the countries on the aspect. The talks continued the next day and even though the issue was not fully resolved we had surely taken a major step further towards its resolution.

On both the days, our Pakistani hosts had arranged sightseeing tours, during the evenings, which included a visit to Shakar Parian, *Daman-e-koh* and Katas Raj Temple.

The drive to the Shakar Parian Hills, in particular, was thrilling. The hills are located in between the twin cities of Islamabad and Rawalpindi. It has two beautiful viewpoints; one is called the 'Eastern View Point' and consists of cascades and terrace lawns from where we had a beautiful view of Islamabad from there. The other the 'Western View Point'; provided us a bird's eye view of the historic city of Rawalpindi.

*Daman-e-Koh* is a conjunction of Urdu and Persian words. *Daman* means 'centre' and *Koh* means 'Hill' and together it means 'Centre of the Hill'. It is about a twenty minutes' drive from Islamabad and is located in the middle of the 'Magalla Hills'. It is at a height of about 2400 feet above sea level and relatively about 500 feet above Islamabad. From here, we had a panoramic view of the forest and the city of Islamabad.

We were also taken for a visit to 'Katas Raj Temple'. We were told that Pakistan had started a drive to renovate old Hindu temples, some of which are in ruins and Katas Raj Temple was one such temple. We saw a renovation stone laid by the Prime Minister of Pakistan inside the temple where one of the rooms had then been partly tiled. It was probably the same temple where Sh. Advani had initiated renovation work, under the good will gesture of the Govt. of Pakistan. A tour that ended up costing him a lot of flak back home on account of a remark made by him on Mr. Jinnah, the founder of Pakistan.

It is said that Katas Raj Temple is dedicated to Lord 'Shiva' and it existed much before the Mahabharatha. Apparently the 'Pandava brothers' spent more than a third of their exile in this area. The place also has the sanctity because it is said that on the death of 'Satti', Lord Shiva's wife, the Lord cried so hard and so long that it led to the creation of two holy ponds, one the Pushkar Lake located at Ajmer and the other the lake at Katas Raj Temple.

We were well received at the temple gate by representatives of the hosts and were entertained with tea and snacks under a new 'shamiana'.

On the evening of 18th June, 2007, the Deputy High Commissioner of India hosted a dinner in honour of the Indian Delegation. Here we were told that our Pakistani hosts had decided to send us back, from Lahore to India by road and not by air as was scheduled earlier. It was a good gesture on their part that would allow us to see life on the road between Lahore to Attari and the Wagah border posts. Wagah is the only road-crossing border between India and Pakistan and lies on the Grand Trunk (GT) Road, which connects the two Punjabs, of India and Pakistan.

The next morning, we flew to Lahore and were received by the same Brigade Commander who had received us earlier. Here too they had arranged sightseeing, which included a short visit to 'Anarkali', which we had missed the last time. We also visited 'Lahore Fort', 'Lahore Badshahi Mosque', 'Shalimar Gardens' and also saw Dr. Iqbal's[9] Tomb and I remembered some of the couplets of the famous poet. In school, I would recite his *Sarey Jahan Se Achha* . . . poem daily in the morning prayers while I was part of the 'Prayer Group'.

I also remembered a couplet by Zauq[10] which my father would generally sing:

'Laayi hayaat aaye kaza le chali Chale
Apni khushi se aaye na apni khushi Chale'
(We are brought to this world by life while death comes
and takes us away,
Neither we come on our own will nor do we go back
from here out of our own choice)

After the sightseeing tour and lunch at Pearl Continental Hotel, we left for the Wagah border by car. While traveling by road I couldn't help feel as though we were traveling in India. There was hardly any difference with regard to people, culture, the shops and everything else. We reached Attari, the Pakistani Border Post and the Brigade Commander, in accordance with the protocol, received us and we were given a farewell as we left for 'Wagah', the Indian Border Post. Here we were received by BSF officers. Thereafter, we left for the Amritsar airport to fly back to Delhi. A memorable and somewhat historic visit thus ended.

---

9     Dr. Mohammad Iqbal (1873-1938)
10     Mohammad Ibrahim 'Zauq' (1789-1854)

# Chapter 31

# PROUD MOMENTS

B ack at the office we were summoned by Mr. Shiv Shankar Menon, the Foreign Secretary, Govt. of India. During our meeting he saw the 'Joint Survey Maps' that we had exchanged with utmost attention and appeared fully satisfied. I told him that nothing much had happened, as the issue could not be fully resolved. He on the other hand emphasised that something very good has happened adding that so far, discussions were merely token in nature quoting various records, which did not make much sense. However, this time round there was an authenticated, jointly surveyed map exchanged which now enabled both the sides to objectively state areas of difference. He went on to say that it was a job very well done. He asked the Surveyor General to be ready to give a presentation to the then

Foreign Minister, Honourable Sh. Pranab Mukerjee, who then went on to become the President of India.

After a few days, we went to the main conference hall of the MEA and awaited the arrival of the Foreign Minister. After a brief introduction, the Surveyor General of India and the Chief Hydrographer made their presentations. The Foreign Secretary told us to show the jointly surveyed maps, to the Honorable Minister, which were exchanged between the two countries. Sh. Pranab Mukerjee was very happy and applauded the Surveyor General and the Chief Hydrographer for an excellent job.

As regards the 'Sir Creek; issue, I am very clear in my mind that whatever remains is doable and can be resolved with a little flexibility on either side. It is best advised not to couple it with other issues, which will only result in unwarranted complexities. I am of the opinion that the issue of 'Sir Creek' could have been best resolved during the time of General Pervez Musharraf for, as the President of Pakistan he had an overwhelming command on the politics of the time. Moreover, he had support of the Army, which as we all know is vital. Above all, he possessed the requisite ingredients of inclination and the will to resolve this particular issue.

As I conclude, with many more experiences to share, I would like to mention in particular a touching scene that has left a mark on my mind. While I crossed the Attari and Wagah border posts and looked behind, the huge and strong iron gates were being closed and secured strongly, as usual. This was to ensure that no humans could cross over. At that moment I couldn't help notice the gushing winds that blew across briskly, birds that flew across freely at will, both probably smiling ironically at us humans.

I expressed this feeling in the poem 'Who Laid the Barbed Wire'. I reproduce the poem below:

# Who Laid the Barbed Wire?

The morning chirps, the blue sky, the soothing wind that sweeps across
and brushes the plains and the hills, dressed in that green attire,
From the top of the hill, the water shed, as I enjoy the artist's delight,
my eyes sore, as I see, along the water shed, a misplaced barbed wire.

I see a bird enjoying its tune, soaring high and diving down,
as it approaches, I warn it, "Oh! Dear don't cross that barbed wire, else
you may invite their ire, Oh! Dear don't cross that barbed wire
for, cannons may roar, guns may fire if you cross that barbed wire".

It gives me a dirty look, flies across and yells, devoid of any fear,
"I don't care for your barbed wire, I don' t care for your barbed wire,
I don' t curse you but I don' t care, to hell with your barbed wire,
it pricks my mind, it pricks my soul, I don't care for your barbed wire".

You humans divide your bodies; divide your souls and your minds,
we create with our minds and souls; you destroy with your anger and ire,
You humans have nothing to do, day and night you plan the cannon fire,
let the cannons roar and guns fire, I don't care for your barbed wire".

The author (extreme right) with General Musharraf,
President of Pakistan and his wife, Maj Gen Gopal Rao,
Surveyor General of India (2nd from left) and
Rear Admiral B.R. Roa, Chief Hydographer (3rd from right)

The author being received by Rear Admiral Tanveer
Faiz, Additional Secretary Ministry of Defence,
Govt. of Pakistan in the Defence Headquarters in Rawalpindi.

The author signs the Jointly Surveyed Map on behalf of India.

The author and his Pakistani counterpart exchange the
Jointly Surveyed Maps on behalf of their respective countries.
Standing behind are the leaders of the two delegation.